MARX
His Theory and its Context

MARX

His Theory and its Context

Politics as economics

An introductory and critical essay on the political economy of Karl Marx

ANGUS WALKER

SECOND EDITION

Rivers Oram Press
London

First published in 1978,
second impression 1979 by
the Longman Group Limited, London

This edition published by
Rivers Oram Press
144 Hemingford Road, London N1 1DE

Published in the USA by
Unwin Hyman Inc
8 Winchester Place, Winchester, Mass

Printed in Great Britain
by T.J. Press, Padstow

British Library Cataloguing in Publication Data
Walker, Angus
 Marx
 1.Marxian economics
 335.4'12'0924 HB97.5 78-40017

ISBN 185489 003 4

For my Mother in memory of my Father

Frederick William Walker
1892-1943

Contents

Preface to the second edition

The chances are that the browser will take this book down in a bookshop from a shelf in the section marked 'Marxism'. This section is likely to be separate from others marked 'philosophy', 'economics' or 'political thought'. This distinct label for books on Marx represents an acceptance of the idea that those who are interested in Marx have an attitude towards his work which differs from that which is normally brought to bear on studies of social issues. 'Marxist' books are expected to be read by those who 'believe' in him and who are *a priori* persuaded that the texts of his work will, like the sacred writings of the world's religions, yield new insights to the devout. This book is not for them.

It is this book's more modest ambition to find a place in the bibliographies of secondary sources for the history of political and economic thought. It is addressed to those who approach the work of Marx with the same disinterested curiosity with which they study the work of Machiavelli, Locke, Mill, Marshall, Spencer or Keynes. What is it that has tended to prevent booksellers from displaying this book in the place where it is most likely to catch the eye of such readers?

Three decades ago Marxist theory had apparently ossified. It was trapped in the state dogmas of the Soviet Union and its dependencies. It was propagated didactically and in a form which brooked little discussion by communist parties which, while territorially outside the Soviet bloc, were effectively directed from Moscow. These communist parties were already in decline in terms of their political influence. Marxism, as a set of ideas, at least in the advanced market societies of Western Europe, North America and Japan, looked set for a similar process of decay.

The Russian Revolution of 1917 and the triumph of the Red Army in 1945 gave Marxism a standing in the world which it would not otherwise have enjoyed. For the years after the Second World War were not the first period to see a decline in the influence of Marx's ideas. The period before the First World War failed to provide evidence for the truth of Marx's economic predictions and the enthusiasm with which the workers of various European countries took up arms against each other further and seriously reduced the credibility of the notion of the international brotherhood of workers. These experiences prompted attempts to revise Marxist analyses to 'fit' a world of imperialism and technological advance of a kind quite different from what Marx had imagined.

In the 1960s the decline in the popularity of Marxism was reversed, or at least retarded, by various and not dissimilar attempts to adapt the doctrines to the new needs of its audience. It is hard to give a powerful and single reason for this success. It was not something which affected the mass of the population of the 'working classes' but it clearly had much to do with demographic change and the consequent expansion of universities in Europe and North America.

At all events, for this primarily student audience, various adaptations of Marx's ideas were introduced. In America ways were sought to compensate for the failure of the proletariat to fulfil the revolutionary role that Marx had prescribed for it. Substitutes for a subversive and impoverished working class, notable by its absence in all advanced economies, were sought in disadvantaged minorities and the 'Third World'.

Another and more subtle revisionist approach was based on the re-examination of the origins of Marx's idea in the work of the immediate successors of Hegel. Although the connexion between Marx and Hegel had always been understood by Marx's more perceptive readers (including Lenin), it now received a new emphasis. The early work of Marx and especially the notes and manuscripts unpublished in his lifetime received close attention. By 1970, Marx's *Grundrisse*, a difficult and obscure manuscript of one-thousand pages, not widely available until the 1950s, could be described as the 'centrepiece' of his work by one of the popularisers of this new approach.

This interpretation emphasised the 'humanism' and 'voluntarism' of Marx's thinking as a young man and offered them as the 'truths' lying behind the apparent determinism and impersonalism of the theories of social development set out in *Capital*. The purpose of this exegesis is clear. Whether the interpretation is 'true' or not, and without intending to impugn the integrity of those scholars who expounded this approach, it may fairly be said to be designed to rescue Marx from his fate as an evidently failed social scientist and to reinstate him as someone who provides ethical guidance for social analysis independently of the process of the crude empirical verification of data.

For the radical left, especially in Europe, disappointed with the compromises of social democracy and brought up within an intellectual tradition in which revolution had a powerful connotation of dedication and self-sacrifice, the prize was great. The disinterment of the 'young Marx', freed from the taint of 'social engineering' and dissociated from the uncomfortable history of the Soviet Union, enabled them to claim the right to the Marxist inheritance. It is a process not unlike the rediscovery of the Bible by the religious radicals who provoked the Reformation. It was a way of promoting Christ while dissociating oneself from His Vicar on earth.

It would by cynical to say that a generation of neo-Marxists, inconvenienced by what Marx actually wrote, had simply tried to give some textual colour to their wish that he had written something else. Nonetheless, the intellectual world at large has found it difficult to group with other modes of social analysis the study of Marx as pursued over the last twenty years, and has concluded that 'Marxism' is significantly different from other disciplines of social investigation. Booksellers, segmenting their markets have, unsurprisingly, come to the same conclusion. That is why this book may have been found between some uncomfortable neighbours on the shelf from which it has just been taken down.

Ironically Marx himself would have been horrified. The last thing that he had intended to create was a closed and intellectually impenetrable sect preaching a socialist version of Pentecostalism or a political equivalent of Biblical Fundamentalism. He believed that he was making a major contribution to the understanding of the social and economic world and expected it to satisfy the criteria for truth common to educated men.

But it is not the purpose here to argue that Marx has no contemporary interest. It is, no doubt, a sufficient reason for reading Marx that his historical influence is a massive fact. At the same time there are powerful elements in his thinking which are not simply useful as explanations of actions and events in the past. Marx ensured himself a place in intellectual history by his whole-hearted engagement in the critique of the social, political and moral implications of the use of markets for distributing goods and services and for deciding the allocation of investment.

Markets are not natural phenomena. They are sets of rules which can only be effective if they are policed and sanctioned. 'Contracts without the sword' as Hobbes observed, 'are void'. Different markets have different rules in different economies and even within the same economy. The way in which they are constructed and configured, their extent and the freedom with which they can be entered are all the result of political and externally generated decisions. This is as true now as it was when Marx was writing.

Consequently, whatever the theoretical desirability or otherwise, in terms of social justice, of making markets more efficient, less imperfect or more comprehensive, even the most fanatical believer in the perversity of any other mode of distribution cannot escape from the duty to decide and argue, in terms which transcend the values of the market, why markets should be arranged in one way and not another.

Marx's view of markets was ambiguous. On the one hand, under capitalism, men are blinded to the true nature of the economic forces, i.e., the market, which drive them. But, on the other hand, socialism results from the identification and destruction of the market and its associated institutions. It is not clear in Marx on what theoretical basis to what extent men can gain insights in anticipation of autonomous economic change or to what extent, given these insights, they can effect the transition from one mode of production to another. But it is not necessary to subscribe to Marx's version of this dilemma in order to benefit from his analysis of the problem. The importance of market mechanisms in providing the underlying substance of political exchange is sufficient to explain why no student of modern society, of whatever political persuasion, could claim to be completely equipped without a critical understanding of Marx.

It follows that the importance of Marx is strengthened and not weakened by contemporary changes in economic management in countries which have claimed Marx as the inspiration of their policies for development. Although recent developments in the USSR and China have been especially striking, attempts to tinker with the centralised structures of command economies have a long history and there is nothing new in principle in the various changes that have been made or are proposed. The managers of these economies have always been aware of the limitations of planning, of the problems of providing incentives for initiative and efficiency and of the unreliability of the information provided by administered systems. Command economies, even at their most centralised, always retained an important role for markets, especially in the supply of consumer goods and services. The freedom of labour markets has varied over time but in general has been much more extensive, at least in Soviet and Eastern Europe than is often supposed.

Historically, the Soviet economic machinery is only the latest version of a system of economic administration which has been more notable for direct state intervention than for its encouragement of markets. In the broadest perspective Gorbachev's *perestroika* is simply the most recent of successive attempts over the centuries to model Asiatic Europe against a Western template. Peter the Great, Alexander II, Stolypin and Lenin all attempted, in at least one phase of their efforts, to bring Russia closer to a market model of development. These attempts are all tributes to various aspects of the power and attractiveness of the market as a major element in economic management. Policies which are dependent on market solutions have the overall rhetorical appeal of freedom and liberty, promise lower transaction costs for the allocation of resources, offer the possibility of freeing the State from the onus of economic failure, are intellectually attractive as elegant resolutions of resource allocation problems and, above all, are the developmental path chosen by the capitalist economies which communist countries have chosen to attempt to emulate and to overtake.

The success of all these attempts has been qualified by the unpleasant truth that the market is not an institution which can be divorced from the material circumstances in which it has to operate. The poor population/resource ratio of the Soviet Union means that the state imperatives of a Great Power cannot be met by following the consumption preferences of the Soviet population. The Soviet Union is not a political construction which the economic choices of its citizens would, in aggregate, support. The integrity of the Soviet Union can only be maintained by the central imposition of priorities. What the authorities periodically rediscover is that these priorities can be more efficiently met in some circumstances and over some periods of time by allowing, through market mechanisms, local and subjective preferences a greater role in decisions about allocation.

When they do so, however, they find themselves faced with outcomes that may be socially and politically destabilising, or dysfunctional for their primary objectives. When this happens all the considerations inherent in Marx's analysis again reassert themselves on the economic and managerial agenda. However successful Gorbachev may be in stimulating commercial initiative or extending market relations into capital funds and foreign exchange, the physical constraints of Russia's impoverished economic circumstances will, at some point, painfully recur. We have not heard the last of Marx in Russia, or elsewhere.

From an historical and economic point of view the interest of Marx is not, therefore, so much a cause of the appearance of communist regimes and command economies, as it is the effect of attempting to modernise and to organise poor and institutionally backward societies. Although Marx's pitcher has been to different wells more than once and is now very cracked and chipped, its days of holding water may not yet be over.

Marx should be read, therefore, not in the hope that his role can be extended so as to legitimise patched-up attempts to evade the consequences for political ideas of that *embourgeoisement* of the proletariat which Marx himself had so feared. He should be read for his magnificent, albeit failed assault on the fundamental analytical problem of modern society as laid out in the volumes of *Capital*. Wherever there are markets political debate will be about the desirability of their social and economic outcomes. Marx still provides the *locus classicus* for entry into that debate.

Introduction

The purpose of this book is to provide a general introduction to Marx's ideas about society. It aims to locate Marx's theories in the context of the intellectual history on which Marx was nurtured and, as such, is an essay rather than a textbook.

Karl Marx is more commonly thought of as a political theorist than as an economist. The history of the Soviet Union, of modern China, of revolutionary movements in underdeveloped countries and of radical student protest have taught us to think of Marxism as the advocacy of a particular set of political institutions and of the use of violence in the seizure of political power. Indeed, Marx himself was concerned with the realization of a political goal – the liberation of all mankind. Marx's great treatise, *Capital*, to which he devoted the best part of his life, was meant to provide a scientific basis for political action embodying 'the fundamental principles of the great working class movement'.[1]

At the same time, no political theory has ever had so extensive an economic content. Marx's *magnum opus* is, as its title, *Capital*, and its sub-title, *A Critical Analysis of Capitalist Production*, indicate, primarily an economic study. Most of its 2,000 pages are filled with the discussion of employment, price determination, income distribution, business cycles, capital accumulation and technical progress. The political theorist will find in it few answers to his questions about political organization, the dissection of political institutions, political sociology or revolution.

That a work with political intentions should devote so much space to economics did not appear paradoxical to Marx or to his contemporaries. 'Politics' and 'economics' did not yet have the connotations that they do today. Although both these words were in common use at the time that Marx wrote, 'economic' was often used to refer to matters thought to be the proper concern of 'political economy'. In Marx's day, political economy, although primarily concerned with problems we would now describe as economic, also dealt extensively with the consideration of social organization and legislation. The arguments of political economists play a very important part in the fierce political discussions in early nineteenth-century England and their influence is to be seen in the work of all the reforming parliaments of the time. Nineteenth-century English politics were about economics. The intellectual armoury on which its protagonists drew were supplied by political economy. Marx's *capital* was intended as a contribution to, and transformation of, this discipline.

But even as Marx wrote, new tools of economic analysis were being developed which were for some important purposes greatly to exceed in analytical power the kind of concepts with which Karl Marx, in common with the other great political economists, was accustomed to work. Moreover, since his death the growth of universities and the institutionalization of knowledge have led to the compartmentalization of learning; the vast plains of scholarship across which Marx strode and from which he freely harvested the philosophy, economics, politics, sociology and statistics of which his mighty synthesis is composed have now been fenced in and hedged about into the sub-divisions of half a dozen separate areas of inquiry. Political economy, as a field of study, has regrettably disappeared under a complex of academic zoning regulations; the intellectual context of Marx's ideas is one which few students are, by the nature of their studies, trained to see whole.

Hence, and paradoxically, Marx has attracted a great and increasing amount of academic interest at a time when intense specialization inhibits most scholars from straying from their professional paddock. The results are to be seen in the literature; there are books on Marx's philosophy, on his political theories, on his ethics, on his social ideas and on his economics; there are few which contrive or even intend to relate all these aspects of his theories to each other. Yet, unless it is understood that Marx's theories are the product of a particular philosophical tradition applied to a particular and historically located set of economic doctrines and that the result has an intimately related political purpose, the whole point of Marx's great effort will be missed.

Apart from the need to assimilate an unfamiliar intellectual frame of reference a reader coming to Marx for the first time is faced with other difficulties. Of these perhaps the most obvious is constituted by the enormous bulk of Marx's output – we have been left not too little of his writings but too much. At the same time what he has to say is not always clearly and unequivocally expressed. Marx made, over a long and active intellectual career, a great number of statements about the nature of economic change and the connexions between the constituents of the social fabric; many of these are easily misunderstood when taken out of their complex context and some are difficult to reconcile with each other.

Marx is, at the same time, a very powerful writer. Part of the compelling nature of what he had to say stems from his own passionate reaction to what he felt to be the sheer hypocrisy of commercialized society, which proclaimed liberty but enslaved its members economically. His presentation is, at its most powerful, highly dramatic, and he wrote passages of persuasive prose which have passed into the collective subconscious of whole generations of economists, sociologists and historians, Marxist and non-Marxist alike. Thus, while the apparently unquenchable force of what he had to say demands explanation, at the same time the philosophically and economically technical nature of what he wrote, together with the sometimes fragmentary and incomplete character of the form in which it is expressed, makes it difficult to offer the kind of neat and consistent account which an introduction to his work seeks to provide.

This book is an attempt, in the face of these admittedly daunting obstacles, to provide an entry into Marx's intellectual world. It cannot pretend to be the only way nor claim necessarily to be the best: it is hoped that it is one that many will find useful.

In the first two chapters, which amount to a prelude, I have tried to identify what seems to me to be a fundamental source of tension in Marx's ideas. In this section it is argued that while Marx attributed the development of the modern world to the rise of capitalism, his notion of capitalism can be rendered as the predominance of market relations in society. This is a controversial point of view, vigorously contested by Marx himself. Nonetheless, the reduction of capitalism to the market is made, not in a polemical spirit, but in order to suggest an approach to Marx which makes him easier to understand without, in my opinion, seriously detracting from the force of the most important things he had to say.

This treatment of Marx's capitalism serves as an introduction to the rest of the book which falls into three parts. The first, formed by Chapters 3–8, attempts to show how market concepts and a critique of them bind together the apparently disparate ideas of political economy, Hegelianism and early nineteenth-century socialism. It constitutes an account of the intellectual and historical antecedents of Marx's ideas which, it is hoped, will make them more comprehensible by showing that his theories did not spring from Marx's mind without root or precedent but were a perfectly explicable outgrowth of the most important and powerful intellectual currents of his time.

This first part provides the basis of the second section, formed by Chapters 9–14, in which an exposition and critique of Marx's leading theoretical notions are set out.

Chapters 15–16 attempt further to illuminate the basic structure and fertility of Marx's work by discussing the part played in it by his understanding of nineteenth-century industrialized England and nineteenth-century unindustrialized Russia.

It is not possible to write about Marx without being controversial; for many sincere and intelligent men his words have a special significance greater than that which they would accord to any other text; for others Marx's name is anathema. As will be clear from what I have written, I am not one of the latter but I cannot hope for the approbation of the former. Nor can I claim, as a sceptic, to know that the views set out here are certainly and immutably right. They are offered as a way into a difficult but fascinating subject. I hope that they will make Marx more accessible, more readable and more read.

Note 1. Frederick Engels, 'Preface to the English edition' (1886) in Karl Marx, *Capital* (Moscow 1965), vol. 1, p. 5.

Acknowledgements

In the text of this book there are virtually no references to secondary sources. This is not because I wish to claim that what I have written is entirely original but because I have tried to set out my own understanding of what Marx actually wrote without becoming directly involved in the many and complex controversies which Marx's works have provoked and to which they continue to give rise; if I had tried to document every idea and interpretation of Marx which I have mentioned or discussed, the text would have been much shorter than the footnotes. What I have done is to attempt to put in order my own thoughts about those aspects of Marx's intellectual development which appear to me to be most important and about those of his ideas which seem to me to be most fertile. At the same time I have tried to ground my account in the primary sources. I have put forward some notions which, right or wrong, have as yet no supporters and I have expounded some ideas arrived at independently of but after others. However, and of course, many of the things I have to say have been suggested or directly inspired by secondary works and I am conscious of having absorbed ideas, interpretations, illustrations and even telling phrases from a wide range of sources. The bibliography given at the end of this book is, I fear, an inadequate indication of the extent of my intellectual debts. Everyone familiar with the literature will understand my difficulty and I hope it will be realized that any failure in attribution is a failure of performance and not intention.

Like all authors I owe much to conversations with and the forebearance of my friends. I have also learnt much from my students. I wish especially to record my thanks for criticism, encouragement and stimulation to Victoria Austin, John Bush, Roger Butler, Cecilia Dick, Graham Gardiner, Patrick Gardiner, Stanley Jones, Michael Kitch, Herminio Martins, Patrick O'Brien, Beverly Phillpotts and Bill Wagner.

I am particularly indebted to Keith Jefferis for his patience and understanding in the preparation of this, second, edition. His help was all the more useful and his forebearance valued because not all his views of Marx are coextensive with those explicitly or implicitly expounded here.

Chapter 1

History and the market

It is possible to represent the history of modern European society as the history of its commercialization. Everywhere, over the last 700 or 800 years, agrarian societies have been suffused and then transformed by the spread of market relations. Where this development has been carried furthest the world has changed from one in which the social status and function of men were inherited and hard to change, to a fluid social system in which men are notionally equal and their standing and employment are determined primarily by the price they can command in the market-place. The political institutions of customary society, and even attempts to change them, were legitimized by appeals to the Church and to God; political obligations were conceived as ethical imperatives. Commercialized societies have developed moral systems in which ethics are explained in utilitarian terms and right behaviour seen as being ultimately derived from self-interest; their political thought is rooted in a term derived from the vocabulary of commerce – the social contract. This transition to the market is not complete. It has been, and still is, resisted. It has been counter-attacked with great success. But the struggle which it has engendered lies at the root of all modern political, social and economic conflict.

This internal process has had its counterpart in European expansion overseas. The steady exploration, annexation, conquest and colonization by Europeans of Africa, the Americas, Australasia and Asia, since the fourteenth century, have been carried out for a variety of motives: religious, strategic, commercial and political. Whatever the initial purpose of these European undertakings they have always brought in their train a culture, a mode of social organization, and sets of political norms, which are individualistic, materialistic and essentially market oriented. It can be argued that the importation of these European practices and ideas has been beneficial; it can also be argued that their effect has been catastrophic. Whatever view is taken, there is no doubt their effect on the societies into which they have been infused has been revolutionary. In the conflicts to which European penetration has nearly always given rise, different forms of social organization have been broken up, religions dissolved, nations destroyed, and old patterns of behaviour rooted out.

It is his perception of this process, a process which is not complete nor universally successful, which lies at the heart of Marx's theories. And it is because this process has been so spectacular in its effects and because its political epiphenomena have been and still are so startling that Marx's work, over a century after the publication of *Capital*, still reverberates and echoes across the world.

The market: meaning and function

What do we mean by commercialization? Here this term is used to refer to a steady increase in the practice of ordering economic activity and social institutions in accordance with values derived from the market.

The term 'market' is employed in its less colloquial and more specialized economic sense. As such, it denotes an institution which is designed to facilitate the exchange of goods and services among people. The essence of this institution is that the terms on which exchanges are made are accepted voluntarily by those who buy and sell. The vital function of the market is to establish the identity of these terms: this is achieved in the course of competitive buying and selling. An auction, at which items are sold to that person from among a group of competing buyers who is prepared to pay the highest price, is a one-sided market where the competition is, as it were, among buyers only. The competition for a contract among suppliers establishes who is prepared to offer the lowest price for its fulfilment and a one-sided market where only the sellers are competing with each other. These are, one might say, partial markets, because implicit in the arrangement is the choice of buyers between particular auctions and of suppliers between particular contract competitions. The full market is one in which both buyers and sellers compete with each other, on the one hand to maximize the price at which things are sold, and on the other to minimize the price at which they are bought.

Really, and given the truth of some assumptions which are examined later, the analytical beauty of the market lies in the way in which, if permitted to work properly, it subsumes and integrates the various preferences of those who come to the market and by their participation in fact 'make' the market. Individual buyers come with needs differing in kind and in intensity, while sellers have commodities which are for sale in various quantities, acquired and produced at differing costs, and have been transported over differing distances. The process of bargaining reduces all these varying differences of circumstance, appetite and necessity to the common denominator of a market price. When the market is sufficiently large, transactions are numerous and competition widespread. The addition or subtraction of one participant will make no appreciable difference to prevailing price levels and market prices constitute a record of the terms on which bargains are currently struck. These prices then indicate to new buyers, sellers and producers their most profitable areas of activity, given their own needs and circumstances. In this way, at least ideally, production and services are directed to the satisfaction of the most intense demand, and the maintenance and extension of activities which are unwanted are discouraged.

Implications of the market: expansion, specialization, communication

It is in the interest of both buyers and sellers that the numbers of those in the market should be as large as possible. Buyers will want to face as many sellers as possible in order to keep the price down; sellers will want the greatest possible number of potential buyers in order to keep the prices as high as is consistent with disposing of their stocks. Entry to the market should be as free as possible.

By the same token – and this is really another aspect of the argument for free entry to the market – efficient operation requires the wide dissemination of market information. Sellers will wish to advertise their willingness to sell and buyers will want as much knowledge as possible about the prices at which previous bargains have been concluded.

It also follows that the effectiveness of the market depends on the state of physical transport, both of men and goods.

In ordinary usage a market is usually understood to mean a collection of stalls or shops in a particular place; but it can easily be seen that the application of modern technology gives rise to very large markets indeed. Since the nineteenth century, advances in techniques of communication together with rapid, capacious and cheap systems of transport, have made it possible to speak not only of national markets where toothpaste is sold at similar prices in Maine and in California, but also of international markets where the price of Arabian oil helps determine the level of output and employment throughout the world.

As we have said, the function of the market is to facilitate exchange. In doing so it matches buyers with sellers and enables men to fill wants and dispose of surpluses. But it does more than that. The facilitation of exchange encourages specialization so that a man is no longer obliged, as he is in a poorly articulated society, to provide for many or most of them himself. He can specialize in the production of the good or service which he finds most profitable or congenial, consume some of it if it is of use to him, and dispose of the rest in return for the other goods and services which he requires. It is intuitively obvious that specialization tends to make for greater efficiency. It follows that one of the expected consequences of the spread of market and exchange relations is an increase in production. The hypothetical originators of a market in an economically primitive society would first meet simply to match up their accidental deficits and surpluses. This in itself is a benefit. In addition, the knowledge derived from the experience of the market would enable them to exploit their own personal advantages in knowledge and skill to hunt those animals and raise those crops of which there was a shortage or in the snaring and cultivation of which they were especially skilled. The more extensive the market the greater will be the number of resources, land, material and labour, which will be mobilized.

The size of a market is determined by the volume of goods exchanged and the number of those who participate in it. The immediate limiting factors are the limiting factors of human existence: space, time and the extent of the available resources. The restrictive effect of these factors is further determined by the speed and capacity of the available means of communications and transport. Initially, in a new or primitive community, the efficiency and accessibility of transport will be determined by geography and the climate. Once these have been fully exploited the market will have reached limits which can only be overcome by improvements in communications and productive techniques. But the increase in output which previous expansion has promoted will make it easier to find the resources necessary to make such improvements. The market is inherently dynamic. It may not be very obvious in economically underdeveloped and poor societies, where such change may be very slow and where indeed, external factors in the shape of climatic catastrophes, disease, war, demographic changes and political misfortunes may set the process back or even lead to its extinction. Elsewhere, however, its progress may be dramatic and, at least in Western Europe, its effects have been all-pervasive.

What is true of communications and technology is true of all those other institutions on which market size and efficiency depend. To many nineteenth-century thinkers and theorists the market seemed to be the obvious mode of economic activity and to be 'natural' in the sense that, when men were left to their own devices, they would inevitably fall to bargaining and exchanging and creating markets. In fact, of course, a modern market, even the market of the nineteenth century, is the expression of a very complex social system. It depends, among other things, on stable political institutions able to deploy a police force to guarantee the security of property, on courts of law to enforce property rights and contracts, on a currency the acceptability of which is guaranteed by the State, on the public financing of the maintenance and improvement of communications, and on the public provision of education to maintain and improve the quality of all those engaged in commercial activity.

Implications of the market: selfishness and political conflict

The working of the market also depends on the truth of some psychological assumptions. The mainspring of market expansion is a desire, on the part of individuals, for gain. A man compares the cost to himself of a particular economic activity with the price which the resulting product commands in the market. Implicit in the market schema is the assumption that the wider the difference, the greater the incentive to undertake the enterprise in question. The success of the market depends on there being a sufficiently large number of people for whom the principal aims of their activity can be expressed in terms of price and material advantage. Success in the market only comes from bettering one's competitors. The higher gains of the successful are reflected in the lower profits or losses of the less successful or failures. To win is to defeat. The defence of the market as a device for determining the nature, quantity and distribution of goods and services rests on the assertion that the effect of competition is to maximize the welfare of all those involved by encouraging the most productive use of resources and ensuring their allocation in terms of rewards for productive effort. The motives for participation and the calculations made in the course of participation, ought, for the proper operation of the system, to be entirely selfish.

The existence of a market has obvious legal implications. As we have seen, among the preconditions of a market are freedom of movement and choice of economic activity and these in turn imply the absence not only of physical constraints but also of personal legal disabilities. In fact, legally, a market is a set of personal rights and, from the same viewpoint, the size of a market is constrained by the extent and distribution of these rights among people. The development of the market in a society where productive activity has hitherto been carried on on some other basis will involve the enlargement of existing civil rights and their extension to classes of people which have not enjoyed them before. In societies not yet fully commercialized, where some occupations are reserved on religious, social, racial or simply political grounds, or where economic obligations and relationships are not chosen but inherited the introduction or expansion of a commercial system is likely to generate social conflict and almost certainly to excite political struggle.

The indeterminacy of market outcomes

The converse is also true; attempts may be made to roll back the market, with similar consequences. Even in the best of cases no market is perfect; nobody has perfect knowledge of the market situation and neither labour nor commodities are perfectly mobile, not always readily substitutable one for another. Such imperfections handicap some and bestow 'unfair' advantages on others. Moreover, the justice of the perfectly operating market is less than self-evident. Ideally rewards are determined by the values evolved in a fully competitive market. Returns are proportionate to contributions in the economic process. But egalitarian notions of justice usually abstract from differences in skill, physical strength, accumulated or inherited wealth and so on – and yet these things are of crucial importance to success in market competition. If a buyer is in a position to demand very large quantities relative to his competitors then he may have a disproportionate effect on the market.

Similarly a monopolistic seller can sell at prices above those which would prevail if there were more competition. Both success and failure are self-reinforcing. The equality of the market is the equality not of individuals but of individual units of account – one dollar, one vote, as it were. The differences in wealth and income generated by market competition are usually justified as incentives to efficiency, rewards available to all market competitors. As long as these differentials are relatively small and can reasonably be held to be playing a part in increasing output and promoting rational allocation they will not excite much attention; but when disparities are extreme, and when, as a result of the working of the market, whole sets of occupations become suddenly redundant or entire regions are blighted by economic decline, the political result may well take the form of attempts to limit the operation of commercial forces.

This indeterminacy in the effects of commercialization is everywhere demonstrable in European history. Consider for example, the vicissitudes of servile labour. At the beginning of the millenium a relatively stable system of social and economic organization had been established after the barbarian invasions and migrations had destroyed the political structure and disrupted or eroded many of the economic and social formations characteristic of the Roman Empire. In simplified terms this was an arrangement whereby land, together with the labourers who tilled it, was distributed to subordinates in return for an obligation to military service (sometimes called the 'feudal' system). In this system economic relationships were indistinguishable from judicial and political relationships. Its foundation was the obligation of the unfree labourer, serf or villein, to spend a portion of his time working the land for the feudal lord and only the remainder in raising crops for the support of himself and his family. In this way the surplus productive power of the villein was secured directly, without the intervention of the market, its appropriation sanctioned by law and assured, where necessary, by force. In short, it was not a society of the kind implied by the description of the market given above. However, throughout the Middle Ages, although initially at a low level and limited in geographical extent, exchange and commerce persisted. With increased political stability commercial relations were extended. The growth in towns, the development of non-agricultural production and the slowly increasing vigour of inter-regional trade all testify to the widening of markets in this period. Relations between landlord and serf became increasingly monetized. But the effect of the opportunities for commercial agriculture was to lead the landlords to try to strengthen the legal ties and obligations which bound the serf to the soil and assured them of a supply of labour for the working of their estates. By the beginning of the fourteenth century, however, even before the impact of the bubonic plague hastened the process, the serf was beginning to shuffle-off the various disabilities which prevented him from acquiring and alienating land, which hindered the free disposition of his children in marriage, which hampered his mobility and which hindered his productive choices – which, in a word, prevented him from exploiting the benefits with which participation in the market would provide him. In Eastern Europe, on the other hand, across the Elbe, the growth of the international grain markets led directly to the multiplication of labour dues. This reinforcement of servile status could be seen in Russia as late as the period immediately before the Emancipation of the Serfs in 1861. Commercialization was not an irreversible process.

Nor was the speed and intensity of commercialization uniform. For example, the geographical location of Flanders and the density of its population enabled it to specialize in the manufacture of cloth in the Middle Ages to such an extent that, by the thirteenth century, it had developed an urban proletariat, its supply of raw materials and the sale of its product depended on the existence of long-range commercial links, and the organization of its labour and the management of its enterprises were of a kind which, although their scale must not be exaggerated, are normally associated with the industrialization of later centuries. Again, and even more spectacularly, the commercial revolution in Northern Italy, well established in Venice and Genoa by the twelfth century, flowered vigorously in the thirteenth century, anticipating, before the Middle Ages were over, much of what we customarily think of as achievements of the modern age. It freed the peasants; it fostered the secularization of society, promoting individualism in politics and religion: it created a new class of the rich; it brought forth a new literature and a new art; it established the study of science and law; and it discovered the principles which underly some of the most important techniques of modern trade and finance. And yet elsewhere in Western and Eastern Europe some sections of agriculture were not to be permeated by market relations for hundreds of years, while others were to be affected only feebly.

The market and the Industrial Revolution

Nonetheless it remains true, whatever the internal logic or explanation of the development, that in anything longer than a short view of its history the envelopment of European society by a thickening tissue of monetary and market relationships is a steady and progressive process. Nowhere is an account of social and political change in terms of the penetration of, and adaptation to, the market more persuasive than in the case of the United Kingdom. The explanation for the commercial transformation of England comprises many factors. To all economic intents and purposes villeinage had disappeared by the end of the fifteenth century. By the sixteenth century, England was politically unified and there were no internal customs barriers. England was the largest single market in Europe. London grew and by providing a great market for food constituted a powerful national economic stimulus.

English internal communications were excellent by the standards of the day and nobody in England lives more than seventy miles from the sea. A temperate climate and long growing season contributed to English economic precocity; in the seventeenth century it was possible to claim that England was the most prosperous country in the world. As has been stressed already, the process by which England grew rich was a slow one. There were no sudden changes in attitudes or techniques. Industry and trade advanced without any striking inventions. In spite of the political upheavals of the seventeenth century, English society of the eighteenth century was still clearly related to English society of the sixteenth century. Market penetration seems to have been slow, steady and inexorable.

In the latter part of the eighteenth century this gradual development was quite suddenly accelerated. Industrial output started to grow more rapidly. More than 75 per cent of the increase in the trade in textiles in the United Kingdom, for example, was concentrated in the last two decades of the eighteenth century. In the same period the country saw more than half the century's growth in the shipment of coal and the mining of copper. The immediate causes of these changes were the more extensive application of old techniques and the rapid development of new ones, at first in textiles and soon right across the whole range of industry. This sudden and maintained improvement in industrial output transformed the United Kingdom. And indeed, not only the United Kingdom but the whole world. The political structure of England was radically altered, the nature of its relations with the rest of the world was changed, the European social order was revolutionized and the path set for the Europeanization of the world's civilizations. By 1850 the United Kingdom was a model for the world, culturally, politically and economically.

Apart from a rise in output the two most striking visible manifestations of this change into economic top gear were the large buildings and concentrations of plant which constituted the factory system, and its corollary, the rapid growth of large towns which housed a new sociological phenomenon – the industrial proletariat. To meet the demand which helped to create, and which was in turn created by, the increased productive powers of industry, it was necessary to exploit many of the new processes on a large scale. By means of wheels and bellows one steam engine was able to drive a large number of machines standing under one roof. Old processes could be carried out more quickly and extensively and it became profitable and technically feasible to increase the size of machinery. In order to exploit these advances it was necessary to assemble large numbers of workers, and discipline them for factory routines. Because the new equipment depended, for its effective use, on being concentrated, the new workers, recruited from the countryside, were uprooted from their old environment, cut off from the patterns of rural life and labour, made wholly dependent on a wage and turned into town-dwellers.

Described in this way the Industrial Revolution appears as an economic social and demographic discontinuity. And there is no doubt that such a description is useful for some purposes – especially the sociological – even if it overstates the abruptness of changes which took more than a generation to develop fully in the United Kingdom. The problems created by the emergence of a large wage-earning, industrially dependent class, and by urbanization on that scale and at that speed, were unprecedented and have formed the stuff of English politics from that day to this.

However, it was only with hindsight that the economic development of the United Kingdom was seen as a 'revolution'. As a term, 'Industrial Revolution' was current in France in the 1830s and Marx frequently refers to the 'revolutionizing' of production by the introduction of machinery. But this was fifty years after the onset of the jump in English industrial output and the changes in the economy which accompanied it, although more rapid, were no different in kind from those which had accompanied the introduction of a monetized exchange economy from the beginning, nor were they thought of as such by contemporaries. Urbanization, capital accumulation and technological innovation were all phenomena as old as money itself.

It is true that the great surge of industrialization from the end of the eighteenth century onwards worked such immense changes in society that our historical vocabulary would be severely impoverished if we denied ourselves a phrase with which to label it. It is also true that, in one sense, the 'causes' of the Industrial Revolution remain to some extent mysterious. It appears to be the case that at some moment or over some particular time-span the relationship between food-supply, financial institutions, the rate of population growth, international trading opportunities, civil order, education and technical knowledge resolved themselves in such a way that the economic mass 'went critical' and began spontaneously to regenerate itself more rapidly.

At the same time few economic historians doubt that the factors making for this sudden growth were mediated through the market and that it was the pressure of demand which forced suppliers to break through existing bottle-necks in productive techniques, and richly rewarded entrepreneurial skill, skill which involved the mobilization and diffusion of existing techniques as well as the invention of new ones. The Industrial Revolution was the natural child of the interplay of supply and demand – the offspring of the market.

Chapter 2

Marx's 'capitalism'

The history of economic thought has been a series of attempts to comprehend theoretically the phenomena of the market, and we have seen how the development of the modern world of cash-relationships, with its great technological achievements and its transformation of rural societies into populations of town-dwellers, can be plausibly explained in terms of the market. Marx, however, was not satisfied with this interpretation. He set out to account for his contemporaneous world as the outcome of 'capitalism'. This chapter is intended to demonstrate that there are certain difficulties inherent in his view of capitalism, and that these are connected with a fundamental dualism in his work. Marx could not adopt the view that the market as an institution could explain anything, since it was part of his basic attitude that market phenomena are only the superficial manifestations of deeper forces at work in the world. At the same time his own 'capitalism' looks very much like the market in disguise.[1]

Marx and the market

At first sight Marx's view on the nature of economic development and the means by which it is brought about appear to be very similar to those outlined in Chapter 1 above. There are famous passages in which it is the market which is adduced to explain the great economic and social changes of the nineteenth century. The Middle Ages were brought to an end by the expansion of commerce: 'The East-Indian and Chinese markets, the colonization of America, the trade with the colonies, the increase in the means of exchange and in commodities generally gave an unprecedented impetus to commerce, shipping and industry. This in turn entailed the rapid growth of the revolutionary element in the tottering social structure of feudalism.'[2] This extension of markets led, in turn, to the development of industry which has finally unified the world in a universal web of commercial relationships. 'Meantime the markets kept ever growing, the demand ever rising. Even manufacture no longer sufficed. Thereupon, steam and machinery revolutionized industrial production. . . . Modern industry has established the world market.'[3]

For Marx 'capitalism' was not simply an alteration in the productive techniques of 'feudalism'; it also entailed the appearance of a new class, the 'bourgeoisie'. Marx's description of this new ruling class emphasises that they are men who recognise no social relationships except those which are expressible in cash and whose whole understanding of the world is dominated by the market and all of whose actions are directed to the realization of commercial aims:

> *The bourgeoisie, wherever it has got the upper hand, has put an end to all feudal, patriarchal, idyllic relations. It has pitilessly torn asunder the motley feudal ties that bound man to his 'natural superiors', and has left remaining no other nexus between man and man than naked self interest, than callous 'cash-payment'. It has drowned the most heavenly ecstasies of religious fervour, of chivalrous enthusiasm, of philistine sentimentalism, in the icy water of egotistical calculation. It has resolved personal worth into exchange value and in place of the numberless chartered freedoms acquired by due process has set up that single, unconscionable freedom – Free Trade. In one word, for exploitation, veiled by religious and political illusions, it has substituted naked, shameless, direct, brutal exploitation.*
>
> *The bourgeoisie has stripped of its halo every occupation hitherto honoured and looked up to with reverent awe. It has converted the physician, the lawyer, the priest, the poet, the man of science, into its paid wage-labourers.*
>
> *The bourgeoisie . . . has reduced the family relation to a mere money relation . . .*[4]

Marx and 'Capitalism'

But the striking aspect of Marx's economic theory is that it professes to be concerned directly with neither commercialism nor yet the Industrial Revolution. What makes the modern period what it is is neither its technological achievements nor yet the transmutation of social relations by the cash nexus. Marx's economic theory is devoted to the explanation of the rise and mode of operation of 'capitalism'. It should be stressed that capitalism is, for Marx, not *industrialization* because the word is often loosely used by both Marxists and non-Marxists to mean just that. Capitalism, according to Marx, is a phenomenon which appears in England in the middle of the sixteenth century, quite independently of the steam-engine and the mechanical innovations of the late eighteenth century.

Marx, in common with many social theorists of his day, conceived of social history as proceeding by stages. The modern capitalist or bourgeois stage was immediately preceded by 'feudalism'. He and his contemporaries thought of this as a rigid version of the social system sketched on pages 7 and 8 above. In it the agricultural labourer is attached to the soil 'the slave, serf, or bondman of another'.[5] Non-agricultural productive activities are carried on in an institutional framework which is less than free – 'the regime of the guilds [with] their rules for apprentices and journeyman, and the impediments of their labour regulations'.[6]

Marx never provides an extended discussion of the nature of feudalism but its chief characteristics, apart from its institutional arrangements, might be summarized as the absence or poverty of commodity markets, the absence of a developed market for labour, and a relatively poorly differentiated population in terms of the distribution of wealth.

About Marx's 'capitalism' it is possible to be more exact. It appears about 1550.[7] It is not clear whether feudalism is replaced by it gradually or suddenly – a point taken up again below – but it is clear that the one results in the other: 'The economic structure of capitalist society has grown out of the economic structure of feudal society. The dissolution of the latter set free the elements of the former.'[8] The transition from the one to the other 'can only take place under certain circumstances that centre in this, *viz*, that two very different kinds of commodity possessors must come face to face and in contact; on the one hand, the owners of money . . . on the other hand, free labourers'.[9] The commodities possessed by the owners of money are capital, the means of production; the 'commodity' possessed by the free workers is their own labour. It is a further condition that these free labourers should be very poor and, in particular that they should be unencumbered by any means of production of their own.[10] Moreover, capitalism can only begin when the individual entrepreneur 'employs simultaneously a comparatively large number of labourers; when consequently the labour-process is carried on on an extensive scale and yields, relatively, large quantities of products'.[11]

The conditions for the existence of Marx's capitalism may thus be stated as follows:

(a) a market in commodities and land;
(b) a poor but free labouring population;
(c) a number of men who have accumulated wealth in the form of raw materials, buildings and tools – the means of production;
(d) a market in labour;
(e) the use of productive techniques depending on the physical proximity of large numbers of workers.

Commercialization and the transition to capitalism

Marx's definition of capitalism is examined again below (pp. 18–20), but at this point it is the problem of the way in which capitalism, according to Marx, makes its appearance which needs attention.

What is the nature of the mechanism which transforms feudalism into capitalism? In the passages from the *Communist Manifesto* quoted above Marx offers a simple and persuasive explanation; feudalism is dissolved in an acid bath of commercial relations. But elsewhere Marx insists that this account of the emergence of capital is inadequate.

Marx admits that even in economic formations before capitalism trade is carried on and that money is employed in this activity. This money Marx identifies as a separate economic category which he calls 'merchant's capital' and to which he ascribes an important place in capitalism itself. He declares that merchant's capital is 'older than the capitalist mode of production, is, in fact, historically the oldest free state of existence of capital'.[12] As such, one would have expected trade to be the obvious candidate for consideration as the seminal origin of capitalism but Marx is categorical about its inadmissibility. 'Its function', we are told, 'consists exclusively of promoting the exchange of commodities', and unlike capitalism 'it requires no other conditions for its existence . . . outside those necessary for the simple circulation of commodities and money',[13] while . . . 'its development . . . is incapable by itself of promoting and explaining the transition from one mode of production to another'.[14] The money employed in trade, and its turnover, are quite distinct from the producers who trade with each other; (it) represents the separation of the circulation process from its extremes, and these extremes are the exchanging producers themselves. They remain independent of the circulation process just as the latter remains independent of them.'[15] So much is this the case that 'the independent development of merchant's capital . . . stands in inverse proportion to the general economic development of society'.[16]

At the same time and in the same chapter, and on the same pages, Marx says a number of things which are difficult to reconcile with these assertions. The existence of the market *does* affect the producers: 'commerce imparts to production a character directed more and more towards exchange-value'.[17] It does play an important part in the transition to capitalism: 'its existence and development to a certain level are in themselves historical premises for the development of capitalist production';[18] 'commerce will have more or less of a counter-effect on the communities between which it is carried on';[19] 'Commerce . . . has a more or less dissolving influence everywhere on the producing organization . . . in the modern world, it results in the capitalist mode of production';[20] 'the sudden expansion of the world market, the multiplication of circulating commodities, the competitive zeal of the European nations to possess themselves of the products of Asia and the treasures of America, and the colonial system – all contributed materially toward destroying the feudal fetters on production'.[21]

Marx tries to reconcile this contradiction. The extent to which commerce transforms society, he writes, 'depends on its solidity and internal structure. And the direction taken by this process of dissolution, i.e. what new mode of production replaces the old one, depends not on trade but on the character of the old mode of production itself'.[22] Marx was too good an economic historian not to know that commercialization varies in its effects on different societies. (See pages 5–7 on indeterminacy of market outcomes.) As he writes,

In the ancient world the effect of trade and merchant's capital always resulted in a slave economy. Because of the basis from which it started it simply changed a patriarchal system of slavery devoted to the production of the means of subsistence into a patriarchal system of slavery, devoted to the production of surplus value. In the modern world, however, it results in the capitalist mode of production. It follows from this that these results themselves were determined by factors other than the development of merchant's capital.[23]

But this is only to describe things in terms of themselves. Marx is attempting to explain the origins of European society, but what he actually does is only to suggest that the ancient world was different from the modern world; different in a way not exactly specified but which prevented it from producing the capitalist mode of production. However, it is precisely why this was so which needs to be explained.

At the end of Chapter xx of volume III of *Capital*, Marx describes the transition to capitalism as being secured essentially when the merchant becomes a producer as well as a trader or, alternatively, the small producer 'himself becomes merchant and produces directly for the wholesale market'.[24] Eventually 'commerce becomes the servant of industrial production'[25] and Marx concludes by declaring that 'The real science of modern economy only begins when the theoretical analysis passes from the process of circulation to the process of production.'[26] But to say that 'capitalism' appears when production is somehow more important than distribution (whatever that may mean) is not to tell us why this transition takes place.

It is difficult to deduce an entirely coherent account of the part played by commercialization in the transition to 'capitalism' from Chapter xx of volume III of *Capital*. What does seem to be clear is that Marx wanted to say that commercialization could not be the only explanation of the development of modern civilization and yet could not identify any other coherent cause. Unable to deny the importance of trade as the initiator and developer of the nineteenth-century world he was therefore inclined to try to minimize its role as a causal factor in the emergence of the 'bourgeois mode of production'.

The accumulation of capital

Part of Marx's purpose in denigrating commercialization and the development of markets as the vehicle of historical change was to strengthen his assertion that the transition from stage to stage in the history of civilization is a shock, a developmental jump, or revolution. Marx maintained that the accumulation of the resources necessary for the large-scale productive enterprises of capitalism was something carried out suddenly and with violence. This 'primitive accumulation', Marx thought, was the disruption which marked the transition from feudalism to capitalism.

Before turning to Marx's own statements let us first examine the connexion between market relations and capital accumulation. There is, of course, something intuitively appealing in the idea of prior accumulation. *Before* the textile mills can begin to operate the buildings have to be erected and the machinery manufactured and installed. *Before* a man can launch out into business he must have saved some money – or else he must borrow someone else's savings. The industrial enterprise presents itself as an undertaking in which men are employed in the operation of plant which represents the embodiment of great, and previously accumulated, quantities of wealth. Where does the money come from which finances the outlays necessary before production can begin?

In the context of a market economy, however, further reflection will show that the problem is only apparent. It is not the case that, say, weaving is industrialized because a number of thrifty outworkers toiling away in their cottages gradually accumulate gold under their beds and then at some concerted moment, go out and buy a factory. If savings are thought of not as a hoard, or a stock, in the hands of one particular person or set of people, but as a *flow* of resources within the economy as a whole, the situation becomes plainer. Savings are simply what is not consumed out of what is produced. The most important form of commercial saving both before, and until the Industrial Revolution was well under way arose from the profits of the activities of the firm itself. Part of the income of an enterprise would be used to pay for accommodation, for raw materials, and for labour some would be distributed to the owners of the firm, and some would be ploughed back to buy more materials, labour, and so on in order to expand the firm's activities. In this way the firm saved to finance itself. It can be seen that, although in some accounting sense the savings of one year go to finance the activities of the next, in fact there is a continual flow of money and resources from the proceeds of commercial and productive activity into the means of sustaining and financing the activity itself. The flow of investment, the purchase of the means of production, depends on the flow of resources not consumed. The vast capital outlays of a great firm are to be explained in terms of the simultaneously saved resources within the firm and the economy as a whole. The ability of a firm to invest and expand depends on its income and its consequent credit-worthiness, not on how many tons of steel and cement it has been able to save over the years.

Of course, all action involving the mobilization of resources requires the prior existence of those resources and the prior existence of someone to mobilize them but, in the context of large streams of material, this is a trivial point. It is also true, of course, that there is an historical element in accumulation. Present wealth and productivity are themselves the product of the operation in the past of a particular set of property rights and of productive activity, but, within a market economy taken as a whole, they are an unalterable given; the future is determined by what is done now, not by what was done yesterday.

The part played by capital in economic growth is one which constitutes a very important problem both for economic historians and for economic theorists. Historiographically attention has been concentrated on the connexion between the Industrial Revolution and capital formation in the eighteenth century. Theoretically, writers have argued, as Marx did, that the accumulation of capital is a vital step in an increase in production; it has also been argued that it is not the quantity but the quality, of capital that is important – that is to say, whether or not it embodies improved productive techniques (a point on which Marx's own view is ambiguous; see Chapter 13). The evidence available for the eighteenth century is not very satisfactory but it can be said that improvements in the size and productivity of capital were the result rather than the cause of growth, and the extent of the resources diverted from consumption to investment do not appear to have been very large. From this point of view the part played by capital accumulation in the origins of the Industrial Revolution is a spontaneous outcome of the development of the market, not the effect of factors external to the commercial process.

This, as will already be clear, Marx wished to deny. His description of capital accumulation – the concentration of the means of production in the hands of a group of rich men, condition (c) for capitalism on page 12 above – falls into two parts. The first is concerned with the wresting of property in land from peasants and the second with the sequestration of resources overseas. In his description of both processes the importance of commercial institutions is minimized. In both developments 'it is notorious that conquest enslavement, robbery, murder, briefly force, play the great part'.[27]

For Marx, it is the existence of 'free labourers in the double sense that neither they themselves form part and parcel of the means of production, as in the case of slaves bondsmen etc., nor do the means of production belong to them, as in the case of peasant-proprietors',[28] that is a precondition for capitalism. Marx insists that this impoverishment and their need to work for wages is not the result of ordinary market forces. According to Marx, in the fourteenth and fifteenth centuries in England 'the immense majority of the population consisted . . . of free peasant proprietors'. As such they still enjoyed economic advantages which the feudal system provided; 'they . . . enjoyed the usufruct of the common land, which gave pasture to their capital, furnished them with timber, fire-wood, turf, etc.'[29] The transformation of this happy state of affairs was the result, in part, of the increasing strength of the centralized monarchy which broke up the 'bands of feudal retainers', in consequence of which 'a mass of free proletarians was hurled on the labour-market'.[30] But the principal cause lay in the way in which the landlords then 'created an incomparably larger proletariat by the forcible driving of the peasantry from the land'.[31] Arable land was transformed into sheep-grazing and the peasants evicted in various underhand ways. The expropriation of Church property at the Reformation gave a 'new and frightful impulse' to 'the process of forcible expropriation',[32] of the former Church tenants. This process was carried on in the fifteenth and sixteenth centuries 'by means of individual acts of violence against which legislation, for a hundred and fifty years, fought in vain' and the enclosure Acts of the eighteenth century shows that even 'the law itself becomes now the instrument of theft of the people's land'.[33] 'The English working class was precipitated without any transition from its golden into its iron age'.[34]

The acquisition of capital is also a violent process in other ways;

The discovery of gold and silver in America, the extirpation, enslavement and entombment in mines of the aboriginal population, the beginning of the conquest and looting of the East Indies, the turning of Africa into a warren for the commercial hunting of black-skins signalised the rosy dawn of the era of capitalist production. These idyllic proceedings are the chief momenta of primitive accumulation. On their heels treads the commercial war of the European nations with the globe for a theatre. It begins with the revolt of the anti-Jacobin War, and is still going on in the opium wars against China etc.

The different moments of primitive accumulation distribute themselves now, more or less in chronological order, particularly over Spain, Portugal, Holland, France and England. In England at the end of the seventeenth century, they arrive at a systematical combination, embracing the colonies, the national debt, the modern mode of taxation, and the protectionist system. These methods depend in part on brute force, e.g. the colonial system. But they all employ the power of the State, the concentrated and organized force of society, to hasten, hothouse fashion, the process of transformation of the feudal node of production into the capitalist mode and to shorten the transition. Force is the midwife of every old society pregnant with a new one. It is itself an economic power.[35]

'Capital' Marx goes on to declare, 'comes [into the world] dripping from head to foot, from every pore, with blood and dirt'.[36]

Marx, then, is at pains to stress that the accumulation of capital is brought about by factors external to the continuous flows and adjustment of market changes. But to adduce force, as Marx does, as an 'economic power' is only to play with words. Indeed, it is evident, even from the passages cited, that Marx was less than certain that the change he discusses was as sudden as much of the language he uses implies. The expropriation of the peasants is a process lasting, according to Marx, for at least 150 years, while the process of the colonization of the world by Europeans had lasted, as Marx knew, for centuries. Thus even in his description of capital accumulation, where Marx is at his most lurid and graphic, he is haunted by the consciousness that single acts of sudden violence are not enough to account for the phenomena he is attempting to explain and that the transition he wants to present as a discontinuity can more readily be seen as, at best, a long process of attrition, in which market calculations play a vital role.

'Capitalism' and the conceptual tension in Marx

Marx's 'capitalism', at least as he describes it and as rendered on page 12 above, is even on his own showing, a difficult concept. If there is (a), a market in commodities and land, then the operation of the market may well produce an uneven distribution of wealth. Markets are competitive, winning consists of getting more out of the commercial process that one's rivals. That markets do work in this way is empirically observable; if a customary society is commercialized, considerable economic differentiation may be expected. Many people will then be poor, as in (b). This would account for the existence of propertyless labourers after the gradual dissolution of 'feudal' tenures. The weakness of peasants against enclosing gentry was an economic as well as a political disability. The propertyless of one section of society implies the existence of another group who are not propertyless, as in (c); there must be winners if there are losers. That labourers work for a wage follows from their propertylessness and accounts for the existence of the labour market, (d). Simple market rationality would explain the division of labour and the organization of workers in groups as in (e). What Marx calls 'capitalism' is simply inherent in or, at least, a very probable outcome of the extension of commercial relations.

In the first chapter of this book a simplified account of the economic history of the modern world is set out which stresses that even the very great changes which typified Western European economic development in the eighteenth and nineteenth centuries can be represented as a quickening of the pace of development rather than a qualitative 'revolution'. This is a view which is widely but not universally accepted. Some Marxist writers, certainly, would say that this was incorrect. While I find the interpretation of the 'Industrial Revolution' which sees it as a continuum more persuasive that that which seeks to show that there is some kind of economically disruptive break, it is not necessary for my argument to be dogmatic about the claims of either; the point to be made is that the text of Marx's writings contains the elements of both. Marx insisted that the agent of change was 'capitalism', a discrete social system which owed its existence to factors external to the market and which makes its appearance suddenly and violently. On the other hand, much of what he writes seems to suggest that he found the most convincing vehicle of social and political change, in spite of his vehement assertions to the contrary, in the market.

The uneasy coexistence of these two points of view in Marx's book both needs explanation and is in itself significant for the understanding of his work as a whole. The explanation is to be found in the fact that Marx's thinking about purely political thinking was shaped, like that of his contemporaries, by the momentous upheavals in France which, from 1789 onwards, transformed the political structure both of that country and of Europe. Marx's basic assumption was that social development proceeded by discontinuities of which the French Revolution and the English Civil War of the seventeenth century were characteristic. The social inequities and abuses which he saw in the nineteenth century could only be alleviated, he thought, by a political upheaval, by a revolution. Marx did not take up his economic studies, as we shall see later, simply to learn a new analytical technique; he did so to find support for ideas which he had already developed about the nature of social change. Before Marx began any rigorous formulation of his ideas about economic development, he was certain that industrialization, as exemplified in England, was evil and the generator of social unrest which would result in the overthrow of the existing political system.

If, as seems to be the case from what we know of his intellectual biography, Marx came to economics looking for the theoretical basis of an already formulated social and political prognosis, his dilemma is easy to understand. The only economic theories available to him were deeply rooted in market assumptions. The analysis which he derived from these theories tended to suggest that social development is a continuous process which proceeds by continuous adjustments of the kind which typify market operations. At the same time Marx felt that the Industrial Revolution was not only historically unprecedented but, as such, required some new and special explanation different from that advanced to account for earlier events in history. In his search for this explanation Marx realized that he could not attribute it to the development of trade alone. Trade would not provide him with a mechanism which would produce predictable and irreversible outcomes. Commercialization as a rough reductionist account of modern economic development may be helpful as a descriptive generalization; Marx knew that it would not provide him with the theoretical precision which he sought. As he knew for example, and as we have noted, an intensification of cash relationships in a society can give rise to the forcing of labour in various forms of slavery as well as to the liberal ideal of the politically emancipated individual. If trade and monetary exchange were the sole vehicle of social transformation then they explained not too little but too much.

Marx sought, then for particular and socially distinct institutional preconditions for the rise of capitalism. In doing so he read back into English history the two great social novelties of the nineteenth century: an impoverished, industrial and wage-dependent working class on the one hand, and the mass organization of workers in the factory system on the other. His description of 'capitalism' as a social system which precedes the Industrial Revolution and which dates from the sixteenth century with its wage labourers, its factory owners, and its poverty is simply the Industrial Revolution without the steam-engine. 'Capitalism' remains a description; it is no more powerful as an explanatory device than is 'commercialization'. Economic theory suggested to Marx that change was continuous, political events that it was discontinuous. When he discusses the more purely economic data deployed in support of his theses he tends to rely on explanations of continuity derived from the market. When he turns to exclusively political phenomena, although he asserts that they are dependent on economic change for their dynamism, he is inclined to revert to explanations in terms of force and revolution.

This dualism runs right through Marx's work, is difficult to resolve and easily gives rise to confusion. Its significance lies in the fact that this difficulty does not arise from mere chance but is related to Marx's philosophical approach to social problems the special nature of which will emerge in the course of the following chapters.

References and Notes

1. In fact Marx never used the expression 'capitalism' but referred to the 'capitalist' or 'bourgeois mode of production'; the use of the shorter term 'capitalism', however, does no violence to his notion.
2. Karl Marx and Frederick Engels, 'Manifesto of the Communist Party' in *Selected Works* (Moscow 1958), vol. I, p. 35; Marx and Engels, *Werke* [*MEW*] (Berlin 1956–73) vol. IV, p. 463.
3. Ibid., vol. I, p. 35; *MEW*, vol. IV, p. 463.
4. Ibid., vol. I, pp. 36–7; *MEW*, vol. IV, pp. 464–5.
5. *Capital*, vol. I, Ch. xxvi, p. 715.
6. Ibid.
7. Ibid., vol. I, Ch. xiv, p. 336.
8. Ibid., vol. I, Ch. xxvi, p. 715.
9. Ibid., vol. I, Ch. xxvi, p. 714.
10. Ibid.
11. Ibid., vol. I, Ch. xiii, p. 322.
12. Ibid., vol. III, Ch. xx, p. 325.
13. Ibid.
14. Ibid., vol. III, Ch. xx, p. 327.
15. Ibid., vol. III, Ch. xx, p. 328.
16. Ibid.
17. Ibid., vol. III, Ch. xx, p. 326.
18. Ibid., vol. III, Ch. xx, p. 327.
19. Ibid., vol. III, Ch. xx, pp. 331–2.

20. Ibid., vol. III, Ch. xx, pp. 332–3; *MEW* vol. 25, p. 344.
21. Ibid.
22. Ibid., vol. III, Ch. xx, p. 332.
23. Ibid., *MEW,* vol. 25, p. 344.
24. Ibid., vol. III, Ch. xx, p. 335.
25. Ibid., vol. III, Ch. xx, p. 336.
26. Ibid., vol. III, Ch. xx, p. 337.
27. Ibid., vol. I, Ch. xxvi, p. 714.
28. Ibid., vol. I, Ch. xxvii, p. 717.
29. Ibid.
30. Ibid.
31. Ibid., vol. I, Ch. xxvii, p. 718.
32. Ibid.
33. Ibid., vol. I, Ch. xxvii, p. 721.
34. Ibid., vol. I, Ch. xxvii, p. 728.
35. Ibid., vol. I, Ch. xxvii, p. 719.
36. Ibid., vol. I, Ch. xxxi, p. 751.
37. Ibid., vol. I, Ch. xxxi, p. 760.

Chapter 3

Political economy: Adam Smith

Marx was not an economist; the first volume of *Capital* was published in 1867 but 'economics' as an academic discipline in the modern sense does not make its appearance until nearly the end of the nineteenth century. Until then, and for a hundred years before the publication of *Capital*, what is now called 'economics' had been comprehended within a much broader set of concepts commonly referred to as 'political economy'. As the expression indicated, 'political economists' were concerned with the connexion between economic processes and the political and social institutions within which these processes were carried on. By contrast, a modern 'economist' has a much more narrowly defined view of his field of study. He is concerned only with the rigorous analysis of the production and distribution of goods and services. The data with which he works are mainly statistical and some would even hold that the contemporary economist is really a particular kind of mathematician. He has little interest in the environment of economic activity; the study of the social and political matrix within which economic activity is contained is the province of other social studies, especially sociology and political science.

But the political economist was not familiar with the distinctions we now make between the various branches of the social sciences. For him, economic processes were deeply embedded in, and took their meaning from, the social systems which they sustained; social, political and economic relationships were thought to be more or less indistinguishable. As John Stuart Mill wrote in 1848,

In so far as the economical condition of nations turns upon the state of physical knowledge, it is a subject for the physical sciences, and the arts founded on them. But in so far as the causes are moral or psychological, dependent on institutions and social relations, or on the principles of human nature, their investigation belongs not to the physical, but to moral and social science, and in the object of what is called Political Economy.[1]

Political economy was not a social science, it was *the* social science.

The political economists are sometimes treated in histories of economic thought as if they represented nothing more than the earliest and clumsy efforts of men groping their way toward, but falling far short of, modern economic methods. But political economy was more than a hodge-podge of poorly articulated ideas about economic and social development; men like Adam Smith, David Ricardo, John Stuart Mill and Karl Marx shared assumptions, concepts and theories in such a way as to make it possible to speak of political economy as a discrete and historically defined school of social theory. It is true that like all theories, the ideas of the political economists had their originas in the work of earlier writers. None of their seventeenth- and eighteenth-century predecessors, however, had such a comprehensive or clearly articulated account of social development to offer. Adam Smith's *The Wealth of Nations* marks a new departure in the history of social thought. At the same time political economy is distinguished from subsequent work in 'economics' not only by virtue of the broader range and purpose of political economy but also by a number of analytical differences which, especially in the case of their views of the fundamental economic problem, the nature of value, constitute a theoretical discontinuity.[2]

The first step to understanding Marx lies in realizing that he wrote *Capital* within an intellectual framework quite distinct from modern economics. He intended it to be the consummation and transformation of the theories of the British political economists. Marx's understanding of the structure of society, the dynamism of his theory of revolutionary change and the content of his theory of exploitation are all derived directly or indirectly from the work of the political economists. Without them his understanding of the world would have been different, the analytical power of his ideas would have been greatly weakened and the most distinctive characteristics of his ideas, the labour theory of value and the vision of capitalist society as an organism in decline, would have been absent; Marxism is a version of political economy.

The origins of political economy: Locke, Montesquieu and Quesnay

What then were the origins of political economy? Political economy was the product of a brilliant set of savants, the Scottish Historical School, whose ideas constitute the most formidable achievement of the eighteenth-century enlightenment. The members of the group, of whom Adam Smith himself is the best known, shared a belief that a principle, or set of principles, which would explain and make coherent the apparently diverse and unconnected activities of man in society, which would provide, in short, a theory of social change, was to be found through the study of history. The scientific revolution of the seventeenth century had unleashed a passion for the collection and ordering of data about the physical world. Smith and his friends could look back upon a hundred years of endeavour which, in the work of Newton, Locke, Montesquieu, Linnaeus, the Physiocrats[3] and others, had produced great advances in philosophy and scientific method, in physics and botany, in political thought and jurisprudence, in technology and in economics, but which had produced no synthesis subsuming these achievements into a general account of human progress. It was this lacuna which the Scots hoped to fill. They attempted to apply science to the study of the human community itself and provide a theoretical account of the rise of modern civilization.

The reasons for this historical interest are to be found in history itself. The 200 years from the middle of the sixteenth century had wrought great changes in society. Commercialization had transformed political institutions and social structures. The growth of overseas trade brought Europeans into contact with civilizations different from their own. These changes prompted responses in the form of fresh political assumptions and theories, and new sociological and economic insights. It was these intellectual ephiphenomena of commercial society that provided the Scottish Historical School with the raw material for its theoretical endeavours – and it was the rise of commercial society which they strove to explain.

The commercialization of Europe had been accompanied by the appearance of political ideas and theories which were man-centred rather than God-centred. The mediaeval Church had taught that salvation was the fruit of incorporation into the community of saints rather than the result of personal endeavour. A model for secular, political and social stability had been sought in the idea of a City of God, a community created, sustained, differentiated and ruled by the Almighty. Machiavelli and other Renaissance thinkers began the secularization of politics. The Prince replaces the Divinity as the central figure in the political schema. The sovereign no longer seeks explicity to execute the Will of God but endeavours to manipulate his citizens and to trade off political concessions against personal advantage; politics becomes a managerial problem. The humanists of the Renaissance were succeeded by the theologians of the Protestant Reformation who, by their elevation of the importance of the individual conscience, helped to shift the focus of political thought from the sovereign to the subject. Protestant theory and the political upheavals of the sixteenth and seventeenth centuries encouraged a belief in the equality of all men in the eyes of God. The exact connexion between the development of market-relationships and the growth of individualistic political theory remains a vexed question, but clearly, the competitive behaviour which constitutes the market helped to give substance and force to the arguments of those who advocated political theories in which the individual and his rights were central considerations.

Although the maximization of individual liberty is in one sense a precondition for the fullest working of the market, in another sense individual freedom presents a problem both for political and economic organization. On the one hand, the operation of the market requires that individuals should be able freely to dispose of themselves and their property and should be able to acquire the labour and property of others; the smaller the constraints on acquisitive behaviour the more effective and attractive the market system becomes to the able and the ambitious. On the other hand, the market cannot operate without financial, legal and social institutions for the enforcement of market rules and property rights and these in turn cannot be maintained without the subordination of individuals to a sovereign political authority. John Locke (1632–1704), building on theoretical foundation laid by Thomas Hobbes (1558–1679) developed a theory which provided a rationale for the political requirements of market society. Locke bridged the gap between liberty and subordination with the use of a concept borrowed by analogy from commercial practice–the social contract. Locke sees the political arrangements of a commercialized society as depending on an agreement between the citizens and the central political authority in which the citizens exchange obedience for the protection of life and property. The individual allows his natural rights of self-assertion to be curtailed to the extent necessary to make social institutions operable and to facilitate the working of the market. Locke's political theory makes it possible to defend a political system, the purpose of which is to secure obedience to the laws which defend property, in terms of the liberty which it affords. At the root of his propositions is the belief that participation in the market maximizes welfare. This is the origin of liberal political theory and it is within this political tradition that the political economists work. One might say that, politically, the function of political economy was to exemplify the truth of political liberalism.

Hobbes and Locke, because they lived in the century of the English Revolution, when even the authority of the king was bloodily and successfully challenged, were obsessed with the problem of securing the stability of, or orderly change within, the political order. But later writers began to see certain self-generating elements of stability in society which survived independently of the exact nature of the political superstructure. Charles Louis de Secondat, Baron de la Brede et de Montesquieu (1689–1755) undertook a comparative study of societies, ancient and modern, which was published as *De l'esprit des lois* in 1748, and which was greatly admired by the Scots. In it he discusses systems of law and government, fiscal arrangements, military organization, religious and social institutions, and demonstrates their interrelationship with each other and with geography, climate and economics. Montesquieu contends that the forces at work in society together produced an *esprit général* which both expresses and conditions the nature of social development. His *esprit général* is really the sociological intuition. It is the apprehension that society is more than the sum of its parts, that the individual elements, classes, legal systems, institutions of all kinds take their meaning from their interrelationships with each other. On this view, social arrangements are no longer the result of political decisions deliberately taken, the residual in the history of royal houses. Rather, politics is organically related to the structure of society in general; men's activities in society are interdependent and, in part, determined by factors inherent in the social structure and physical environment, and hence beyond human control.

Adam Smith and other eighteenth-century writers used a special term when referring to society in this sense. They employed the expression 'civil society'. This is to be understood as a sociological concept which for Smith and his contemporaries denoted the social phenomena of the commercial system. A description of the development of civil society in modern terms might go as follows; as the market widens, the principal ties in a community change from those determined by custom and tradition to those more closely related to the fluid relationships engendered by the market, relationships which are typically expressed in contractual form; political and administrative institutions become more complex and their behaviour more predictable; social functions are more and more differentiated; as political institutions are adapted to the needs of an exchange society the relationship between State and citizen becomes less direct; the central authorities themselves meet more and more of their requirements by buying in the market as the fiscal system improves so that there is less need for direct intervention and sequestration; the increase in the extent of the market and in the volume and variety of commodities and services exchanged makes more and more of social activity independent of political considerations; gradually more and more aspects of social behaviour including family relationships and religious activity are assimilated to the basic contractual notion. In this complex of processes private individuals are seen to be pursuing private and conflicting ends and yet, at the same time, society appears to be held together by forces which transcend the actions of the individuals which make it up. It was the operation and articulation of this *social* system which Adam Smith and his colleagues set out to explain.

Montesquieu was not the only French social theorist of the period whom the Scots of the eighteenth-century enlightenment admired. Indeed, it has been argued that the credit for the invention of economic science should go to the French Physiocratic School rather than to Adam Smith. This claim is based on the coherence and penetration of their analysis of the process of production and the *circulation* of resources within the economy which it entails. They were the first to see and to integrate theoretically the idea that the source of wealth lies in the *surplus* which economic activity generates. Other writers, like Adam Smith's fellow countryman and contemporary, Sir James Steuart (1712–80), saw profit, i.e. the surplus, as arising when something is sold at a price above that paid for it–the advantage drawn from buying cheap and selling dear. This was a notion heavily attacked by Marx who thought the notion of 'profit upon alienation' vacuous and, like the Physiocrats, sought for a deeper origin for profit. Their analysis was based on the realization that economic exchange is a continuous and circular process. They saw that production and consumption are interdependent, that every producer produces in order to exchange his product for other products, that every man's income is someone else's expenditure, and that any act of exchange is part of a circular chain of transactions, the maintenance of which is the perpetuation of the economy. They saw that exchange takes place not just simultaneously in a given market but extends over time. In this remarkable prefiguration of what is now called 'macroeconomics' the Physiocrats sought for some key variable in the flow of output between manufacturers and farmers. They thought that they had found it in the 'net product' of agriculture. In farming, so much capital is laid out or advanced for labour, seed and equipment, and then, with the passage of time, the harvest is sold at a price which not only covers the costs of the original outlays but also yields a surplus. This surplus is the only source of new resources, since by definition all the rest of income is devoted to replacing the resources used up in production. It follows that the strength of society is to be measured in terms of this surplus. If it fails, society fails. If it is large, then it can be deployed to employ more men, finance more exchange and the general level of economic activity and welfare will rise. The Physiocrats sank into obscurity because of their peculiar insistence that only agriculture would generate a surplus, a fault that Smith was to rectify by extending the idea to cover manufacturing, but in their discovery of the 'circular flow' and the identification of the origin of profits they constituted perhaps the most important single influence on Adam Smith.

The most famous of the Physiocrats was Francois Quesnay (1694–1774). Adam Smith met Quesnay and other members of the Physiocratic School when travelling in France some ten years before the publication of *The Wealth of Nations*. The importance of Quesnay stems not only from the part he played in the development of Adam Smith's concept of capital accumulation but also from the fact that his work inspired an important section of Marx's *Capital*. Quesnay's *Tableau Économique*, a diagrammatic representation of his theory, published in 1758, fascinated Marx and prompted some of the most difficult and precocious of his speculations (see page 183, Chapter 14).

The work of the Scottish Historical School was thus, in part, a synthesis and development of the political ideas of Locke, the sociology of Montesquieu and the economics of Quesnay. Others in the eighteenth century had sought to propound theories of history, but the originality of the Scots consists in the importance which they attached to the economic factor in social organization and change. As Adam Ferguson, a writer referred to by Marx as 'the teacher of Adam Smith', declares, 'In every enquiry concerning the operations of men when united together in society, the first object of attention should be their mode of subsistence. According as that varies their laws and policy must be different.'[4] In what we now think of as a characteristically Marxist fashion they identified different social structures with particular kinds of economic organization; they considered that the progress of human society consisted in its passage through stages of social development in an historical and economically determined order. Adam Smith's *An Inquiry into the Nature and Causes of the Wealth of Nations*, published in 1776, represents the fullest exposition of their ideas and is the first and greatest essay in political economy.

The purpose of *The Wealth of Nations* is to demonstrate the connexion between the welfare of society and the expansion of the market. It is both a positive account of how mankind's progress has always consisted in the development of the activities and attitudes which underly modern commercial behaviour and is also an exercise in persuasion, an attempt to show that the wellbeing of the community is best advanced by minimizing the constraints put upon personal freedom. As such, it became the grounding charter for the advocates of *laissez faire* in the nineteenth century. In this way, its political implications, its hostility to governmental economic interference and its justification of the pursuit of gain reinforced the influence of its technical analysis, and Smith's work established the vocabulary and framework for a discipline that was to survive more or less unaltered in essentials for a hundred years. The ambition of the Scottish Historical School to produce something worthy to rank with the finest intellectual achievements of the modern world was fulfilled.

The stages of social development

Adam Smith's theory of historical development assumed that the 'four stages of society are hunting, pasturage, farming and commerce'.[5] In each of these stages the different ways in which men win the means of existence are associated with different property arrangements. The hunting stage is egalitarian and property is minimal. When men turn to pasturage the herding of livestock creates a need for government 'for the defence of the rich against the poor'.[6] The third, agrarian, stage is characterized in Europe by the concentration of the ownership of land into the hands of a few great proprietors. This inequality of wealth and the lack of alternative means of employment makes large numbers of the population dependent on the landowners for employment, either as agricultural labourers or as members of the retinues of these landlords. It is this economically generated dependence which constitutes the basis of feudalism. This feudal system, in turn, is broken down by the improvement of communications, the growth of towns, and the development of a market for the exchange of agricultural produce against manufactured[7] goods. The appearance of the market provides the landlords with an alternative use for the surplus from their farmlands which they have hitherto used to maintain their retainers. The market in luxury goods provides the feudal lords with an incentive to monetize their relationships with their dependents and to shake off surplus feudal subordinates. As the country is thus drawn into a web of market relationships, emanating from the town, the feudal lords gradually lose the judicial authority which, in pre-market conditions, was produced by the dependence of their followers on them for their livelihood. The arbitrariness of feudal justice is superseded by a regular and rational system of law and order. In this way, according to Smith, the modern era, the commercial age, is ushered in. The historical sections of Karl Marx's *Capital* discussed in the previous chapter betray strikingly similar notions of the inevitability of social progress through various stages and the same order of importance is attached to economic circumstances as the agent of change; and the distinction between Marx's 'capitalism' and Adam Smith's 'commercial society' is one which rests on no real difference (see Chapter 2).

Exchange and the market

The basic assumption in *The Wealth of Nations* is that the main-spring of each man's economic behaviour is the pursuit of his own advantage. This is expressed in 'the propensity to truck, barter, and exchange one thing for another'.[8] Men strike bargains with one another, not out of fellow-feeling, but because it is in their mutual interest to do so. 'It is not from the benevolence of the butcher, brewer, or the baker, that we expect our dinner, but from their regard to their own interest. We address ourselves, not to their humanity, but to their self-love, and never talk to them of our own necessities but of their advantages.'[9] This 'propensity to exchange' gives rise to the division of labour. To illustrate what he means by this, Smith gives his famous description of pin-making. One man working by himself, drawing out the wire, straightening it, cutting it, pointing it, grinding it to receive the head, making the head, putting it on, whitening it, and putting it into the paper in which it is sold, asserts Smith, could not 'make twenty, perhaps not one pin in a day. But when, say, ten men are employed, each performing two or three distinct operations, they can, if they exert themselves, simply because the labour is divided up between them, make among them 48,000 pins a day.'[10] The 'division of labour' is the very heart of technical progress and it should be noted that the introduction of machinery is not the *cause* of efficient economic organization but only one of a number of *consequences*:

This great increase of the quantity of work which, in consequence of the division of labour, the same number of people are capable of performing, is owing to three different circumstances; first, to the increase of dexterity of every workman; secondly, to the saving of the time which is commonly lost in passing from one species of work to another; and lastly, to the invention of a great number of machines which facilitate and abridge labour, and enable one man to do the work of many.[11]

This principle applies not only to individual commodities like pins but also to whole sectors of the economy. Greatly increased output per man follows from specialization in particular trades. 'In every improved society, the farmer is generally nothing but a farmer; the manufacturer nothing but a manufacturer'.[12] Exchange promotes specialization which, in turn, increases output and the growth of the wealth of nations. At the same time, this specialization explains the division of society into groups or classes. For Smith, these classes are the owners of land, the owners of capital, and the labourers.

Smith stresses that it is the market which both gives rise and sets a limit to the growth of output: 'As it is the power of exchanging that gives occasion to the division of labour, so the extent of this division must always be limited by the extent of that power, or, in other words, by the extent of the market'.[13] It follows that the development of overseas markets is important in overcoming these limits:

The discovery of America ... by opening a new, an inexhaustible market to all the commodities of Europe ... gave occasion to new divisions of labour and improvements of art, which, in the narrow circle of the ancient commerce, could never have taken place for want of a market to take off the greater part of their produce. The productive powers of labour were improved, and its produce increased in all the different countries of Europe, and together with it the real revenue and wealth of the inhabitants.[14]

The market is thus a system which can be extended to cover the world and draw all nations into its operation.

Money

In one sense, the whole of Smith's great treatise, *The Wealth of Nations*, is an exercise to persuade the public of the iniquity of another economic doctrine – mercantilism. Whether there ever really was such a doctrine, or whether it was a theoretical device, an Aunt Sally invented by Smith to make points about his own theory, is still a debatable question, but not one that need detain us here. The point is that mercantilism, according to Smith, was a theory, the fallaciousness of which consisted in its confusion between money – pieces of gold, silver, copper or banknotes – and *real* wealth. Smith, throughout *The Wealth of Nations* is indefatigable in his insistence that it is not the amount of gold or silver that a man has that constitutes his wealth but the power which the ownership of these pieces of metal confer on him. Money is a commodity like any other manufactured item and, as such, has an intrinsic worth. But it is not to this intrinsic worth that we normally refer when we talk about money and it is not normally for its intrinsic worth that it is valued but for the goods and services for which it can be exchanged. The distinction between, as Smith puts it 'the guinea's worth and the guinea' is clearest when it is in the form of a paper bill. If a person's weekly income 'was paid to him, not in gold, but in a weekly bill for a guinea, his revenue surely would not so properly consist in the piece of paper, as in what he could get for it. . . . If it could be exchanged for nothing, it would, like a bill upon a bankrupt, be of no more value than the most useless piece of paper'.[15] Money is simply a device for facilitating the exchange of commodities which would otherwise be 'very much clogged and embarrassed in its operations'.[16] Money is 'the great wheel of circulation',[17] 'and though the metal pieces of which it is composed, in the course of their annual circulation, distribute to every man the revenue which properly belongs to him, they make themselves no part of that revenue'.[18] Smith stresses that money has no active role; that its supply is determined by the demand derived from the need to make the exchanges which the level of production allows, and that therefore it cannot be overproduced: 'The whole paper money of every kind which can easily circulate in any country never can exceed the value of gold and silver of which it supplies the place, or which (the commerce being supposed the same) would circulate there, if there was no paper money.'[19] Smith was trying to combat what we would now call 'money illusion'. The price of a single commodity tells us nothing if we do not know the price of any other commodity. Prices are relative, they have no absolute significance and are valuable only as a means of telling the worth of one commodity in terms of another. We must continually be alive to this relativity and not allow the movement of a *single* price to cause us to lose sight of the underlying relationships between commodities which are shown by the relative levels of *all* prices. Money is merely a veil which tends to obscure the real pattern of connexions between the elements of economic activity. Smith's theory of money might almost be said to be designed to demonstrate the importance of neglecting it. Money and prices are simply the surface manifestations of deeper and more important 'real' forces.

Value and labour

This attitude to money forms the background to Smith's approach to the problem of value and his explanation of the nature of the 'real forces' which determine prices. Value is the central and most difficult problem in economics. Its resolution is the crux of Marx's theory. Smith himself found this issue the most complex of those with which he deals and apologetically observes 'after taking the utmost pains that I can to be perspicuous, some obscurity may still appear to remain upon a subject in its own nature extremely abstracted'.[20] This, as someone once said, is one of the greatest understatements in the history of economic thought and the difficulties of Smith's theory of value are such as to preclude an extended discussion of it here. What follows is intended, at the risk of caricaturing what he actually said, to emphasize two things about what he had to say. The first of these is that Smith's theory was not designed to account for the way in which the price of any unit of any commodity is determined by the interaction of subjective utility and relative scarcity as in modern price theory (see further discussion of price in Chapter 9). Smith actually provides no theory of price determination for a *particular* item of production. Secondly, in seeking to establish an absolute standard beyond price, he made a number of statements about the importance of labour in arriving at a criterion of value which are readily misrepresented or misunderstood as an imperfect prefiguration of Marx's own thorough-going 'labour theory of value'.

First, then, Smith fails to discuss the determination of the prices of individual things offered for sale, as opposed to the average or long-run price of units of a particular *kind* of commodity. He starts out by firmly distinguishing between 'value in use' and 'value in exchange';

The things which have the greatest value in use have frequently little or no value in exchange; and, on the contrary, those which have the greatest value in exchange have frequently little or no value in use. Nothing is more useful than water: but it will purchase scarce any thing; scarce any thing can be had in exchange for it. A diamond, on the contrary, has scarce any value in use; but a very great quantity of other goods may frequently be had in exchange for it.[21]

Having made this distinction, Smith confines himself to studying 'the principles which regulate the exchangeable value of commodities'. It is clear that in referring to 'use-value' he means *social* utility as opposed to the subjective preferences of individuals at particular moments in time. But in *The Wealth of Nations* he makes no extended attempt to integrate either of these notions into a theory of price. He is not concerned to account for changes in taste or how demand varies as a *function* of supply, but proceeds on the assumption that demand is *given* and that explanations of price are to be sought in an examination of the conditions under which production takes place. Smith's central concern is with production, not consumption.

What he has to say about labour is more difficult. 'Labour', he writes, 'is the real measure of the exchangeable value of all commodities'.[22] By this he means that, *given the variable and interdependent nature of prices*, the only meaningful measure of value is the amount of labour which the possession of a particular commodity enables one to command. In other words, Smith is again trying to dispel money illusion, and to make it clear that what it means to be rich is to be able to oblige other people to perform services or provide goods. What wealth conveys is 'a certain command over all the labour, or over all the produce of labour which is then in the market'.[23] The extent of this command is measured by the amount of labour of which the owner of wealth can, by virtue of his ownership, dispose. Smith is not trying to deny the convenience or necessity of money as a measuring device, but only to make plain that behind the veil of money there stand real-world relationships of work and the production and distribution of goods.

Labour also plays a prominent part in Smith's analysis of price. It is, in some sense, the first and most important of the factors of production; 'It was . . . by labour that all the wealth of the world was originally purchased.'[24] Before the invention of money, before capital had been accumulated to generate profits, and land appropriated on which rent must be paid,

the proportion between the quantities of labour necessary for acquiring different objects seems to be the only circumstance which can afford any rule for exchanging them for one another. If among a nation of hunters, for example, it usually costs twice the labour to kill a beaver which it does to kill a deer, one beaver should naturally exchange for or be worth two deer. It is natural that what is usually the produce of two days or two hours labour, should be worth double of what is usually the produce of one day's or one hour's labour. . . . In this state of things, the whole produce belongs to the labourer; and the quantity of labour commonly employed in acquiring or producing any commodity, is the only circumstance which can regulate the quantity of labour which it ought commonly to purchase, command or exchange for.[2]

But when society has developed into its agricultural and commercial stages and rent and profit make their appearance:

In this stage of things, the whole produce of labour does not always belong to the labourer. He must in most cases share it with the owner of the stock which employs him. Neither is the quantitity of labour commonly employed in acquiring or producing any commodity, the only circumstance which can regulate the quantity which it ought commonly to purchase, command, or exchange for. An additional quantity, it is evident, must be due for the profits of the stock which advanced the wages and furnished the materials of that labour.[26]

Thus, in Smith's modern society, labour is not the sole determinant of supply price. Rather, price is made up of the cost of each of the three factors of production, labour capital and land. All prices must represent at least one of these elements and most are made up of all three. This is a 'cost of production' theory of price, not a simple labour theory of value.

Nonetheless, for Smith, labour plays the vital role in production. The very first sentence of *The Wealth of Nations* reads: 'The annual labour of every nation is the fund which originally supplies it with all the necessaries and conveniences of life which it annually consumes, and which consist always, either in the immediate produce of that labour, or in what is purchased with that produce from other nations.'[27] Smith's anxiety to make it clear to his readers that gold and specie are not the essence but only the manifestation of wealth led him repeatedly to stress that it is the employment of labour which generates the output in which trade is carried on and of which wealth is composed; it is easy to see how his various statements can be construed by the unwary as a declaration that prices are determined by labour. Indeed, labour does play an important part in all the political economists' theories of price and value; Marx's own labour theory of value is an extreme version of a set of assumptions and arguments common to them all.

The market: the 'long run' and equilibrium: social welfare and individualism

The essence of any 'cost of production' theory is that it is a long run theory. In other words, it is not contended that the price of a good will necessarily equal the cost of production in the short run, but only that the operation of the market has a tendency over time to bring price into equilibrium with costs. Adam Smith's account of how this takes place is perhaps the most famous part of his thesis. In order to accommodate the fact that market price clearly varies from place to place and from day to day for things produced at the same cost of production, Adam Smith distinguishes between 'nominal price' and 'real price'. The nominal price is the short term market price which fluctuates but is ever tending towards the long run or real price which exactly covers production costs.

Smith explains market price as the result of supply and demand. When the supply of a particular good is insufficient – i.e. when there is less of it than will satisfy, at the cost of production, the demand represented by the amount of money which people are prepared to offer for it – its price rises. Conversely, when more is offered than is demanded, in order to dispose of all their stocks, sellers will need to sell at a price below the cost of production. This deviation between the market price or going rate and the real price or cost of production provides incentives and disincentives for producers. In branches of production where the real price is higher than the market price, production will fall because producers cannot cover their costs, the supply to the market will diminish, and the market price will tend toward the real price. Where the real price is below the market price more producers will be attracted into that sector, the supply to the market will increase and this will reduce the market price until it coincides with the real price. By following the indications provided by prices, investing his capital where it will command the greatest return and transferring it away from less profitable enterprises, the producer ensures that what is demanded is supplied and that, in the long run, it will be provided at the 'real price' in terms of the cost of production.[28]

Smith drew an important lesson from this. When a man chooses a more profitable branch over a less profitable one for investment he is not simply making more money. This is because, as Smith so strongly stresses, more money is simply another way of saying more real goods, more labour, in short, more output. The pursuit of profit, therefore, increases the total output of society.

As every individual, therefore, endeavours as much as he can both to employ his capital in the support of domestic industry, and so to direct that industry that its produce may be of the greatest value; every individual necessarily labours to render the annual revenue of the society as great as he can. He generally, indeed, neither intends to promote the public interest, nor knows how much he is promoting it.

So that, although, 'By directing that industry in such a manner as its produce may be of the greatest value, he intends only his own gain . . . he is in this, as in many other cases, led by an invisible hand to promote an end which was no part of his intention.'[29]

Adam Smith thus portrays the market as a mechanism which reduces to order the conflicting activities of the individuals of which it is composed. But it does more than resolve the apparent mystery of how it is that individual self-seeking can be reconciled with the existence of a constant social framework; it shows how such activity actually promotes the good of society as a whole. In the resolution of this paradox Smith had apparently solved the whole problem of the coherence of commercial society; he had provided the economic key to the problem of order and subordination and had shown how the centrifugal forces of an individualistic structure were countered and controlled by the centripetal forces of price.

This furnished him with a powerful weapon against policies which he attributed to 'mercantilists' and others – policies which advocated state interference in the economic process and the distortion of market forces by the use of duties on imports and bounties on exports. He was able to show that

every system which endeavours, either by extraordinary encouragements to draw towards a particular species of industry a greater share of capital of the society than what would naturally go to it, or, by extraordinary restraints, force from a particular species of industry some share of the capital which would otherwise be employed in it, is in reality subversive of the great purpose which it means to promote. It retards, instead of accelerating, the progress of the society towards real wealth and greatness; and diminishes, instead of increasing, the real value of the annual produce of its land and labour.

All systems either of preference or of restraint . . . being . . . taken completely away, the obvious and simple system of natural liberty establishes itself of its own accord. Every man, as long as he does not violate the laws of justice, is left perfectly free to pursue his own interest his own way, and to bring both his industry and capital into competition with those of any other man, or order of men. The sovereign is completely discharged from a duty, in the attempting to perform which he must always be exposed to innumerable delusions, and for the proper performance of which no human wisdom or knowledge could every be sufficient; the duty of superintending the industry of private people, and of directing towards the employments most suitable to the interest of the society.[30]

It was in his exposition and advocacy of these ideas that Smith ensured for himself what was perhaps the most important place in the formation of the nineteenth century's understanding of the world. The market was a stabilizing mechanism which promoted individual *and* social interests. It followed that the role of government could and should be minimized. Although it is true that, according to Smith, government has duties of 'great importance' and that he devotes the whole of one of the five books of *The Wealth of Nations* to the problems of government finance, it is nonetheless the case that the State is relegated by Smith to the periphery of society, and that *The Wealth of Nations* can be and was read as a treatise extolling the rights of the individual at the expense of the regulatory powers of the State.

Smith's notion of the market was, and still is, a very powerful idea – perhaps the most powerful and persuasive ever produced by social science. At the same time it is important to note how much it *assumes*. Only a few pages of *The Wealth of Nations* are devoted to an explicit examination of market operations and that largely in order to *explain away* 'short term' fluctuations in price. Smith does not say how long the short term might be – a fact of clear and crucial importance to any assessment of the market as a promoter of welfare; unemployment is endurable if it is rapidly followed by redeployment in a more profitable occupation, it is unendurable if it lasts indefinitely in a society without adequate arrangements for social assistance. But Smith was not interested in 'the higgling and bargaining of the market', only in the patterns of real factors of which market phenomena are merely the surface manifestations. Smith's theory is concerned with social and economic change over long periods of time. In his analysis the market is very largely a convenient device for dealing with the untidy and theoretically inconvenient 'accidents' and 'aberrations' in the largely smooth progress of change. It is this assumption of the 'long run' which was to be challenged by later critics and which was to be used, with ambiguous effect, by Marx.

Capital accumulation and progress

To recapitulate our discussion for a moment: Smith establishes labour as the most important of the three determinants of price – labour, capital and land. He then shows how price, through the market, provides indicators for private and social profit. We now go on to look at the way in which he says the prices of these three elements and especially the price of capital are themselves determined and how these prices are in turn integrated into a theory of social development.

Rent is easily disposed of. Smith has no real theoretical account of the reasons for which the ownership of land attracts an income, although he devotes a chapter to the subject. The reasons for this are not important and we shall in any case see how the deficiency was supplied by his successors.

His theory of wages is quite straightforward. Wages are the outcome of 'disputes' between workmen and employers. In these, 'the workmen desire to get as much and the masters to give as little as possible'.[31] Because the employers are rich they are able to stand out for a low price for longer than the workmen can stand out for a high one. The worker's wage therefore tend downwards toward the level 'sufficient to maintain him'.[32] The level ' sufficient to maintain him' is the level of wage which is related to the level of the price of food and, in particular, wheat. Although Smith is clear that wages in England and in any rapidly growing economy are above the level of 'the lowest which is consistent with common humanity'[33] the long trend is nonetheless toward such a level. Although it was not Smith's intention this can easily be read as a theory of chronic poverty. Subsequent writers, including Marx, were to bring this out.

The price of capital plays a key role in Adam Smith's theory. To appreciate this it is first necessary to examine the part assigned to it in economic growth. As I have already explained, Smith thought that the division of labour and the expansion of the market were the prime causes of economic growth. The third and equally vital element in the expansion of output is, according to Smith, the accumulation of capital. This is the Physiocratic idea of the 'net product' expanded so as to include manufacturing as a generator of the surplus. For Smith, however, the idea of capital accumulation is much more closely integrated with the system of price incentives afforded by the market. Smith explains the problem historically:

In that rude state of society in which there is no division of labour, in which exchanges are seldom made, and in which every man provides everything for himself, it is not necessary that any stock should be accumulated or stored up beforehand, in order to carry on the business of the society. Every man endeavours to supply by his own industry his own occasional wants as they occur. When he is hungry, he goes to the forest to hunt; when his coat is worn out, he clothes himself with the skin of the first large animal he kills; and when his hut begins to go to ruin, he repairs it, as well as he can, with the trees and the turf that are nearest it.

But when the division of labour has once been thoroughly introduced, the produce of a man's own labour can supply but a very small part of his occasional wants. The far greater part of them are supplied by the produce of other men's labour, which he purchases with the produce, or, what is the same thing, with the price of the produce of his own. But this purchase cannot be made till such time as the produce of his own labour has not only been completed, but sold. A stock of different kinds, therefore, must be stored up somewhere sufficient to maintain him, and to supply him with the materials and tools of his work, till such time, at least, as both these events can be brought about.[34]

The division of labour depends therefore on the availability of capital, and the division of labour both creates a larger surplus by increasing efficiency and generates a demand for more capital.

As the division of labour advances, therefore, in order to give constant employment, to an equal number of workmen, an equal stock of provisions, and a greater stock of materials and tools than what would have been necessary in a ruder state of things, must be accumulated beforehand. But the number of workmen in every branch of business generally increases with the division of labour in that branch, or rather it is the increase of their number which enables them to class and subdivide themselves in this manner.[35]

There are two points to be made here. First of all, it was this Physiocratic and 'historical' account of capital accumulation on which Marx was to seize. Secondly, it should be noted that although Smith gives an *historical* account of capital to make his point about its crucial importance in the production process and in the development of the economy over time, his more detailed account of the process of accumulation, to which we shall now turn, is a much more 'market' or 'simultaneous' account (see pages 15–16). This potential ambiguity in Smith survives, as we shall see, in Marx (see Chapter Fourteen).

By 'capital' we are accustomed to refer to the bulky and permanent items in industrial resources – buildings, machines, fixed investment of all kinds. Smith certainly included fixed capital under the heading of stock, but, as one would expect from the financial needs of the rapid turnover typical in the business of his day, what he called 'circulating capital' played a much more important part. By circulating capital Smith means the raw materials which are worked up in the manufacturing process and the food which constitutes the wages of the labourer. The ownership of 'fixed capital' is constant. Circulating capital passes from hand to hand. Circulating capital is capital which is used to buy raw materials and labour which are then, as it were, incorporated in a manufactured commodity, and sold to some other person. The manufacturer's money goes from him to obtain ownership of goods and labour, the goods and labour are combined in a new good, which is then in turn sent out and its ownership transferred to someone else in return for money which comes back to the manufacturer. Fixed capital is put into land improvements or tools which are used in production but which remain the property of the manufacturer. Most of a manufacturer's outlays are, in this way, 'circulating capital'.

When Smith comes, therefore, to describe the nature of investment, what he has in mind is not a *stock*, something stored up, but a *flow*, a stream of continuous expenditure. According to him, all income is either consumed or invested. Like all the other political economists he does not take seriously the possibility of hoarding. All income is spent productively or unproductively. Unproductive expenditure includes consumption in the ordinary sense, i.e. on food, on clothing and also in the employment of people unproductively – e.g. as servants. Productive expenditure is devoted to the payment of 'productive hands'. The whole income of a nation can be divided into these two streams of spending: one devoted to the purchase of commodities and the hiring of labour for the purposes of consumption, the other employed to set in motion the labour and raw materials which constitute productive activity and generate a further surplus. 'The proportion between those different funds necessarily determines in every country the general character of the inhabitants as to industry or idleness'[36] and the relative size of these two streams of expenditure is therefore of vital importance in determing the rate of growth of an economy. As a country consumes less it spends more on providing employment and increasing output. Hence the crucial role of what Smith describes as capital accumulation.

Having established the crucial role of capital, the importance of its price becomes immediately apparent. The private reason for setting capital to work is, of course, that it yields a profit. But profit is the price of capital just as wages are the price of labour; and, as we said above, an increase in the supply of anything tends to lower its price. An increase in the supply of capital therefore tends to lower the rate of profit. A steady decline in the rate of profit is the key to a general theory of socioeconomic change in which Smith relates to each other the division of labour, the incomes of the various classes of society, the accumulation of capital and the rate of profit. All these relationships are equilibrated through the workings of the market price system and are shown to constitute the very laws of motion of civil society. As society advances, as it must inevitably, 'the increase of stock . . . tends to lower profit. When the stocks of many rich merchants are turned into the same trade their mutual competition naturally tends to lower its profit; and when there is a like increase in stock in all the different trades carried on in the same society, the same competition must produce the same effect in them all.'[37] It follows therefore that

in a country which had acquired that full complement of riches which the nature of its soil and climate, and its situation with respect to other countries allowed it to acquire; which could therefore advance no further, and which was not going backwards, both the wages of labour and the profits of stock would probably be very low. In a country fully stocked in proportion to what either its territory could maintain or its stock employ the competition for employment would necessarily be so great as to reduce the wages of labour to what was barely sufficient to keep up the number of labourers and, the country already being fully peopled, that number could never be augmented. In a country fully stocked in proportion to all the business it had to transact, as great a quantity of stock would be employed in every particular branch as the nature and extent of trade would admit. The competition, therefore, would everywhere be great, and consequently, the ordinary profit as low as possible.[38]

Progress is therefore an ambiguous affair. It means abundance, but abundance means a reduction in the wages of labour as well as in the price of output, and the owners of stock, although receiving only a small rate of return, would monopolize wealth.

Such, in outline, is Adam Smith's majestic economic theory of social change. Before we go on to look at subsequent amendments to the discipline which he invented, it should be noted that although he was widely read and provided the economic education for a country passing through the Industrial Revolution, Smith himself was writing before the great economic changes to which we give that name and at a time when the economy was still predominantly agrarian. It is true that Smith improved on the Physiocrats by declaring that manufacturing as well as agriculture generated a surplus, but throughout *The Wealth of Nations* he continually stresses the overwhelming importance of the development of agriculture as a condition for economic growth in both sectors of the economy. Indeed his knowledge of those technological innovations in manufacturing which we associate with the great upsurge of the English economy in the late eighteenth century seems to have been remarkably deficient. He appears to have been ignorant of the metallurgical advances of his own day and does not mention the inventions which revolutionized the textile industry before his death. James Watt was a friend, but Smith makes no mention of the commercial possibilities of his development of the steam-engine. This is not in itself remarkable. What is to be noted is that the economic theorist who provided a framework of thought for all educated men who lived through the coming of the machine age, thought of technology as the result, rather than the cause of progress.

References and Notes

1. John Stuart Mill, *Principles of Political Economy with Some of their Applications to Social Philosophy*, ed. W. J. Ashley (London 1909), p. 21.
2. The reference is to the 'marginalist revolution', and the widespread

acceptance of a 'subjective' theory of value which that entailed; see pp. 121–123.

3. The word 'Physiocrat' was a neologism derived from Greek roots meaning 'the rule of nature'. Like the Scottish Historical School and in common with many other eighteenth-century thinkers, the Physiocrats felt that society was, or ought to be, governed by natural laws, the exact identity of which they sought to establish.

4. Adam Ferguson, *Works*, vol. V, p. 111. Quoted in Andrew Skinner, 'Economics and history – the Scottish enlightenment', *Scottish Journal of Political Economy*, vol. 12, February 1965, p. 7.

5. Adam Smith, *Lectures on Justice, Police, Revenue and Arms*, ed. Edwin Cannan (Oxford 1906), p. 107. Quoted in Andrew Skinner's introduction to his edition of Adam Smith, *The Wealth of Nations* (Penguin Books, Harmondsworth 1970), p. 31.

6. Adam Smith, *An Inquiry into the Nature and Causes of the Wealth of Nations*, ed. R. H. Campbell, A. S. Skinner and W. B. Todd, 2 vols. (Oxford 1976): (Book V, Ch. i, Part 2), vol. II, p. 715.

7. 'Manufactured' in the sense of having been produced and worked up – not necessarily by a machine.

8. Ibid. (Book I, Ch. ii), vol. I, p. 25.

9. Ibid. (Book I, Ch. ii), vol. I, pp. 26–7. Smith did not think selfishness was the only motive of human behaviour but he did think that selfishness was the exclusive basis of rational *economic* action.

10. Ibid. (Book I, Ch. i), vol. I, pp. 14–15.

11. Ibid. (book I, Ch. i), vol. I, p. 17.

12. Ibid. (Book I, Ch. i), vol. I, pp. 15–16.

13. Ibid. (Book I, Ch. iii), vol. I, p. 31.

14. Ibid. (Book IV, Ch. i), vol. I, p. 448.

15. Ibid. (Book II, Ch. ii), vol. I, p. 290.

16. Ibid. (Book I, Ch. iv), vol. I, p. 37.

17. Ibid. (Book II, Ch. ii), vol. I, p. 291.

18. Ibid.

19. Ibid. (Book II, Ch. ii), vol. I, p. 300.

20. Ibid. (Book I, Ch. iv), vol. I, p. 46.

21. Ibid. (Book I, Ch. iv), vol. I, pp. 44–5.

22. Ibid. (Book I, Ch. v), vol. I, p. 47.

23. Ibid. (Book I, Ch. v), vol. I, p. 48.

24. Ibid.

25. Ibid. (Book I, Ch. vi), vol. I, p. 65.

26. Ibid. (Book I, Ch. vi), vol. I, p. 66.

27. Ibid., 'Introduction and plan of work', vol. I, p. 10.

28. Ibid. (Book I, Ch. vii), vol. I, pp. 72–5.

29. Ibid.

30. Ibid. (Book IV, Ch. ii), vol. I, p. 456.

31. Ibid. (Book I, Ch. viii), vol. I, p. 83.

32. Ibid. (Book I, Ch. viii), vol. I, p. 85.

33. Ibid. (Book I, Ch. viii), vol. I, p. 86.
34. Ibid. (Book II, Introduction), vol. I, p. 276.
35. Ibid. (Book II, Introduction), vol. I, p. 277.
36. Ibid. (Book II, Ch. iii), vol. I, pp. 333–4.
37. Ibid. (Book I, Ch. ix), vol. I, p. 105.
38. Ibid. (Book I, Ch. ix), vol. I, p. 111.

Chapter 4

Political economy before Marx

The history of political economy after Adam Smith and before Marx has two main features. The first of these is a process of analytical refinement in which certain aspects of the theory, especially those referring to population and rent, were tightened up. The second, which is not quite distinct from the first, is the development of rather less optimistic views about the long run tendency of economic development than those implied in *The Wealth of Nations*.

Malthus and population

The connexion between the development of more restrictive assumptions and consequently more constrained reasoning on the one hand and the emergence of gloomier expectations about the future of commercial society on the other is well exemplified in Thomas Malthus's (1766–1834) *An Essay on the Principle of Population* first published in 1798. His sobering reflections on the relationship between food supply and the growth of population is simple, powerful and easily stated: 'Population, when unchecked, increases in a geometrical ratio. Subsistence increases only in an arithmetical ratio.. . . This implies a strong and constantly operating check on population from the difficulty of subsistence.'[1] Malthus's *Essay* immediately obtained great notoriety and it was expanded and republished in five further editions from 1803 to 1826. The elements of Malthus's idea can be found in *The Wealth of Nations* but are nowhere expressed so starkly. According to Malthus, optimism about the future of society is incompatible with the knowledge that the sexual drive of mankind is greater than its ability to produce food for the offspring which result from his procreative urge. The working population is and must always be poor because it is always faced with the fact or prospect of starvation. The assumption fundamental to the theory is that the possibility of increasing output in agriculture is very limited. To his contemporaries, such an assumption appeared very reasonable; the revolution in agricultural productivity, the real rise in yields per unit of land, although often ascribed to the eighteenth century, does not come until the nineteenth century, with the introduction of fertilizers and mechanization. Malthus's assertion cast a shadow over the study of political economy and was the first blow in a debate which is still alive and to which *Capital* was the most famous contribution: do the workers benefit from economic progress?

Ricardo: rent and labour

The theory of rent developed to repair the inadequacy of Smith's own account was a more technical achievement than Malthus's theory of population but proved to have strong political implications. Although evolved independently by others, including Malthus, it was David Ricardo (1772–1823) who integrated it into Smithian political economy. Ricardo, a close friend of Malthus, is the most important political economist after Smith and his book, *On the Principles of Political Economy and Taxation* was published in 1817. He accepted Malthus's theory of population as a theory of wages so that it could be assumed that, in the long run, wages would be determined by the price of food necessary to maintain the life of the labourers and his family. The price of food would, in turn, be determined by its cost of production. This cost would be composed of the profits of the capital employed in farming, the wages of the labourers employed, and the rent paid for agricultural land. In this cost, rent, the landowners' income, was the crucial variable. Over time, population tends to grow. As it grows it presses on the margin of subsistence and more and more land must be taken into cultivation in order to feed the extra mouths. But the land taken into cultivation will be less and less fertile because farmers will have ploughed up the most productive soil first. Therefore, as population increases, the cost of producing the extra, or marginal unit of wheat, will also increase. This extra cost of the marginal wheat will raise the price of all wheat brought to the market because the equilibrating effect of the market brings *all* the units of a commodity up to the price necessary to bring the *last* unit into the market-place. However, the costs of production of the more fertile land taken into cultivation earlier have not risen, and intra-marginal wheat will now command a higher price without any extra effort being put into its production. This means that the owners of non-marginal land first put to the plough will be able to demand higher and higher rents. Now, according to Smith, the price of corn is made up of wages, rent and profits. In real terms, wages remain constant and irreducible, because of Malthus's theory of population; rent rises as extra land is taken up, and therefore the share of profits in price must fall. The progress of society impoverishes the capitalist and enriches the landlord. This is Ricardo's theory of rent. Deployed in this way it presents the theory of the declining rate of profit in a new form and with a new note of urgency.

Ricardo did not, however, view the long term future of society with alarm, provided that the restraints on the importation of food were removed. He certainly felt that, with the abolition of the tariff, the availability of large reserves of cultivable land in Central Europe,

America and elsewhere would put off the day of stagnation indefinitely. At the same time the idea that the rate at which the economy progresses is one that will lose impetus over time, that the return on capital does tend to diminish and that economic development *cannot* be indefinitely prolonged is deeply embedded in his logic. The clear implication of his work is that economic activity is governed by rigid laws which cannot be circumvented.

This deterministic element reinforced the less encouraging social implications of his theory. His adoption of Malthus's population principle to explain the level of wages did nothing to encourage a belief that there was hope for much improvement in the lot of the working class. Even if economic expansion tended to drive the market price of labour above its natural price the longer term effect of this was to increase the population and so, by increasing the supply of labour, hasten the return of wages to their lower, natural level.

Nonetheless, like Smith, Ricardo subscribed to a labour theory of value and emphasized that labour is both the origin and measure of worth, writing

That [labour] is really the foundation of the exchangeable value of all things . . . is a doctrine of the utmost importance in political economy . . . If the quantity of labour realized in commodities regulates their exchangeable value, every increase of the quantity of labour must augment the value of that commodity on which it is exercised, as every diminution must lower it.[2]

This potential contradiction in the Ricardian theory of value between labour, as the source of value, and the labourer, as a man whose income was driven by inexorable economic law towards subsistence while others, who had not laboured in the production process, enjoyed a disproportionate share of the labourer's output, was to be seized on by radical critics and lies at the heart of Marx's theory of political economy.

Ricardo and technical progress

One of the most interesting parts of Marx's *Capital* is the section dealing with invention in the Industrial Revolution. He found it very hard to assimilate technical advance to his general theory of capitalist collapse (see Chapter Thirteen). The origins of his difficulty are to be found in the general approach of the political economists to technological change. Adam Smith's theory quite coherently accounts for technical advance as the fruit rather than the root of progress. But Ricardo's theory is markedly inferior to Smith's and there is hardly a place at all in it for technical innovation.

Ricardo certainly considered that capital accumulation is the vehicle of economic growth. In speaking of capital accumulation he has in mind, as does Smith, mainly the increase in *circulating* capital, the quantity of resources of food and raw materials available to set labourers to work. And in the first two editions of the *Principles* Ricardo thinks of economic growth as purely extensive, not intensive. In the first thirty chapters of the *Principles* Ricardo thinks of industry as expanding, not by improving the techniques employed, but by using increased output to set more hands to work with a *proportionately* increased amount of fixed capital using the *same techniques of production.*

In the third edition, however, Ricardo added Chapter xxxi, 'On Machinery'. In this he abandons the idea of an exclusively extensive mode of expansion and assumes that capital accumulation entails improved techniques and the employment of a greater quantity of capital per man. If he had thought through this idea it would have entailed very considerable revision of the rest of his theory for, of course, if the ratio of capital to labour employed continually increases, this enormously complicates his account of distribution and suggests that a rise in wages need not entail a fall in the rate of profit and further implies some inadequacy in his *labour* theory of value. Marx would have done well to study this chapter more carefully.

He, however, like Ricardo's contemporaries, was struck instead by the further grounds that the chapter provided for pessimism about the social effect of economic development. Previously, Ricardo writes, he had supposed that the effect of machinery was simply, as Smith suggested, to reduce the price of output and that increases in output would provide the extra surplus needed to provide employment for anyone displaced by mechanization. Now he fears that new machinery with greatly increased productivity might abruptly render some existing investments unprofitable and that the resulting redundancy might not be taken up. This leads him to the statement that 'the opinion entertained by the labouring class, that the employment of machinery is frequently detrimental to their interests, is not founded on prejudice and error, but is conformable to the correct principles of political economy'.[3] But he then goes on in the same chapter to counter his own argument and to suggest that, in the long-run, it is invalid, writing that 'To elucidate the principle, I have been supposing, that improved machinery is *suddenly* discovered and extensively used; but the truth is, that these discoveries are gradual, and rather operate in determining the employment of the capital which is saved and accumulated, than in diverting capital from its actual employment'.[4] This is an interesting illustration of the theoretical difficulties with which the question of technological change is attended. It is also again showing the importance of the crucial question of whether growth is seen as a continuous market process, or whether it is conceived as a leap and a series of discontinuities.

The reasons for Ricardo's troubles with what now seems to us to be the salient feature of the Industrial Revolution are three-fold. First,

Ricardo's theory is concerned with a problem which is fundamentally agricultural, the role of the marginal cost of food production in determining the rate of profit; the opening paragraphs of the Preface suggest that Ricardo conceived the economic world as one big farm. Secondly, whereas Smith had been concerned with the 'improvement, in the productive powers of labour' as well as 'the order, according to which its produce is naturally distributed among the different ranks and conditions of men in society'.[5] Ricardo's emphasis was almost exclusively on distribution:

The produce of the earth – all that is derived from its surface by the united application of labour, machinery, and capital, is divided among three classes of the community; namely, the proprietor of the land, the owner of the stock or capital necessary for its cultivation, and the labourers by whose industry it is cultivated . . . To determine the laws which regulate this distribution, is the principal problem in Political Economy.[6]

Thirdly, as Ricardo's observations about the possibly deleterious effect of mechanization show, the world which Adam Smith had observed, with a predominantly agrarian economy in which trade was the principal and overwhelmingly important source of growth and in which growth itself was a slow, almost imperceptible and smooth process, was passing away.

The aftermath of the Napoleonic Wars, which were concluded in 1815, was attended by agrarian and industrial unrest as patterns of hitherto interrupted international trade were re-established and industrialization forced big structural changes in the economy; the growth of the factory system reduced a whole class of textile workers, the handloom weavers, to destitution. But these were new phenomena for Ricardo and his contemporaries. As the middle of Ricardo's Chapter xxxi shows, they did not lend themselves readily to explanation by political economy with its emphasis on the long run. Their significance for its future had not been fully grasped either theoretically or imaginatively by 1821. The very expression 'Industrial Revolution' was still unknown.

Ricardo's influence

Ricardo's work has theoretical shortcomings and was criticised by other political economists, but his version of Smith's great theory was to survive as orthodox thinking well into the second half of the century and was taken by Marx as received wisdom. Most of the elements which make Smith so fascinating as a social theorist are still there. Like Smith, Ricardo is concerned with the class distribution of income. Like Smith, he finds it in labour. Like Smith, he propounds a theory which provides a total explanation for the movement of society and its possible stagnation. Like Smith, he has a view of mechanical invention and change, which with hindsight seems inappropriate to the century in which England was to become the industrial centre of the world.

The coherence and logical power of Ricardian political economy made it a powerful analytical tool the force of which helped to secure the prolongation of its influence. The industrial development of England gave it an enormous economic advantage over other countries. It soon became clear, at least to industrialists, that England's economic interests were best served by importing food and raw materials and exporting manufactured goods. England had a vested interest in the widening of the international market and the greatest possible freedom of foreign trade. In the decades after the end of the Napoleonic Wars there was a struggle for the abolition of agricultural protection which had been afforded to British wheat when the ending of protection again made it vulnerable to foreign competition. This helped to fuel a general campaign for free trade in all goods and by the 1840s such arguments had become first the centre of political debate and then finally assumptions common to all political parties. The work of Smith and Ricardo gave powerful theoretical support to the arguments of those who felt that industrial development was vital both for the maintenance of capitalist incomes and for the provision of employment. The triumph of free trade with the repeal of the Corn Laws in 1846 was associated with the unprecedented economic achievements of Britain by the middle of the century, and a belief in free trade became a touch-stone of right-minded economic thought. Whatever uneasiness may have been felt about those aspects of Ricardian theory which suggested that economic development led to conflict between classes was drowned by the evident success of those who had used his ideas to justify their attack on the tariff.

Say's Law

In spite of Ricardo's premonitions that economic progress might not be an unadulterated good, these are no more than faint suspicions on his part; he is in general unequivocal about the need to remove all barriers to the process of economic expansion and the possibly catastrophic effects of failing to do so. For explicit attacks on the idea that maximum freedom in pursuing self-interest in the market necessarily promotes social welfare, it is necessary to turn to 'underconsumptionist' doctrines. But before the force of these ideas can be assessed, the political economists' theory of money must first be briefly considered.

We have seen now Adam Smith's primary concern with money was to fight the 'illusion' which it creates. For Smith, the function of money and banks is simply to cheapen the cost of transacting business which would otherwise involve time-consuming barter. The political economists gave a more exact expression to Adam Smith's belief. This was given by Say's Law. Jean Baptiste Say (1767–1832), a French popularizer of Smith, was especially impressed by Smith's demonstration of the superficiality of monetary phenomena. His 'Law of Markets' was meant to show the logic underlying this idea. His proposition that 'supply creates its own demand' is an answer to the problem of why it is that what is produced can always be sold, and how it is that manufacturers can be sure that their output can be disposed of without loss, although they cannot, before they take their goods to market, identify the purchasers. Say's theory states that output will always be sold at a price which covers its cost of production because the cost of production is made up of rent, wages and profits and these, when spent, will exactly cover the prices of the goods offered for sale. The payments which make output possible reappear as the means by which output is disposed of. Once again, this is a long term truth rather than a short term one. All the political economists knew that disruptions to trade and crises were possible and had seen years in which not all goods could be sold and in which confidence fell, banks crashed, firms were bankrupted and men were turned off work. Nonetheless they all felt that Say's Law held in the long run. By this, they meant that whatever disturbances in the flow of economic activity there might be over a short period as a result of wars and the disruption of international trade, the failure of harvests at home or abroad, a sudden contraction in the supply of raw materials or a drop in foreign demand, nonetheless, in the end, all incomes derived from production would be spent on the goods produced and activity would revive and return to 'normal'.

The crucial assumption was that people do not hoard money. This was an article of faith and was based on the belief that hoarding was irrational when there existed a market for loans – why hoard when interest could be obtained for lending? Of course, if not all income is spent, if some of it *is* hoarded, then demand will be less than supply and goods will be sold at a loss. But given the assumption that nobody simply holds on to cash for the sake of it, Say's Law is self-evidently true.

Say's Law was also deployed in two ways in support of arguments against the government's interference with the supply of money. It was argued that for the government to try to intervene in the market for money and credit would either be disastrous, by upsetting the natural coincidence of supply and demand, or, alternatively, that to interfere was simply a waste of time since the demand for money was simply a reflection of the underlying real forces as expressed in Say's Law and to increase the amount of cash available by, say, coining or printing, would not affect the demand for it; any surplus would simply lie unwanted in the banks.

Underconsumption

Underconsumptionism, in its strict sense, is a denial of the truth of Say's Law. As such, it is a logical fallacy. However, it is a fallacy which has a perennial attraction – how *do* manufacturers know that they will be able to sell all that they produce so blindly? – and one long associated with Marxist beliefs. At the same time it is an idea that often appears in company with criticisms of market systems which have greater weight and are much more persuasive. We can illustrate these two strands of underconsumptionism, the narrower and fallacious one, and the broader and more pertinent one, with reference first to Malthus and second to Sismondi, both of whom were read and noted by Marx.

In its purest form underconsumptionist doctrine holds that in 'capitalist' society, i.e. where the means of production are not owned by the workers, there is a persistent tendency towards glut and unemployment. This was Malthus's view and according to it, since the workers are not paid the full value of their product, there will be a chronic difficulty for manufacturers in disposing of their output. Intuitively, the idea that some people save might seem to suggest that some money is indeed withdrawn from the spending stream. But given that, according to the political economists, money that is saved is invested, or, as Smith would put it, 'spent productively' then there is no diminution of the circular flow, and the incomes to land and capital will reappear in the market to purchase all output, whether of consumer goods or of investment goods and raw materials designed to further production. Even if there is a shift in the ratio of consumption to investment and there is initially a fall in demand for consumer goods and an increase in the demand for investment goods, on the second and subsequent rounds, producers will respond to the new pattern and alter their production plans accordingly, so that, in the long run, a new equlibrium will be established in which, once again, all output will be sold at prices covering the cost of production.

Curiously enough, although Malthus engaged in a long dispute with Ricardo about this idea, he expressly denied that gluts could be explained monetarily, and without a monetary explanation underconsumptionism is logically untenable. It may seem a trivial and inconsiderable argument but it is one which has had a perennial attraction for the critics of the commercial system, which tempted Marx and which recurs in the work of later Marxists.

The Frenchman, Jean Charles Leonard de Sismondi (1773–1842) is sometimes spoken of as an underconsumptionist, but he had other and stronger grounds for his misgivings about political economy. At first a disciple of Smith, he subsequently became disillusioned with the social effects of commercialization and instead of seeing commercial upheavals and crises as exceptional he became convinced that they were endemic in the modern economic system. In other words, he lost his faith in the 'long run' of the political economists and came to consider the short term difficulties as insuperable barriers to the general social progress supposedly entailed by the theories of Smith and Ricardo. He fastened on the institutional arrangements of the contemporaneous economic system, stressing the difficulty of accurately predicting the demand for output, the comparative immobility of skilled labour and the real immobility of investment in fixed plant and machinery. He made central to his critique this idea only previously touched upon in Ricardo's chapter 'On Machinery'. Innovations and changes in patterns of consumption may render not only machinery but whole occupations redundant. Adam Smith and the political economists based their theory on the idea that the factors of production, labour, equipment and raw materials could be moved and transferred freely; Sismondi was impressed with the 'stickiness' of economic arrangements, and the destructive effects and costs to others of the private search for gain. He also thought that the unequal distribution of property between capitalist and worker which the modern system had produced was inimical to the very ends which the political economists predicted that it would further:

We are now, and it has never been sufficiently noted, in a condition of society which is absolutely new and of which we have as yet no experience at all. We are tending to separate completely every kind of property from every kind of labour, to break the whole connection between the day-labourer and the master, and to take away from the first every kind of participation in the profit of the second.[7]

Ricardo persuaded Sismondi of the falsity of his underconsumptionist ideas, but his structural criticisms of the effect of the working of the market have proved to be very durable.

The characteristics, then, of political economy, as it presented itself to Marx when he came to study it in the 1840s may be summarized as follows:

Social and economic development is the product of forces beyond the control of any individual.

The history of social development is the history of the spread of commercial relationships.

The fundamental motive in economic behaviour is the selfish and rational desire for gain.

Social welfare is best promoted by allowing the market to operate freely.

The economy is divided into two sectors, industry and agriculture.

Society is divided into economically defined classes.

Monetary problems are not, in principle, important.

There is a chronic surplus of population which depresses wages.

The wages of labour are the most important factor in the determination of price.

Economic growth depends on the accumulation of capital.

Technical progress is subordinate to the accumulation of capital.

With economic growth the rate of profit tends to decline and society to stagnate.

Before Marx began to write, political economy had been criticized on theoretical, underconsumptionist, grounds and also for what were alleged to be its unrealistic and overoptimistic assumptions about the ability of a commercial society to stabilize itself in response to the pressure on its institutions which the working of the market itself generates.

Marx read many more works on political economy than those cited in this and the preceding chapter, but those which have been discussed here were written by its most important expositors and critics. It was in the political economists that Marx, while frequently disagreeing with their conclusions found the analyses and economic theories which helped him to construct his critique of capitalism. To say this is not to deny Marx's originality; few thinkers, and certainly none of the political economists, can claim to have produced ideas which were without precedent.

A note on 'political economy'

It is, of course, by definition, only with the benefit of hindsight that a distinct and historically defined school of 'political economists' beginning with Adam Smith and ending with Karl Marx, can be identified. The economic thinkers of the eighteenth and nineteenth centuries did not know that their analytical framework would be superseded and were not conscious of its distinctiveness; even Marx thought that it would eventually simply be redundant. In the nineteenth century, therefore, the expression 'political economy' was not used with the same exactness with which it has been employed in this book. Adam Smith and Marx both thought of political economy as beginning *before* Adam Smith's time, in the seventeenth century. Indeed, the expression was first used as early as 1611. They included as exponents of the subject writers like William Petty (1623–87) whose central interests, while they may be described as 'economic' were different from, and less systematically expressed than in, Adam Smith's writings. If there is a generally accepted term for the work of the writers with whom this chapter has been concerned it is perhaps 'classical political economists'. John Maynard Keynes (1883–1946), however, used the word 'classical' to describe virtually all economists who wrote before him, and especially those whom he accused of naively subscribing to Say's Law. On the other hand, Marx himself reserved the epithet 'classical' for writers who 'investigated the real relations of production in bourgeois society' of whom Adam Smith and Ricardo were 'the best representatives'; other, lesser, lights, who dealt in a superficial way 'with appearances only' were designated 'vulgar'.[8] Because of these possible sources of confusion and because, in any case, 'classical political economy' is so clumsy an expression it has here been shortened to 'political economy'.

The reader should also be cautioned that contemporaneously 'political economy' is sometimes used to describe certain kinds of social analysis and prescription precisely because the expression has a Marxist connotation and the users wish to draw attention to their claim to some sort of socialist sanction for their ideas.

Again the term is sometimes employed in another and even looser sense to refer to the general political problems entailed in modern economics, e.g. the political considerations affecting the choice between different types and rates of taxation.

References

1. Thomas Robert Malthus, *An Essay on the Principle of Population* and *A Summary View of the Principle of Population*, ed. Antony Flew (Penguin Books, Harmondsworth 1970), p. 71.
2. David Ricardo, *On the Principles of Political Economy and Taxation, The Works and Correspondence of David Ricardo*, ed. Piero Saffa (Cambridge 1970): (Ch. i, Sect. 1), vol. I, p. 13.
3. Ibid. (Ch. xxxi), vol. I, p. 392.
4. Ibid. (Ch. xxxi), vol. I, p. 395.
5. *The Wealth of Nations* 'Introduction and Plan of the Work', vol. I, pp. 10–11.
6. Ricardo, op. cit., Preface, p. 5.
7. Jean Charles Leonard de Sismondi, *Nouveaux Principes d'Economi Politique* (1819), vol. II, p. 434. Quoted, in part, in *Capital*, vol. I, p. 762 n, and, in full, in R. L. Meek, *The Economics of Physiocracy. Essays and Translations* (London 1962), p. 330.
8. *Capital*, vol. I, Ch. i, Sect. 4, p. 8n.

Chapter 5

Hegel and Adam Smith

In 1914 Lenin was reading and making notes on Hegel's *Logic*. As he did so the importance of Hegel in the development of Marx's thought became clearer and clearer to him. He suddenly saw that Marx's method has been to '*apply* Hegel's dialectic in its rational form to political economy'.[1] This led him to the observation that 'it is impossible fully to grasp Marx's *Capital* and especially the first chapter, if you have not studied and understood the whole of Hegel's *Logic*. Consequently, none of the Marxists has understood Marx for the last half century!!'[2] Lenin's two exclamation marks were justified. Not only had he himself been a Marxist for twenty-five years but Marxism had always been presented as a straightforward, commonsensical and virtually self-evident set of doctrines. Neither Marx nor Engels made any secret of the fact that, as young men, they had started their intellectual careers as Hegelians. But they offered the theories of the *Communist Manifesto* and of *Capital* as the product of a simple materialistic philosophy which 'resolved to comprehend the real world-nature and history – just as it presents itself to everyone who approaches it free from pre-conceived and whimsical idealist notions'.[3] Hegel, by contrast, was a German philosopher of great difficulty, whose principal concern was with metaphysics, the 'whimsical idealist notions' condemned by Engels. Worse, his theories had been adopted as a semi-official apologia by the conservative Prussian regime, and in 1831 Hegel was decorated by King Frederick William III. To suggest that Hegel was the *key* to Marxist economics sounded both intellectually and politically improbable. Nonetheless, Lenin's insight was confirmed by the publication, in the 1920s and 1930s, of various essays and notes which Marx had made as a young man while striving for a synthesis of his views on social and economic theory. These early writings show not only what Marx owed to Hegel but also how he arrived at his economic theory. The course of this evolution explains some of the most striking peculiarities of Marx's economic thought – peculiarities which have their origins in Marx's early training as an Hegelian.

What has to be explained is how Marx made the transition from Hegel, an idealist philosopher concerned to find a quasi-religious explanation of the world, to political economy, a social science concerned with the tough facts of industrial life, and with the elucidation of the relationship between wages, prices, profits and economic growth. This chapter is concerned with the nature of Hegel's philosophy and the use he makes in it of political economy.

Modern philosophy: epistemology

To understand the nature of Hegel's philosophical endeavours we need to return to the origins of modern thought in the seventeenth and eighteenth centuries. Thinkers like Hobbes and Locke operated with individualistic assumptions. That is to say, for them it was axiomatic that individuals are in some sense equal, autonomous and comparable, and constitute the ultimate units in political organization. The great scientific advances of the seventeenth century were in mathematics and mechanics. These advances, which revolutionized astronomy and cosmology, by the same token made it difficult to subscribe to the idea of an immanent God. With progress in natural science the world could be seen as a gigantic machine governed by the laws of mechanics. This albeit incomplete secularization of the understanding nonetheless relegated God to the status of a prime mover who was logically necessary as the *ultimate* cause of all things, but who was no longer necessary to explain *how* things happened in the world. That could be done by the examination of natural phenomena and establishing the patterns and laws of their occurrence. With the withdrawal of God to the outskirts of the Universe, man took up the central position. The philosophers now assumed that the behaviour of man was subject to rules and principles identical with or analogous to those which governed the material world. Just as the understanding of the movement of the planets was no longer to be sought in the Bible but with reference to the laws of motion discovered by observation, so now it was hoped to understand human behaviour not with the help of divine revelation but by studying man himself.

This concern with man as an individual meant that philosophers and others were led to take as their first problem the question of the connexion between the individual and his environment – material objects, other minds; how is it that an individual *knows* things and persons external to him? what is consciousness and how does awareness of the world come about? what are the mechanisms which govern the way in which knowledge is acquired? This analysis of whether and how 'mind' knows 'matter' is still a central problem of modern philosophy and is the subject of what is known as 'epistemology' (from Greek, *epistèmè*: knowledge).

The most famous name associated with this problem in early modern times is that of the Frenchman, René Descartes (1596–1650), a contemporary of Hobbes who might be said to have established the dichotomy between mind and other non-thinking 'substances'. But the first Englishman to make an extended philosophical investigation of the problem was John Locke, in his *Essay concerning Human Understanding* (1690). Locke's achievement was to establish a distinctive approach to the issue, that of empiricism. Empiricism is based on the assertion that nothing can be known which is not something which has occurred in experience or which is not some construction based on experience.

David Hume (1711-76), Adam Smith's friend and compatriot, and the greatest of modern philosophers, carried empiricism to its logical conclusion. The core of Hume's speculations is concerned with the uncertain connexion between experienced perception and our beliefs about external objects. Hume argued that the only knowledge we have is through our senses, yet, what we regard as the most valuable objects of knowledge – theories, moral notions, ideas themselves – are not to be found in sense-experience. These intellectual constructions relate various elements of experience in interesting and useful ways but are not themselves perceived by the senses; they are and remain *intellectual* constructions. Even the ideas of 'matter' and the 'real world' are *only* 'fictions' or imaginary constructions and there is no logically satisfactory way of demonstrating their existence. Similarly, crucial doubts are raised about the objectivity of moral notions and beliefs.

In his *A Treatise of Human Nature* (1739-40) Hume takes the concept fundamental to any kind of explanation, 'cause', and demonstrates that it lacks objective status. We cannot discover causes in the real world, we can only *impute* a causal function to particular events. Nothing in the material world is labelled 'cause'; this is simply a term which we use to denote the first of two events which are invariably observed immediately to follow one another. No examination of the events themselves will reveal any casual 'quality' in one of them; 'cause' is a category constructed intellectually. Hume concludes that causation is a concept which 'lies merely in ourselves and is nothing but that determination of the mind which is acquired by custom'.[4]

This conclusion has very serious consequences. For if what Hume says of an idea so fundamental to our understanding of the world is true, then it suggests that all the notions which we use to describe and analyse the world may be, equally, mental inventions and not empirical discoveries. If our notion of necessary connexion is *imputed* to things in nature rather than *discovered from* them then the generation of criteria for truth becomes extremely difficult – the relationship of any one thing to another is always, in principle, questionable. Moreover, if statements about the material world are always questionable, then again, in principle, the nature of statements about right conduct is problematical and the standing of moral philosophy is reduced. What is true of moral philosophy is also true of theology; God is no longer simply held at arm's length; he has been exorcised from a fully secularized world. Man is left in a logically scandalous state faced with an apparently irreparable dichotomy between thought and matter, between 'is' and 'ought'. No universally acceptable resolution of Hume's difficulty has ever been provided.

Kant and German philosophy

From one point of view, German philosophy in the late eighteenth and early nineteenth centuries was an extensive and serious attempt to cope with Hume's dilemma. Immanuel Kant (1724–1804) attempted a resolution by shifting the argument about cognition onto a different footing. For Hume and the British empiricists the material world began, as it were, at the nerve endings. Empirical data came from 'outside' the mind. Kant tried to abolish this distinction by shifting the arena of cognition to the mind itself, and making this the focus of philosophical inquiry. Kant, by virtually identifying the mental and the material world, was able to neglect the problem of the differences in their ontological status and to concentrate on the mental world, as in any case, by definition, comprehending all that can possibly be known. The data directly apprehended by the mind Kant designated 'phenomena'. In Kant's philosophical scheme phenomena are the superficial and imperfect appearance of things; behind them lie 'noumena', another technical term denoting things 'as they really are'. Noumena are not known directly but in some way, which Kant never makes clear, are arrived at by a speculative process to which phenomena are fundamental.

Kant's alteration in the status, as it were, of Hume's empirical world, and the analytical devices he produced in order to examine cognition conceived in this way, represented a set of very great technical achievements which opened up new areas of philosophical inquiry. The reinstatement of the objective existence of ideas, of noumena, beyond the immediately sensible world, also allowed him to re-establish moral philosophy. But Kant's system is beset with a number of logical difficulties, the most striking of which is the problem of how the existence of noumena can be discovered if, by definition, only phenomena represent immediate experience. Either phenomena are the only objects of knowledge or they are not. If noumena can also be known, whether by intuition or in any other way, then phenomena cease to be the sole source of knowledge and Kant's whole system is put in jeopardy.

Kant's difficulty with the connexion between phenomena and noumena, things as they *appear* to the mind and things as they *are in themselves*, is strikingly like the problem that Hume found in attempting to establish the relationship between mind and the objects it perceives. Kant, by his ingenious device of shifting the field of cognitive inquiry from the interface between mind and material things to thought itself, made a powerful philosophical innovation. Nonetheless, the relationship between phenomena and noumena 'sense' and 'things', presents a logically irresoluble difficulty which is the nemesis which awaits all philosophers who presume to solve the epistemological problem.

This weakness in Kant's theory undermines his moral philosophy which might be said consequently to degenerate into a physchological account of the tension between man's consciousness of his behaviour as imperfect phenomenon, and the perfect and unattainable noumenal standards of conduct which he sets himself. Hume's problem remains; the abyss between fact and mental constructions, between the positive and normative, persists.

Hegel's 'philosophy': developmental psychology

Armed with some idea of this fundamental philosophical problem, we are now in a position to give an account of Hegel's ideas, for it was his main purpose to restate man's understanding of the world so as to eliminate the difficulty so starkly put by Hume. Hegel's philosophical system is a gigantic intellectual effort to overcome the abyss between consciousness and the external world and to reconcile man with his material environment and the other minds with which it is peopled. Kant's moral philosophy is based on a tension between 'is', the patchy and imperfect phenomenal nature of our moral experience, and 'ought', the shining perfection of 'noumenal' moral goals. Hegel accepted this tension as a dynamic element fundamental to all existence. Hegel's philosophy is an attempt to dissect this basic dissension in the order of things and show how it contained within itself the elements by which harmony could be restored to the universe.

It can already be seen from these few words that Hegel's philosophical ambition was an extraordinarily far reaching one; it was much more than a technical exercise; it was an attempt to explain the nature of all things. Hegel identifies the duality of the world, as seen by Hume and Kant, as a struggle between mind and matter; the effort of understanding, the mental exertion of knowing, becomes a microcosm of an elemental conflict, the resolution of which makes clear why things are as they are. Hegel's philosophy is a *developmental* account of the world, showing how it has reached its present state through the successive generation and resolution of conflicts which owe their origin to the world's very nature. Hegel claims to show not only how we *know* the world but also *why* its history and the social and political institutions found in it have taken the form which they have. Hegel's purpose was not simply to solve the epistemological problem but also to use the solution for the astounding purpose of achieving absolute knowledge. His thought is thus not merely philosophical in the modern sense, but also implies theories of psychology, sociology, politics and history.

The foundations of Hegelianism are psychological. Marx thought that 'the true point of origin and the secret of Hegelian philosophy'[5] was to be found in *The Phenomenology of Mind* (1807). This, as its title suggests, is a treatise employing the technical vocabulary devised by Kant and is, in large part, an account of the mental experience of cognition. In fact, it is this process, Hegel suggests, which *is* philosophy.

In other words, philosophy is not simply a corpus of logically connected propositions or analytical devices which can be studied like a natural science, but is rather 'the thinking study of things',[6] that is to say, a process and an activity.

Hegel claims, not to give an account of the truth, but to expound what it is like to travel towards the truth, to point to 'the pathway of the natural consciousness which is pressing forward to true knowledge'[7] of which 'the goal . . . is the insight into what knowing is'.[8] Nowhere does he say exactly how he deduced that the cognitive process is as he says it is but he appeals for the confirmation of his theory to the evidence of the reader's own consciousness:

The propositions giving an account of thought . . . are not offered as assertions or opinions of mine on the matter. But . . . any deduction or proof would be impossible, and the statements must be taken as matters in evidence. In other words, every man, when he thinks and considers his thoughts, will discover by the experience of his consciousness that they possess the character of universality.[9]

We must, then, search our own experience for something corresponding to the two concepts fundamental to Hegel's theory – the 'dialectic' and 'alienation'. 'Dialectic' is a term indicating the way in which thought and cognition proceed and 'alienation' refers to an element central to the dialectical process. Hegel's idea seems to be that simple perception, the recognition of a world external to our minds, is initially an uncomfortable and unhappy state. We experience things but do not understand them. The brute aspects of the material world, felt, but not comprehended, are foreign and hostile to us. This is the state of alienation. We then struggle, by reasoning, to overcome this alienation, this foreignness and incomprehensibility. In this struggle, reason works on the same phenomena of the external world, changes them and in the process is itself changed. That is to say, we come to see that the material world is not necessarily hostile, and that in seeing things for what they really are, both our understanding and our perception are themselves transformed. This reciprocal process is the dialectic. Its outcome is the closing of the cognitive breach and the attainment of truth which '. . . consists in the identity between objectivity and the notion'.[10]

This may sound less obscure if we consider the way in which contemporary psychologists conceive of the psychological development and learning process in the child. A newly born infant is thought to be incapable of distinguishing between itself and what it experiences. To all intents and purposes its mother and the warmth and nourishment she provides are an extension of itself. The infant psyche is not only the centre of its world, it *is* its world. Psychological development is a process by which the infant gradually discovers that its universe is not coextensive with its own consciousness but is made up of discrete and autonomous objects. This discovery consists of painful experiences in which the recalcitrance of physical objects and the absences of its

mother lead to the understanding that the satisfaction of its appetites
cannot always and simply be willed, and that it is not omnipotent. This
discovery of the 'otherness' of the world corresponds to Hegel's idea of
'alienation'. But the infant goes on to discover that the hostility or
'otherness' of its environment is not random. It learns that the objects of
its experience exhibit certain regularities and patterns, are responsive to
particular kinds of manipulation and can, under certain conditions, be
exploited. Similarly, the distressing discovery that there are other
persons in the world with whom it must be shared is tempered by the
subsequent realization that they too are predictable and that a
consideration of their responses can suggest ways in which they can be
recruited to the infant's own interests. As the child learns of the limits to
its own powers and of the existence of other objects and personalities
potentially opposed to its own desires it also learns how to
accommodate itself to this external world, to comprehend the rules by
which it is governed, to appropriate this knowledge to itself and to use it
for its own ends. One of the most explicit descriptions of some such
process is to be found in the introduction to the *Phenomenology* and
concludes with the sentence: 'This dialectic process which consciousness
executes on itself – on its knowledge as well as on its object – in the sense
that out of it the new and true object arises, is precisely what is termed
Experience.'[11]

What is true of infant development is true of learning in general. The
subject becomes aware of the existence of a problem or cognitive
difficulty which cannot be accommodated to its existing knowledge. An
active effort of understanding is made, the problem broken down and
rearranged, understood, resolved and absorbed into a corpus of
knowledge which is itself in the process organized. The subject is then
ready with improved analytical equipment to face up to problems of yet
greater complexity. The process is repeated and the understanding
proceeds through progressively higher stages.

History

The difficulties which lie in the way of understanding Hegel – and this is
a task on which many a commentator has broken his teeth – stem
mainly from a failure to see that Hegel's 'philosophy' is the extension to
all known phenomena of an analytical process derived from a primitive
but persuasive notion of developmental psychology. Hegel's 'philosophical' enterprise is, admittedly, extraordinary, and his logical leaps
hard to credit without some knowledge of the intellectual background
against which he wrote. In this connexion it is especially important to
remember that the discussion of moral philosophy in the late eighteenth
and early nineteenth century still had implications for religion, while a
preoccupation with 'wholeness' and the 'integration' of the personality
was a characteristic of German philosophy from Kant onwards.

Since Hegel was concerned to provide a developmental account of the world he was always concerned with history. His work is devoted to the assimilation of the history of the world to this concept of mental development. The *Phenomenology* is itself both psychological and, albeit obscurely, historical in content. Various phases in the history of European cultural development are identified and then described as manifestations of the development of the whole of mankind through progressively superior stages of consciousness. These stages reveal themselves in the actions and the social and political institutions of successive civilizations.

This fusion of history and psychology looks very arbitrary to modern eyes. But it was a widespread belief in Christendom that, in some very literal sense, God made the world. According to the assumptions of Christian theology God antedates all other beings whatsoever so that whatsoever exists is his creation and is, in its very existence, sustained by him. Accordingly, there was a very strong tendency for Christianity to encourage a belief in an immanent God of whom all natural phenomena were a manifestation. Moreover, and correspondingly, since consciousness is the highest thing of which we can conceive then consciousness must itself be a manifestation of the supreme consciousness. *Our* consciousness is an aspect of *God's* consciousness.

The original creation of the world is an act of alienation. God makes the world from his own substance: 'Spirit . . . becomes an other to itself.'[12] Thus the Spirit initially exists separately and apart from his material creation. But there is a dialectical relationship between Spirit and matter, they are distinct, and yet matter is sustained by, owes its existence to, Spirit, and the world is in fact the manifestation of the activity of God. The history of the world is an account of the process in which, by successive degrees, Spirit, as manifested in the mind of man, overcomes its original alienation from its creation in successive acts of comprehension which are worked out in the development of successive civilizations. The final goal of history is a state in which the whole material world is again reconciled with the Spirit. By this Hegel appears to mean a situation in which men, whose minds are the expression of the divine Spirit, come to understand and fully comprehend the material and social world which they have themselves created, and in so doing achieve absolute knowledge and identification with God himself.

Hegel's theory of cognition is thus made coextensive with and indistinguishable from a theory of progressive history. The activity of reason in working on, transforming, and itself being transformed by, sense phenomena can also be seen in the process by which man works on, transforms and realizes himself in his material environment through labour: 'this activity giving shape and form, is at the same time the individual existence, the pure self-existence of that consciousness, which now in the work it does is externalized and passes into the condition of permanence'.[13] The dialectical process is thus not simply a mental development; it is the very nature of change and development itself, a development in which man both makes the world, and is made by it. Since the world is Spirit, the processsses which we know by introspection to constitute the development of the mind must also constitute the developmental processes of society and the world.

In *The Philosophy of History* (lectures delivered 1830–31) the history of the world is explained as a succession of civilizations,. Oriental, Greek, Roman and European, which each constitute a stage in the attainment of spiritual maturity. 'The political life of the East . . . is the childhood of History'; 'the Greek world may then be compared with adolescence'; The Roman State is 'the Manhood of History'; while the European world is 'Old Age' conceived not as a period of decay but as one of 'perfect maturity and strength'.[14] The rise and fall of these civilizations is seen by Hegel as a series of cognitive acts in which the Spirit attains more and more complex levels of rationality in sets of less social, political and cultural institutions. Decay sets in once each new principle of rationality is firmly established; it is then undermined and eventually superseded by a new and superior one.

In this process of social development moral philosophy is transmuted. The problem of constructing a theory of ethics is profoundly modified by positing the whole of the history of the world as the development of God's knowledge of himself. That is to say, the moral dilemmas which arise between individuals are seen quite differently when it is asserted that the relationships in which they are involved are in fact *internal* to the personality of God himself. Once this is understood, Hegel implies, it is naive to be dismayed by the fact that history is 'a display of passions, and the consequences of their violence'[15] and 'the slaughter-bench at which the happiness of peoples, the wisdom of States, and the virtue of individuals have been victimized'.[16]

If all things and men are simply aspects of God then conflicts between them are, in some strained and peculiar sense, morally innocuous. Hegel claims indeed that it is the atrocities and sufferings of mankind as

the very field *which we, for our part, regard as exhibiting only the means for realizing what we assert to be the essential destiny – the absolute aim, or – which comes to the same thing – the true* result *of the World's History. We have all along purposely eschewed 'moral reflections' as a method of rising from the scene of historical specialities to the general principles which they embody.*[17]

Hegel emphasizes that 'merely individual conviction, individual views, individual conscience'[18] are subordinate to a higher purpose.

This vast congeries of volitions, interests and activities, constitute the instruments and means of the World-Spirit for attaining its object; bringing it to consciousness, and realizing it . . . those manifestations of vitality on the part of individuals and peoples, in which they seek to and satisfy their own purposes, are, at the same time, the means and instruments of a higher and broader purpose of which they know nothing – which they realize unconsciously . . .[19]

The great men of history, Alexander, Caesar, or Napoleon Bonaparte, the agents of the Spirit's realization are beyond moral reproach; whatever they do 'It is even possible that such men may treat other great, even sacred interests, inconsiderately; conduct which is indeed obnoxious to moral reprehension. But so mighty a form must trample down many an innocent flower – crush to pieces many an object in its path.'[20] Hegel does not reconcile 'ought' with 'is'; he is declaring that in the last analysis moral judgements are irrelevant; what is, *is* right.

This element in Hegel's thought has often been adduced as evidence of the sinister implications of his ideas. Certainly, if one was searching for an historical origin of the 'hard-headedness' and apparent moral callousness evident in some of Marx's observations on the costs of political struggle or in the sentiments and actions of Russian Marxist leaders like Lenin or even Stalin, then one might well locate it here. More interesting, however, is the reflection that it is the logic of Hegel's theoretical endeavour that forces him into these unlikely statements about God and morality.

If Hegel wished to evolve a theory encompassing the whole of social development he could only do so by making mere human morality internal to that theory. If 'moral reflections' are allowed to provide judgements of history then history itself ceases to be a development theory and becomes mere narrative description. History loses its unique authority and can be criticized with reference to criteria derived from something other than the process of the world's spiritual development. For Hegel to do this would be for him to admit that his historical philosophy was less than a universal explanation. This intellectual *impasse* is of some significance in the formulation of Marx's own social theories (see Chapter 8).

German philosophy, individualism and social integration

Hegel has long enjoyed, or been cursed with, a reputation as a philosopher who pursued a line of speculative inquiry which is quite alien to the great Western and Anglo-Saxon tradition of liberalism and empiricism. He has been damned as the ideologue of Prussian militarism, and branded as the intellectual progenitor of Russian Bolshevism and German National Socialism. It needs to be stressed, therefore, that his intellectual concerns were much more closely related to those which preoccupied the thoughts of Smith, Ricardo and other liberal thinkers than such analyses have suggested. As we have seen, the mainspring of his theories was provided by a psychological theory which itself stems from an individualist, anthropocentric tradition, and which was designed to meet a philosophical difficulty also resulting from individualist inquiry.

Indeed, the 'idealist philosophy' evolved by German thinkers, of which Hegelianism is the most outstanding example, was itself in part a response to the social and economic changes of eighteenth-century Central Europe. Hegel's preoccupation with the reintegration of man and the world, with the restoration of 'wholeness', was a concern which was shared by many of his German contemporaries. In the eighteenth century, Germany was in a politically incoherent state. The Holy Roman Empire, when it was finally swept away by Napoleon in 1806, was hardly more than a name. Germans were split up among a variety of political units with overlapping jurisdictions and rights. The political constituents of the Empire included the kings of Austria and Prussia, 94 spiritual and lay princes, 103 counts, 40 prelates and 51 free towns. Central Europe was divided between Catholics and Protestants, while the lack of cultural unity was both the cause and effect of the late development of a German national literature. In fact, one of the main concerns of the generation of literateurs among whom Hegel grew up, was that of finding or creating an audience for their work. Writers like Goethe and Schiller were conscious of the cultural backwardness of Germany as compared with France and England, and the lack of social homogeneity in Germany as well as of its political heterogeneity. They cast longing eyes back toward what they conceived to be the cultural integration of the Greek city-state or even the superior cultural structure of a mediaeval unity.

Searching for an explanation of their socially fissured situation they turned naturally to social and historical theory. Jean-Jacques Rousseau (1712–78) helped to make notions about the debilitating effect of social and political development fashionable. According to these the progress of society and the increased complexity of social institutions were corrupting influences which inhibited man in the free exercise of his faculties and the development of his personality. The Germans sought confirmation of this idea in the works of social analysis produced by the Scottish Historical school. Adam Ferguson's *An Essay on the History of Civil Society* was translated into German in 1768 and its popularity subsequently secured election to the Berlin Academy of Sciences for its author. Sir James Steuart's *An Inquiry into the Principles of Political Economy* was translated into German in 1769–72 and John Millar's *The Origin of the Distinction of Ranks* in 1772. Adam Smith's *The Wealth of Nations* was published in German in 1776, the same year that it made its first appearance in English. Goethe was not only familiar with the Scottish writers but declared that their high standing with German scholars was because they provided a better foundation for the understanding of human thought and action than did German philosophers, by combining empirical information more closely with analytical ideas. Although the Scottish writers subscribed to Smith's view that it was the division of labour which impelled society towards greater wealth and diversity of activity, economic, social and intellectual, they were all, like Smith himself, well aware that the division of labour, by making jobs repetitive and undemanding, and by dividing social functions among technicians, could have adverse social effects. This negative aspect of progress is never the major theme of their work, even for Ferguson, who expresses it most strongly, but it was an idea that helps to account for their popularity in Germany. What, in Scottish hands, was a reasonably optimistic account of progress was used by German writers as an explanation of their own social fragmentation. The division of labour was seen as the reason for the stratification of society, for the specialization of man's activities which deprived him of that full exercise of all his powers, mental and physical, for which nature had destined him. It accounted for the weakening of social and personal bonds and for a decline in the coherence of society.

Hegel's economics

It is not surprising therefore, that Hegel, in his own endeavour to provide an account of social and political development, should have drawn on the work of the most advanced social thinkers of his day, the Scottish Historical School, and on the work of the greatest of the political economists, Adam Smith. Ideas about the nature of society and the way in which it functions can be found in *The Phenomenology* as well as in his other less directly social work, but they are most extensively elaborated in his *The Philosophy of Right* (1821).

The purpose of this treatise was the exposition of 'the science of the state'.[21] Hegel applies his developmental method to show that political and social organization is itself the product of a process. Just as successive civilizations in world history represent increasingly the superior levels of consciousness and understanding attained by man, so political development can be shown to proceed by phases. These are: (a) The *family*, 'natural or immediate' consciousness; (b) *civil society*, 'an association of members as self-subsistent individuals ... Their association is brought about by their needs, by the *legal* system – the means to security of person and property – and by an external organization for attaining their particular and common interests';[22] and (c) the *constitution of the state*, which dialectically subsumes and integrates (a) and (b).[23] We are not directly concerned here with Hegel's political philosophy – what it is important to note is the prominent part which economic categories and especially a general concept closely related to the market – civil society – as the infrastructure of the political community, play in his analysis.

It might be claimed that Hegel attributed an even more important function to property as a fundamental element in society and politics than did earlier social theorists like Hobbes and Locke. Hegel asserts that property is not only basic to social and political activity but also to identity. It is by owning things that a man realizes himself and establishes his position in the world. 'Right is in the first place . . . *property* ownership . . . it is only as owners that . . . two persons really exist for each other.'[24] Contract is the act which establishes social identity,[25] and crime is primarily the violation of contract and of property rights[26]. 'Property is the embodiment of personality'[27] and 'the means whereby I give my will an embodiment'[28]. Hegel even approves of the dissolution of monasteries on the grounds that 'no community has so good a right to property as a person has'.[29]

Hegel's description of civil society is drawn more or less directly from the political economists; by 'civil society' Hegel means primarily the market mechanism and its laws as described by Smith. It is the arena for the pursuit of self-interest: 'In civil society each member is his own end, everything else is nothing to him.'[30] But, just as for Smith the pursuit of self-interest is integrated by the market mechanism so as to promote the common good. So, according to Hegel, 'In the course of the actual attainment of selfish ends . . . there is formed a system of complete interdependence, wherein the livelihood, happiness, and legal status of one man is interwoven with the livelihood, happiness and rights of all.'[31] Again, just as for Smith commercial society is the highest stage of social development, so, for Hegel, 'the creation of civil society is the achievement of the modern world'.[32]

Hegel actually identifies the laws of political economy with the operation of the World Spirit. Hegel sees political economy, as he sees the natural sciences, not as explanations of the world rivalling his own, but as scientifically demonstrated partial truths, which have themselves to be explained and integrated into Hegel's own world theory;

Political Economy is the science which starts from this view of needs and labour but then has the task of explaining mass-relationships and mass-movements in their complexity and their qualitative and quantitative character. This is one of the sciences which have arisen out of the conditions of the modern world. Its development offers the interesting spectacle (as in Smith, Say and Ricardo) of thought working upon the endless mass of details which confront it at the outset and extracting there from the simple principles of the thing, the under- standing effective in the thing and directing it.[33]

The basic concepts of political economy are clearly discernible even through the obscurities of Hegel's philosophical presentation. The market promotes not only exchange but also production – and the essential element in production is labour, which determines the value of the things produced. 'The means of acquiring and preparing the . . . means appropriate to our . . . ends is work. Through work . . . raw material . . . is . . . adapted to these . . . ends . . . Now this formative change confers values on means and gives them their utility. . .'[34] 'Work . . . brings about the division of labour'.[35] This increases output and improves technology 'until finally man is able to step aside and install machines in his place'.[36]

Economic interdependence produces a 'compulsion' which 'presents itself . . . as the universal permanent capital'.[37] At the same time, these 'infinitely complex, criss-cross, movements of reciprocal production and exchange . . . are built up . . . into class-divisions'.[38] Economic activity increases population as well as output. In doing so it has a polarizing effect on society, generating wealth at one extreme and an impoverished and unemployed proletariat at the other; 'When civil society is in a state of unimpeded activity, it is engaged in expanding internally in population and industry. The amassing of wealth is intensified . . . That is one side of the picture. The other is the subdivision and restriction of particular jobs. This results in the dependence and distress of the class tied to work of that sort.'[39] Hegel is an underconsumptionist: 'the evil consists precisely in an excess of production and in the lack of a proportionate number of consumers who are themselves also producers'.[40] This in turn 'drives . . . civil society – to push beyond its own limits and seek markets, and so its necessary means of subsistence, in other lands which are either deficient in the goods it has overproduced, or else generally backward in industry, etc.'.[41] This prefiguring of twentieth-century theories of imperialism is tempered by a belief in the beneficial effects of international trade which 'creates commercial connexions between distant countries and so relations involving contractual rights. At the same time, commerce of this kind is the most potent instrument of culture, and through it trade acquires its significance in the history of the world.'[42]

State and society

Quite clearly, what Hegel knew about economics was derived from his reading of British political economy. The structure of his argument about politics and society is also very similar to those of his Scottish and English mentors. His general thesis, that the State represents a synthesis of the family and civil society, together with his exposition of right and law as the institutional carapace of a commercial interdependence in society, would seem to indicate that he was in some sense an economic determinist. Hegel's belief that the Spirit worked through the market to render the incoherence of individual appetites into a coordinated whole offers the outline of a relationship between economics and politics not unlike Marx's own.

At one point, however, Hegel expressly denies that the State is the functional product of economic activity, writing that the State is the 'true ground' of the family and the market, and 'actually, therefore, the state is not so much the result as the beginning'.[42] This assertion that the State is the primary *cause* of social change rather than the *result* perhaps stemmed from Hegel's apprehensions about how this part of his work would be viewed by the authorities. The political unrest in the German Confederation after the end of the Napoleonic Wars prompted the issue of the Carlsbad Decrees in 1819 which, among other things, increased the powers of the censorship. Certainly the passage in question reads awkwardly and fits unhappily with the general trend of his exposition. Whatever the reason for it, the fact that this account of civil society as the outcome of the State rather than its determinant is somewhat forced only serves to underline the otherwise very close affinity of his arguments about commerce and social institutions with those of Smith and his followers. This is not to say that Hegel was an advocate of *laissez-faire*; his belief in the tendency to underconsumption entailed support for the idea that some force external to the market was necessary to ensure that general welfare was maintained. Moreover, his notion of civil society is not quite that of the Scots; there is a much greater consciousness of the importance of non-market institutions. Nevertheless, any reader of Hegel who comes to him after reading Smith and Ricardo will immediately recognize ideas which, although distorted, are still recognizably liberal and market based.

Metaphysics and the 'real' world

In Hegel, mind is essentially indistinguishable from matter. He is what is technically described as an 'idealistic monist', a thinker who denies the duality of nature and asserts that the substance of the universe is homogeneous with and identical to that which composes ideas and mind. But, as his discussion of economics illustrates, his philosophy is not simply metaphysics – it had a very extensive 'real' content.

But this 'real' and 'material' content is of a peculiar kind. Hegel's phenomenological approach to the world dismissed empiricism as a crude attitude which missed the whole point of the epistemological problem. To take the world as given is to finesse the vital question of cognition; 'reality' is the product of the reciprocal interaction between sense phenomena on the one hand and mind on the other. Hegel's ideas about cognition are thus not premissed on an interest in how we establish the existence of an 'external' and ontologically autonomous world but rather are devoted to establishing what it is that we 'make of' our experience. Thus, in the *Phenomenology* and *The Philosophy of History* he is clearly fitting historical events to *a priori* psychological categories derived from introspection.

Cognition is not merely recognition; it is a creative act.

Accordingly, in *The Philosophy of Right*, when Hegel attempts to explain the nature of political institutions, he does not turn directly to empirical accounts of the German economic, political and social structures which he could see about him, but takes, as a description of the real world, the *theories* of *British* political economy. Hegel's economics are thus not based on the first-hand study of production and distribution as exemplified in Central Europe but on the works of men who were speculating about the nature of social and economic change in a country which Hegel never visited. The 'inner' content of Hegel's 'philosophy' is thus not facts and data as commonly conceived, but other writers' interpretations of them. Hegel's writings on society and politics are, in part, a thinly overlaid reworking of political economy.

References and Notes

1. V. I. Lenin, *Polnoe Sobranie Sochinenii*, 5th edn (Moscow 1973), vol. IXXX, p. 160.
2. Ibid., vol. IXXX, p. 162.
3. Frederick Engels, 'Ludwig Feuerbach and the end of classical German philosophy' in Marx Engels, *Selected Works*, vol. II, p. 349; *MEW*, vol. XXI, p. 292.
4. David Hume, *A Treatise of Human Nature*, ed. Ernest C. Mossner (Penguin Books, Harmondsworth and Baltimore 1969), Book I, Sect. 7, p. 314.
5. Karl Marx, *The Economic and Philosophic Manuscripts of 1844*, ed. Dirk J. Struik (New York 1964), International Publishers, p. 173.
6. *The Logic of Hegel*, transl. William Wallace, 2nd edn (London and New York 1892), Oxford University Press, p. 4.
7. G. W. F. Hegel, *The Phenomenology of Mind*, transl. J. B. Baillie, 2nd edn (London and New York 1949), George Allen and Unwin, p. 67.
8. Ibid., p. 90.
9. *The Logic of Hegel*, p. 86.
10. Ibid., p. 354.
11. Hegel, *The Phenomenology of Mind*, p. 142. The work of the modern developmental psychologist, Jean Piaget, is, in effect, a protracted attempt to provide an experimental basis for a set of insights into child development which are very like Hegel's basic intuitions.
12. Ibid., p. 769.
13. Ibid., p. 238.
14. G. W. F. Hegel, *The Philosophy of History*, transl. J. Sibree (New York 1945), Dover, pp. 105–9.
15. Ibid., p. 20.
16. Ibid., p. 21.
17. Ibid.
18. Ibid., p. 24.
19. Ibid., p. 25.
20. Ibid., p. 32.

21. G. F. W. Hegel, *The Philosophy of Right*, transl. T. M. Knox (Oxford 1952), p. 11.
22. Ibid., para. 157, p. 110.
23. Ibid.
24. Ibid., para. 40, p. 33.
25. Ibid.
26. Ibid., see also paras. 90–95, pp. 66–7.
27. Ibid., para. 51, p. 45.
28. Ibid., no 27, addition to para. 46, p. 236.
29. Ibid.
30. Ibid., no 116, addition to para. 182, p. 267.
31. Ibid., para. 183, p. 123.
32. Ibid., no. 116, addition to para. 182, p. 266.
33. Ibid., para, 189, pp. 126–7.
34. Ibid., para, 196, pp. 128–9.
35. Ibid., para. 198, p. 129.
36. Ibid.
37. Ibid., para, 199, p. 130.
38. Ibid., para. 201, pp. 130–1.
39. Ibid., para. 243, 149–50.
40. Ibid., para. 245, p. 150.
41. Ibid., para. 246, p. 151.
42. Ibid., para. 247, p. 151.
43. Ibid., para. 256, p. 155.

Chapter 6

Marx, Hegel and Feuerbach

In 1837 Marx became a Hegelian. The experience was painful, dramatic and sudden. In fact, Marx's own account makes it sound much more like a conversion experience than the result of cool ratiocination. In 1836, after a year at Bonn University, where he spent his time drinking, duelling, writing poetry and running up debts, Marx was removed by his father to the more sober circumstances of the University in Berlin, capital of Prussia. Here he appears to have led a much more studious life and plunged into law and philosophy. The main feature of his early intellectual development was a struggle occasioned by what he felt to be deficiencies in pre-Hegelian idealist philosophy. In particular he was troubled by the inadequacy of Kant's answer to the problem of knowledge and morality, by his failure to connect the ideal and noumenal with the real and phenomenal.

The 'opposition of "is" and "ought" which is the hallmark of idealism' was, Marx thought, a 'dominating and very destructive feature'[1] frustrating his own attempts to develop a comprehensive philosophy. At the same time, although it is not clear why, he resisted the 'grotesque and rocky melody'[2] of Hegel's philosophy. Nonetheless, he found that, in spite of himself, his own speculation and reading led him inexorably to Hegelian conclusions: 'A curtain had fallen, my holy of holies was rent asunder and new gods had to be installed.'[3] He wrote to his father that 'my fruitless and failed intellectual endeavours and my consuming anger at having to make my idol a view that I hated, made me ill . . .'[4] and that 'my vexation prevented me from thinking at all for several days and I ran like a madman round the garden'[5]. During his recuperation from this shattering experience Marx 'got to know Hegel from beginning to end, together with most of his disciples'.[6] In Berlin, these disciples formed a club of 'Young Hegelians' where, in discussion, Marx attached himself 'ever more closely to the philosophy that I had thought to escape'.[7]

Hegelians: right and left

Hegel died in 1831 and although his philosophy continued to exert a powerful influence throughout the 1830s and into the 1840s the story of this influence is the story of its decay and subversion. Marx adopted Hegelianism therefore, when it was already past its hey-day. He also came to it in the midst of a fierce controversy about its political significance which accompanied and hastened its decline.

Soon after 1831 Hegelians split into two wings: left and right. The Right Hegelians, as the name implies, expounded a conservative view of the master's views, while the left wing sought to put Hegelianism to radical use.

The Right Hegelians had the easier task. As we have seen, Hegelianism was a theory which 'accounted for' the world. Hegel himself was at pains to make it clear that his philosophy was not a predictive science and that he could only provide explanations of human and social developments after the event. In the preface to *The Philosophy of Right* he wrote:

One word more about giving instruction as to what the world ought to be. Philosophy in any case comes on the scene too late to give it. As the thought of the world, it appears only when actuality is already there cut and dried after its process of formation has been completed. . . . When philosophy paints its grey in grey, then has a shape of life grown old. By philosophy's grey in grey it cannot be rejuvenated but only understood. The owl of Minerva spreads its wings only with the falling of the dusk.[8]

As such, Hegel's theory is a conservative doctrine; as we have seen, he expels morality from his theory so that explanation is indistinguishable from justification. Hegel's assertion that 'What is rational is actual and what is actual is rational'[9] was understood by his contemporaries to constitute an assertion that the status quo is in principle defensible *because* it is the status quo. It carried the further implication that Hegelianism *was* absolute knowledge and that further development of his philosophy was excluded.

The problem for the radically minded Hegelian was to find a way out of this impasse. In the event, the battle over the proper meaning of Hegel was fought on religious grounds. Hegel's work is explicitly theological; all things are explained as aspects of the working of the Divine Mind. A book by David Strauss, *The Life of Jesus* (1836), helped to draw the lines of the conflict by suggesting that a study of the Gospels shows that there was no historical Jesus and that the stories told about him are simply myths which, nonetheless, fulfil important religious functions. Religion was thus not the revelation of God but an invention of man. This inspired a train of thought, the purport of which was not to demonstrate the irrationality of religion, but to offer secular explanations of it. This suggested that Hegel's philosophy could be transformed by refusing to take as a literal truth, the position ascribed by it to God and seeking instead some esoteric meaning for the Divine Spirit. Hegel's identification of the human with the Divine Mind offered a point of attack. It was only necessary to suggest that Hegel had in some sense shrunk from or had perverted the truth that the Spirit is man and that history and society are the creations of human beings rather than God for new and radical possibilities to be opened up. As Engels wrote in 1844, 'Hitherto the question has always been; What is God? German philosophy has answered: God is man.'[10]

Bruno Bauer (1808–82), the most important of the Young Hegelians, became a close friend of Marx, who helped him to develop his ideas about the 'atheistic' and secular potential of Hegel. In the preface to his doctoral thesis, which he presented in 1841, Marx declares that philosophy is opposed to all those who 'do not recognise man's self-consciousness as the highest divinity',[11] and that 'the proofs for the existence of God are nothing but proofs for the existence of an essentially human self-consciousness and logical elaborations of it'.[12] In other words Marx thought then that the phenomenological and introspective notions which lay at the roots of Hegel's ideas provided a way of reconstructing the world, albeit still an Hegelian one, at the centre of which stands not God but man.

Feuerbach and 'transformational criticism'

It was Ludwig Feuerbach (1804–72), however, who seizing on the psychological content of Hegel's writings, gave the fullest articulation to left Hegelian ideas. Feuerbach's writings, *The Essence of Christianity* (1841), and *Preliminary Theses on the Reform of Philosophy* (1843) were a watershed in the history of post-Hegelian philosophy. Feuerbach cut through the ambiguity which still resided in the idea of the divinity of man's self-consciousness and proclaimed that 'metaphysics is esoteric psychology'.[13] For Feuerbach, Hegel's assertion that God's creation of the world was an act of 'self-alienation' obscures the real truth. This truth is that man has 'alienated' himself in order to create God. He has taken his noblest qualities and human virtues, his regard for truth, for justice and for love, and projected them onto the Deity. The qualities for which he worships God are in fact his own. Man has divested himself of his own true nature and endowed a mythical entity with it. Theology is simply mystified anthropology. 'In religion', wrote Feuerbach, 'man contemplates his own latent nature'.[14] Feuerbach's message is that man must free himself from the illusions of religion in order to realize the fullness of his own potential as a human being. He has to see that the theology of thinkers like Hegel is a metaphysical exercise which wrongly persuades man of his moral inadequacy and prevents him from realizing his own essential goodness in his relations with his fellows. He must penetrate the veils spread by religion and see that its power depends entirely on his failure to see it for what it really is, the alienation of himself.

Feuerbach claimed that, in contrast to Hegel, he had based himself on 'the real material world'[15] and that the subject of his inquiry was 'empirical' man as he *really* existed. At the same time Feuerbach did not discard Hegel; he could claim, with some justification, to have seen through to the origins of Hegel's philosophy, but, embedded in

Feuerbach's system, the structure of Hegel's thought remains intact. Feuerbach's idea of 'alienation' is, of course, Hegelian and his account of man's 'recovery of himself' is clearly related to Hegel's dialectic. His system is anthropocentric and the implication of his ideas is radical but these new emphases are arranged within an old framework. Indeed, Feuerbach thought that Hegel's philosophy contained essential truths; and the fact that Hegel had *uniformly* distorted these truths made it possible to recover them once the nature of the Hegelian distortion was understood. Hegel's confusion of man with God was, according to Feuerbach, the result of the fact that he had simply inverted the real world. The 'real material world' would therefore readily re-emerge when this was taken into account. 'It suffices to put the predicate in the place of the subject everywhere, i.e. *to turn speculative philosophy upside down,* and we arrive at the truth in its unconcealed, pure, manifest form.'[16] Feuerbach had not dismantled the Hegelian construction, he had subjected it to a 'transformational criticism' which changed its meaning but not its mode of operation.

Because the idea is so basic to the dissolution of Hegelianism and because it was so powerfully to haunt the work of Marx in a variety of ways it is worth dwelling for a moment on the nature of 'transformational criticism'. Above all it implies great concentration on the text of the pronouncements of political and social theory or even on the words employed by agents of social processes. An obsession with words was almost a disease among the Young Hegelians and Marx never completely freed himself from the temptation to argue from the *possible* rather than the *actual* connotation of a word or phrase. It is this which has earned him from his detractors a reputation as the last of the Schoolmen. But it is certainly from 'transformational criticism' and not from any supposed inheritance of Talmudist techniques that Marx's predilection for 'critique' and analysis rather than empirical research arises. At a period when statistical information was unreliable or incomplete such an approach is understandable even if it now appears 'scientifically' defective.

Feuerbach enjoyed only a comparatively brief period of fame and his ideas are ill-served by his own tedious, muddled and repetitive exposition of them; now he is read (although for different reasons) only by students of theology and Marxologists. But in his day, translated into English by George Eliot, his work was the *dernier cri* in the intellectual circle of Europe for a decade or more, and his impact on Marx's generation cannot be exaggerated. Looking back across the years in 1888, Engels described how important Feuerbach's influence had been on his contemporaries in the 1840s. Feuerbach's *Essence of Christianity* freed them from the metaphysical toils of Hegel and restored the real world to them:

it placed materialism on the throne again. Nature exists independently of all philosophy. It is the foundation upon which we human beings, ourselves products of nature, have grown up. Nothing exists outside nature and man, and the higher beings our fantasies have created are only the fantastic reflection of our own essence. . . . One must himself have experienced the liberating effect of this book to get an idea of it. Enthusiasm was general; we all became at once Feuerbachians.[17]

German economic backwardness, Marx, and the *'Rheinische Zeitung'*

During his time as a student Marx thought first of being a lawyer then abandoned this in favour of teaching philosophy. But his hopes for a university appointment came to nothing because Bauer, whose influence was to secure him a post, himself fell foul of the authorities because of the radical line which he had come more and more openly to pursue. In 1842 Marx turned to journalism, and began writing articles, first for the Young Hegelian periodical, the *Deutsche Jahrbücher*, and then for the *Rheinische Zeitung.*

It should not be thought that the Germany of the earlier part of the nineteenth century was undergoing an industrial revolution on the English scale. Contemporary observers were much more impressed with her relative political and economic backwardness. Earlier Goethe and Schiller had thought that economic progress was the cause of German national debility; but by the 1840s political events from the turn of the century had given rise to a new belief that it was the lack of proper policies favouring commercial development which was at the root of its difficulties.

The French Revolution had been carried into Germany on French bayonets and had been both an economic and political stimulus. The introduction of new, rationalized French legal and administrative practices on the left bank of the Rhine had encouraged, under the protection of the continental blockade, the rapid growth of a certain amount of industry. Politically, some of Napoleon's efforts at redrawing the map of Europe were to survive his defeat. The Congress of Vienna in 1815, which brought the Napoleonic Wars to a close, reduced the chaos of pre-Napoleonic Germany to thirty-nine states and four free cities united in a new German Confederation. But after 1815 the continental Allies, Prussia, Russia and especially Austria, were fearful of the political consequences of allowing the Revolutionary and Napoleonic examples to be freely followed, and measures of fairly rigorous political control were applied in Germany. Political frustration had been accompanied by economic weakness. Even the new political boundaries represented hindrances to commerce and 1815 re-exposed German industry to foreign competition.

Haltingly, the German states began to grope their way towards a solution of their problems. The demonstration effect of English economic power prompted public debate in which demands for national unity and internal free trade were mingled with appeals for protection against non-German competition. The foundation of the German Customs Union in 1834, to which all the members of the German Confederation with the exception of Austria were eventually to accede, was a product of the preoccupation of German rulers with economic issues. Nonetheless, although Germany was being gradually drawn into the international market, in the period up to the 1840s it is probable that real income per head in Germany was actually declining because the growth in population was faster than the current not very considerable rate of growth of output. In 1840 the steam power installed in the whole of Germany amounted to about 6 per cent of capacity in the United Kingdom. Even in 1848 two-thirds of the population were still employed in agriculture and, of the rest, only a small proportion worked in what could be called modern industrial undertakings. State regulation of economic activity was extensive, political systems were undemocratic, in many states Jews suffered from legal disabilities, and in many branches of manufacture the guild system was still used to organize the labour force.

Marx's brilliant political intuitions and considerable literary gifts, combined with his energy and organizing talent soon secured for him the editorship of the *Rheinische Zeitung*. The paper's subtitle was 'For Politics, Commerce and Industry' and had been founded to further the interests of businessmen in the Rhineland. Its aims were to encourage the expansion and consolidation of the German market to promote policies likely to aid in the rationalization of administrative practice, to defend the principle of equality before the law, and generally to work for a climate favourable to communal development.

Radical Hegelians had been connected with the paper from the beginning and it was through these contacts that Marx was offered the editorship. Under his guidance the paper rapidly increased its circulation and adopted a more and more radical line. In 1843, after articles on property rights, divorce and poverty had attracted the adverse attention of the authorities, and anti-Russian articles had moved Tsar Nicholas I to make representations to Frederick William IV, king of Prussia, the newspaper was suppressed.

Marx's editorial activity, his tussle with the authorities, and first-hand experience of political commentary had an important effect on him. Some years later he described his time as editor as a key moment in the development of his interest in political economy:

In the year 1842–3, as editor of the Rheinische Zeitung *I experienced for the first time the embarrassment of having to take part in discussions on so-called material interests. The proceedings of the Rhenish Landtag on thefts of wood and parcelling of landed property, the official polemic which Herr von Schaper, then* Oberpräsident *of the Rhine Province, opened against the* Rheinische Zeitung *on the conditions of the Moselle peasantry, and finally debates on free trade and protective tariffs*

*provided the first occasions for occupying myself with economic
questions.*[18]

Marx's transformational critique of Hegel

In 1843 Marx agreed to edit, jointly with Arnold Rüge, another Young
Hegelian, a new journal, the *Deutsche-Französische Jahrbücher*. Marx
felt the need, after his journalistic essays, to attempt to establish a more
rigorous framework for his political views and to evolve a method for
dealing with the economic problems with which he had been confronted
as a journalist. From Feuerbach it was clear to him that the way to
establish a proper political theory was by attempting a 'transformational critique' of Hegel. Just as Hegel had sought to understand the
economic structure of the world by reading Adam Smith, so Marx now
thought to understand political institutions by reading Hegel's political
treatise, *The Philosophy of Right*. Feuerbach's claim to have returned
man to the 'real material world' was a peculiar one – he thought, as we
have seen, that the truth was to be found not in the study of empirical
data, but in a new way of reading Hegel. Marx proved himself a faithful
pupil; the opening sentence of Marx's article in the *Deutsche-
Französische Jahrbücher* of February, 1844, entitled 'Towards a
Critique of Hegel's Philosophy of Right. Introduction', reads 'As far as
Germany is concerned, the criticism of religion is essentially complete,
and the criticism of religion is the presupposition of all criticism.'[19] Now
that religion has been revealed as 'the opium of the people' it is

*the task of history, now that the truth is no longer in the beyond, to
establish the truth of the here and now. The first task of philosophy,
which is in the service of history, once the holy form of human self-
alienation has been discovered, is to discover self-alienation in its
unholy forms. The criticism of heaven is thus transformed into the
criticism of earth, the criticism of religion into the criticism of law, and
the criticism of theology into the criticism of politics.*[20]

In other words, Marx, now that the Feuerbachian method has
established the secular basis of religion, sought to establish the 'real'
basis of social institutions by 'criticizing' the systems in which they were
embodied. He is conscious of the charge that such a 'criticism' ought to
start from the empirical world, 'the real seeds of life'[21] but declares that
the backwardness of German political institutions, and their incoherence makes this impossible. German institutions have only reached a
level which 'is already a dusty fact in the historical lumber room of
modern peoples'[22] and the pettiness and fragmentation of German
political life makes it 'below the level of history and below any
criticism.'[23] Significantly, Marx gives an economic example – 'the
relationship of industry and the world of wealth in general to the
political world is one of the chief problems of modern times'[24] and yet

the German response to this is to resort to a system of protectionism, the very thing which Adam Smith had set out to overthrow. 'Thus we are now starting to begin in Germany when France and England are beginning to end'.[25]

Marx can be seen here coping with the problem implicit in Hegel (see pp 68–69). Contemplating a relatively backward country, Germany, Marx is unable to adduce its empirical realities as the basis for a theory concerned essentially with social advance. Hegel had used Smith and Ricardo without apology; Marx goes further and claims that there is no need to look abroad even though the political and economic facts of German life are so primitive as to be recalcitrant to analysis. German sociological inferiority is compensated, according to Marx, by the superiority of its philosophers who 'have *thought* what other people have *done*'[26] so that 'If, instead of criticizing the incomplete works of our real history, we criticize the posthumous works of our ideal history, philosophy, then our criticism will be at the centre of the question of which the present age says: that is the question.'[27] And since 'the German philosophy of state and law . . . was given its most consistent, richest and final version by Hegel', then it followed for Marx that the extension of the Feuerbachian critique from God to society was to be achieved by moving from *The Phenomenology of Mind* to *The Philosophy of Right*.

Marx's reading of *The Philosophy of Right* can only have strengthened his belief in the primacy of economic factors in determining the nature of the political structure, and, as a corollary, have helped him to see that liberal political theory was an intellectual scheme for facilitating economic competition and guaranteeing security for the fruits of success – property. He was quick to rearrange Hegel's hierarchical order in which the existence of family and civil society flow from the prior existence of the state (see pages 67–68) and to make political institutions posterior to social conditions. 'Hegel', he writes, 'starts from the state and makes man into the subjective aspect of the state' whereas, in fact, 'just as religion does not make man, but man makes religion, so the constitution does not make the people, but the people make the constitution'.[28]

In another essay entitled *On the Jewish Question* in the same issue of the *Deutsche-Französische Jahrbücher*, Marx further develops his critique of Hegel. The question of the admission of Jews to full civil rights in Germany is used by Marx as the basis for a consideration of the nature of rights and civil society in general. He concludes that the great slogans of the French Revolution are in themselves no guarantees of emancipation or freedom. After all, religion is now understood to be a device for the enslavement of man, and yet one of the basic civil rights of modern society is freedom of religion. An emancipation which includes the right to remain enslaved is, Marx suggests, a curious affair. Taking as his text the Declaration of the Rights of Man of 1792, Marx interprets the right to liberty as the right of man to separate himself from his fellows and to own property which 'is the right to enjoy his possessions and dispose of the same arbitrarily, without regard for other men, independently from society, the right of selfishness'.[29] The right to security is 'the highest social concept of civil society, the concept of the police. The whole of society is merely there to guarantee to each of its members the preservation of his person, rights and property'.[30] Expounded in this way political rights, far from transcending the social system, turn out to be mundanely functional for a market in which 'the only bond that holds men together is natural necessity, need and private interest'.[31]

In short, Hegel's political theory is the account of the development of a gigantic social and economic swindle. The French Revolution had brought about the end of the feudal world, with its customary rules and guild regulations, its hierarchy of legal status, seigniorial rights, estates and corporations. In their place it had institutionalized 'liberty, equality and fraternity'. But the rights accorded to the individual in modern society, prove, on closer inspection, to be a delusion. They are rules for enslavement different in kind from that of feudalism, but enslavement just the same; they are the rules which bind man to the chariot of competition and the market, and endow him with a liberty which is only the freedom to be bought and sold, the freedom to participate in an economic struggle for existence in which most men are inevitably the losers.

By undertaking a 'critique' of politics Marx, with the help of Hegel's text, concluded that there was a deeper level of reality underlying and malevolently concealed by them and that this reality was economic. It still remained to analyse and penetrate this substratum on which sanity was apparently built; civil society and political economy had themselves to be dissected.

In fact the first to write a *Critique of Political Economy* was Frederick Engels, who sent it to Marx for inclusion in the *Deutsche-Französische Jahrbücher*. Moses Hess, another Young Hegelian who helped to turn the attention of both Marx and Engels to economics, had already declared that 'The essence of the modern world of exchange, of money, is the realized essence of Christianity. The commercial state is the promised kingdom of heaven, as, conversely, God is only idealized capital and heaven only the theoretical commercial world.'[32] Political economy, when analysed, would reveal the true, unhappy state of social relations, just as Hegel's theology as criticized by Feuerbach had revealed man's spiritual alienation from his own true nature. Engels's essay describes political economy as the mask for the pursuit of private interests. It is the 'science of enrichment', and 'came into being as a natural result of the expansion of trade ... with its appearance elementary, unscientific huckstering was replaced by a developed system of licensed fraud – a complete get-rich economy'.[33] Modern economics is 'the system of free trade based on Adam Smith's *The Wealth of Nations*'[34] But 'it did not occur to economics to question the validity of private property'[35] which constitute 'the premises of the state as such'.[36] The results of the system were 'the factory system and modern slavery, which yields nothing in cruelty and humanity to ancient slavery'.[37] Private property engenders competition, which in turn generates trade crises. Great wealth is generated and yet Malthusians declare that the labouring population is doomed to live at subsistence level. The means of transforming society are at hand but the free competitive market prevents productive power being put to use for the benefit of mankind. Instead, monopolies grow up and

The middle classes must increasingly disappear until the world is divided into millionaires and paupers, into large landowners and poor farm labourers. All the laws, all the dividing of landed property, all the possible splitting-up of capital, are of no avail: this result must and will come, unless it is anticipated by a total transformation of social conditions a fusion of opposed interests, a transcendence of private property.[38]

The *Deutsche-Französische Jahrbücher* closed down after one double issue, banned in Germany, virtually unread in France. Marx found himself in Paris without employment and set about writing a great synthesis – an immense critique of the whole world – a fuller and more complete Feuerbachian transformation of Hegel. Engels's essay on political economy gave him added encouragement to make this subject his starting point. His first notes, unpublished in his lifetime, have survived and are known as *The Economic and Philosophical Manuscripts of 1844*. In the preface, Marx makes it clear that he intended this to be only the first of a series of studies. He confesses that his critique of Hegel' political theory and jurisprudence had been too compressed. He announced his decision therefore to 'publish the critique of law, ethics, politics etc. in a series of distinct, independent pamphlets, and afterwards try in a special work to present them again as a connected whole showing the interrelationship of the separate parts . . . '[39] Marx was to spend the rest of his life elaborating what was originally conceived as the first part – the essay on economics.

The Economic and Philosophic Manuscripts are not complete nor always entirely coherent but they are valuable in showing how intimately connected was Marx's understanding of Hegel with his approach to political economy. Marx deals with the various categories with which political economists operated (wages, profits, rent, capital, property), copying out long sections from the most important political economists including Smith, Ricardo and Say, trying to demonstrate that the theories of political economy represented in disguised form the principle analogous to that enunciated by Feuerbach – that social institutions represent the 'alienated' creations of man. In political economy Marx sees a mystified account of the underlying principle that economic activity in the imperfect world is a process whereby man alienates his labour. Material wealth is created by the labour of men and yet this wealth is not enjoyed by those who produce it. Man is alienated from his product. Poverty is thus explained by, and identified with the philosophical idea of alienation as employed by Hegel and Feuerbach. It also accounts for the paradox that while political economy purports to be about the origin of the wealth of nations, in reality it is about the creation of poverty. Marx summarizes his transformational critique as follows:

We have proceeded from the premises of political economy. We have accepted its language and its laws. We presupposed private property, the separation of labour, capital and land, and of wages, profit of capital and rent of land – likewise division of labour, competition, the concept of exchange-value, etc. On the basis of political economy itself, in its own words, we have shown that the worker sinks to the level of a commodity and becomes indeed the most wretched of commodities; that the wretchedness of the worker is in inverse proportion to the power and magnitude of his production; that the necessary result of competition is the accumulation of capital in a few hands, and thus the restoration of monopoly in a more terrible form; and that finally the distinction between capitalist and land renter, like that between the tiller of the soil and the factory worker, disappears and that the whole of society must fall apart into the two classes – the property owners *and the* propertyless *workers.*[40]

The last part of the third section of the manuscripts is, significantly enough, Marx's attempt to come to terms and reckon up with Hegel; he calls the section 'Critique of the Hegelian dialectic and philosophy as a whole'. He freely admits his debt to Feuerbach who 'is the only one who has a serious, critical attitude to the Hegelian dialectic and who has made genuine discoveries in this field. He is in fact the true conqueror of the old philosophy.'[41] Applying Feuerbach's method to Hegel, Marx discovers the empirical referents of Hegel's idealism. The *Phenomenology* 'is a hidden and mystifying criticism' but 'in as much as it grasps steadily man's *estrangement*, even though man appears only in the shape of mind, there lie concealed in it *all* the elements of criticism . . . of whole spheres such as religion, the state, civil life, etc.'.[42] Although, according to Marx, Hegel fails to see that labour in the real world is alienated, impoverishing instead of enriching man's personality, and that Hegel's labour is only *'abstractly mental labour'*, nonetheless Marx asserts that in Hegel's writings it can be seen to be 'the *essence* of man'. Hence, the importance that Hegel attaches to labour is the same as that which it enjoys in *The Wealth of Nations*, where it is the mainspring of progress, the source and the measure of riches. Marx can thus assert that 'Hegel's standpoint is that of modern political economy'.[43]

To summarize what has been said in this and the preceding chapter: the connexion between idealist philosophy and the theories of political economy is vital to the understanding of Marx. Hegel had made a massive attempt to circumvent one of the basic technical problems in philosophy, the problem of how we know things. His concern with and solution of his difficulty was connected with other interests that were psychological and social. Hegel's answer was to deny the existence of any real or permanent fissure between the observer and things observed. Conceiving cognition as an active and developmental process he tried to show that the gap between mental phenomena and material things could be bridged and eliminated by the understanding. Our alienation from our material surroundings is overcome by understanding their nature and function. This understanding is in turn rooted in and made possible by the fact that our minds and our environment are themselves created and sustained by God. The separation of mind and matter is only apparent; in reality they are nothing more than aspects of the same Divine Mind. Hegel's answer to the epistemological difficulty is a psychological rather than a logical one. The scepticism of Hume and the moral and unsatisfied striving of Kant leave man without any sure connexion with the world. Hegel's 'philosophy' is the reassurance that they are in fact parts of an integrated whole.

This reintegration of man with his world necessarily involved not only what we would now regard as technical deliberations proper to philosophy but also a discussion of the nature of society itself. German writers of the later eighteenth and early nineteenth centuries, troubled by the political and cultural incoherence of German Central Europe, found, in seeking for a theoretical explanation of their social and political condition, help and inspiration in the work of the Scottish Historical School. They saw in their writings support for the belief that commercialization tended to fragment society and destroy the individual and his 'wholeness'. Following them, Hegel found in the political economy of Steuart, Smith and Ricardo, a description of the socioeconomic structure of society which he could not have derived from the splintered and confused state of contemporaneous Germany. Whereas his immediate German predecessors could see only fragmentation, Hegel declared that the State transcended and unified the apparently centrifugal tendencies of Smith's market society; Hegel's political philosophy is permeated with the assumptions of political economy.

Hegel's philosophy, embracing as it did psychology, sociology, politics and economics, was in many ways a descriptive rather than a prescriptive construction. At the same time it implied that understanding was closely linked with justification. If history is the account of 'God's way with the world' then normative statements about it are superfluous. God cannot be the subject of criticism. The distinction between positive and normative, between 'is' and 'ought' disappears. The young German intellectuals of the 1830s and 1840s who inherited the massive and comprehensive apparatus of Hegelianism thus found themselves locked in an intellectual box. Hegel's writing offered no fulcrum on which the lever of political criticism could be rested. And yet, in spite of Hegel's claim to have explained and defended the world by demonstrating its 'rationality', it was clear that the political and social organization of the German states was far from perfect.

It is a tribute to the power and amplitude of Hegel's work that an escape from his interpretation of the world could not be achieved simply by turning one's back on him; the confines of Hegelian philosophy could not be breached – they had to be transcended. Feuerbach, by identifying Hegel's Spirit as the 'alienation' of man's own powers and virtues, invented a powerful device for the reinstatement of man as the centre of a secularized world. At the same time, and unwittingly, in transformational criticism he discovered a solvent with the help of which the economic and technological accounts of society which Hegel had taken from Scottish writers could be recovered from his work.

But Feuerbach's 'transformational criticism' was ambiguous. The 'materialism' and 'empiricism' to which it gave rise was of a peculiar kind. For Young Hegelians like Marx, it had two implications. First, that 'by turning Hegel on his head' the real world would be revealed. Secondly, that all theoretical statements about the world could be similarly transformed. This led Marx to a general position, never explicitly formulated, and not, admittedly, consistently held, according to which the empirical world is to be approached, not directly, but by the transformation of what other social critics have said about it. In 1859 Marx described the path by which he became a political economist; his reading of Hegel's *The Philosophy of Right* led him to the conclusion that

legal relations as well as forms of state are to be grasped neither from themselves nor from the so-called general development of the human mind, but rather have their roots in the material conditions of life, the sum total of which Hegel, following the example of the Englishmen and Frenchmen of the eighteenth century, combines under the name of 'civil society', that, however, the anatomy of civil society is to be sought in political economy.[44]

Lenin thought that Hegel was the key to Marx's political economy; Marx thought that political economy was the key to Hegel.

References and Notes

1. Marx to his father, 10 November 1837, in Karl Marx, *Early Texts*, transl. David McLellan (Oxford 1971), p. 3.
2. Ibid., p. 7.
3. Ibid.
4. Ibid., p. 8.
5. Ibid., p. 7.

6. Ibid., p. 8.
7. Ibid.
8. Hegel, *The Philosophy of Right*, pp. 12–13.
9. Ibid., p. 10
10. In 'Die Lage Englands. *Past and Present* by Thomas Carlyle', *MEW*, vol. I, p. 546. Quoted in Robert Tucker, *Philosophy and Myth in Karl Marx* (Cambridge 1961), p. 73.
11. *Early Texts*, p. 13.
12. Ibid., p. 18.
13. Quoted in Sidney Hook, *From Hegel to Marx* (London 1936), p. 259.
14. Ludwig Feuerbach, *The Essence of Christianity* (London 1854), p. 32.
15. Ibid.
16. Ludwig Feuerbach, *Kleine Philosophische Schriften*, ed. Marx Gustav Lange (Leipzig, 1950), p. 73. Quoted in Tucker, op. cit., p. 86.
17. Frederick Engels, 'Ludwig Feuerbach and the end of classical German philosophy' in Marx Engels, *Selected Works* (Moscow 1951), vol. II, p. 333.
18. Karl Marx, 'Preface to "A Contribution to the Critique of Political Economy" ' (1859) in Mark Engels, op. cit., vol. I, p. 361.
19. *Early Texts*, p. 115.
20. Ibid., p. 116.
21. Ibid., p. 121.
22. Ibid., p. 117
23. Ibid., p. 118.
24. Ibid., p. 119.
25. Ibid., p. 120.
26. Ibid., p. 122. [I have italicized the verbs to bring out the meaning of the sentence.]
27. Ibid., pp. 120–1.
28. Ibid., p. 65.
29. Ibid., p. 102.
30. Ibid., p. 104
31. Ibid.
32. Moses Hess, *Sozialistische Aufsätze, 1841–1847* (Berlin 1921), p. 170. Quoted in Tucker, op. cit., p. 110.
33. Frederick Engels, 'Outlines of a critique of political economy' in *The Economic and Philosophic Manuscripts of 1844*, p. 197.
34. Ibid., p. 199.
35. Ibid., p. 198.
36. Ibid.
37. Ibid., p. 199.
38. Ibid., p. 223.
39. Ibid., p. 63. Interestingly enough, Adam Smith appears to have contemplated a 'grand synthetic system' of which *The Wealth of*

Nations was to be but one part, while the others were to be constituted by *Theory of Moral Sentiments* and an account of 'The general principles of law and government and of the different revolutions they had undergone in the different ages and periods of society'. See 'Introduction' in *Adam Smith. The Wealth of Nations*, ed. Andrew Skinner (Penguin Books, Harmondsworth 1970), p. 13.

40. *The Economic and Philosophic Manuscripts of 1844*, p. 106.
41. Ibid.
42. Ibid., p. 176.
43. Ibid., p. 177.
44. Marx Engels, op. cit., vol. I, p. 362.

Chapter 7

Utopian socialism

Marx's ultimate aim was, in his own words, 'to lay bare the economic law of motion of modern society'[1] and it is his efforts to do this which entitle him to be described as a political economist. At the same time, he did not intend that his work should be merely a politically neutral analytical endeavour – it was designed to demonstrate the truth of *socialism*. Marx, claimed Engels, was 'the first to give Socialism, and thereby the whole labour movement of our day, a scientific foundation.'[2] This chapter will attempt to give some idea of the nature of early nineteenth-century socialism and how Marx himself became a socialist.

Distributive and substantive justice

The exact meaning to be given the word 'socialism' is a vexed question; but it is not one which, in a book about Marx, can be avoided. It is a much abused word, used with systematic vagueness, polemical intent and evaluatively rather than descriptively. A start can perhaps be made by defining it negatively; socialism might be said to be, at least in part, an attack on distributive justice. Distributive theory assumes that individuals are comparable and autonomous and offers sets of rules which, if followed, will coordinate the activity of members of society, assigning each a function and status within a social system. The great political theorists of the seventeenth and eighteenth centuries who dominated the tradition within which Marx worked, Hobbes, Locke and Rousseau, were distributive theorists who devised sets of rules for political behaviour in terms of the rights and obligations of individual citizens. These rules, although based on egalitarian assumptions, generate hierarchical structures in which relative standing and rewards are distributed according to social and political functions. In other words, they reconcile the equal rights of individuals with the subordination without which social systems cannot be sustained. These theories have no empirical content; they are, of course, based on certain *assumptions* about human psychology and the material conditions prevailing in society and these vary from thinker to thinker, but these assumptions are not necessarily explicit and in any case do not form the subject of argument. Such theories are hence abstract, and the principles of obligation, subordination and freedom which they expound, have a relevance which is independent of the specifically physical environment of any particular society or of the distribution of wealth within it.

It is immediately obvious that political economy is not only a theory of economic development and equilibrium but also implies a theory of distributive justice; it puts economic flesh on the liberal political theories of Locke. The basis of Smith's 'optimism' about the course of economic development was the belief that output and happiness would be maximized when market institutions were allowed to function with the greatest practicable degree of freedom. Now these market institutions are themselves sets of liberal political rules dealing with the way in which property is acquired and disposed of, how contracts are entered into and goods and labour bought and sold. And although according to political economy even a thoroughly commercialized society would not be free of inequalities, including in particular a large class of the impoverished, the increase in the wealth of a nation which was thought to result from commercialization not only would tend to increase the power of its rulers and the comfort of its possessing classes but also offered hope that the lot of its least fortunate members might be alleviated. Certainly, it was argued, in societies where restraints were placed on commercial activity the lot of the worker would be even worse than where this were not the case. Political economy seemed to provide not just an explanation but an ethical justification for a market-induced distribution of wealth, for it is the very unevenness in the distribution of material goods which provide the very incentives for the production of these goods; without these inequalities production would be lower and the poor would be even poorer.

'Substantive justice' is a term of my own manufacture which is intended to contrast with 'distributive justice'. Socialism is here identified as a substantive theory because it is characterized by attempts not only to define simply the terms of exchange of justice, that is to say how rewards and disincentives are *proportioned*, but also to prescribe substantively the *physical* content of these relationships. Thus socialism was concerned *directly* with the distribution of wealth and organization of production, attempting to establish the specific conditions of social harmony, whereas, in distributive theory, levels of income and the differentiation between rich and poor are the *outcome* of the *rules* which constitute the theory.

The socialists were concerned with substantive definition because of their dissatisfaction with market outcomes – the same kind of dissatisfaction voiced by Marx and described in the previous chapter. To these social critics, in the early years of the nineteenth century, infected with notions of underconsumption, troubled by the dislocation of slump and boom, disturbed by structural unemployment, horrified by poverty and the squalor of the new towns, liberal theory was simply a hypocritical device for the oppression of the majority of society by a wealthy few.

However, their intellectual position was fatally flawed. The socialists strove to provide for a social arrangement which would guarantee the material welfare of the population and provide for an egalitarianism which avoided the subordination inherent in distributive liberal theory; but they set out to do this on the basis of assumptions about the desirability of both liberty and equality identical to those made by liberal theorists. As a theoretical endeavour, therefore, socialism was, and always has been, doubly doomed. First, liberty and equality can only be reconciled, if indeed they are in principle compatible at all, in the way in which liberal theory reconciles them, making equality anterior to liberty; it is not possible *simultaneously* to ensure equality and liberty. Secondly, if it is correct to describe socialism as a 'substantive theory', then this shows a second logical failing; 'substantive theory' is a contradiction in terms, for it is in the nature of a theory to express *relationships* – the substance of these relationships in terms of particular working arrangements and actual entitlements to goods and services cannot be generated by theory alone. At some point quantities and physical conditions must be directly specified. To make matters worse, it has always been part of the stock-in-trade of socialist propagandists that the socially desirable is self-evident and that social theory is, as Marx also implies, an obfuscation of the *obvious* realities of morality and social relationships.

Moreover, socialist ideas were hardly ever *purely* substantive; they nearly all contained elements of distributive justice and indeed, as thinkers, were parasitic on political economy. Their subscription to the market-generated notions of liberty and equality meant that none of them was able to visualize social organizations which were not individualistic and market derived. They were preoccupied with one or both of two things – property rights and productive organization.

Socialism in France

For Marx's contemporaries, socialism was mainly, though not extensively, a French phenomenon. In his *Socialism: Utopian and Scientific*,[3] Engels associates socialism with the French Revolution but, in fact, the word did not come into general use until the 1830s, and appears to have been used first in England. Nonetheless, in the mythology of socialism, especially in France, the French Revolution occupied an important place.

The French radicals in the Paris of the 1840s were the inheritors of an ambiguous political tradition. The French Revolution was associated with many measures implied by the socialists' own programmes: the confiscation of property, the elimination of the ruling and possessing classes, mass popular participation in political debate, state guarantees of material welfare, and an attempt to spread revolutionary doctrines beyond national boundaries and throughout Europe. Although

Robespierre's Terror had been followed by a conservative reaction, suppressing the mobs which had brought success to the Revolution and eventuating in an imperial and authoritarian regime, Napoleon's installation of himself as emperor did not mean the reinstatement of the old order; he continued the rationalization and modernization of French society and the imperial banners still carried the revolutionary slogans of liberty, equality and fraternity. The Revolution had been put down but some of its most important achievements were institutionalized in the new police state. Even the Bourbons, restored to France by the Allies after the defeat of Napoleon in 1814, were unable and also partly unwilling to put the clock back to 1789. On the other hand, the general political climate was not in favour of thorough-going political transformations either. When Charles X's reactionary inclinations finally provoked a political upheaval in 1830, this 'revolution' replaced him, not with a Committee of Public Safety, but with another monarch, Louis Philippe, the 'citizen-king'. The new July monarchy, uncertain of its legitimacy, sought stability and security in inaction.

By the 1840s, accordingly, radicals, discontented with the indifference to social problems of Louis Philippe and his chief minister, Guizot, were able persuasively to describe the inequities and inadequacies of their society as arising from a failure to bring the Revolution to fruition. Socialists, consequently tended to see their task as that of ensuring that the popular demands of the mobs of the 1790s for complete equality, economically, socially and politically, should be fulfilled at last. Post-Napoleonic France, therefore, produced an extensive radical literature which found its inspiration for the order of society in what they supposed to be the frustrated intention of the upheavals which began in 1789. Thus, when Marx arrived in Paris in 1843, at what was perhaps the most critical period of his intellectual development, he found himself in a milieu in which a tradition of revolutionary and socialist thought was already established.

The most important of the socialist thinkers were, according to Marx himself, two Frenchmen, Saint-Simon and Fourier, and an Englishman, Owen. To these must be added a fourth, also a Frenchman, and well known to Marx, Proudhon.

Saint-Simon

Claude-Henri de Rouvroy, Comte de Saint-Simon (1760–1825), during a colourful career, fought the English in the American War of Independence, was imprisoned during the French Revolution and subsequently speculated successfully in sequestered land. He was also, however, a man of great intellectual ambition, obsessed with a desire to do for social science what Newton had done for mechanics. He was convinced that the scientific and technological knowledge which man had accumulated by the end of the eighteenth century would enable him to transform the world in the interests of a new and superior social order.

According to Saint-Simon scientific advance plays a crucial role in stimulating changes in the social structure, changes which are progressive and which, in recent times, were responsible for a transition from a feudal to an industrial world. There are echoes in Marx, and, more extensively, in Engels, of Saint-Simon's concept of the mechanism of social change, but more significant for the development of socialism was his concept of the ideal industrial society. The most important social group in the modern world was composed of 'industriels', whom Saint-Simon contrasted with unproductive members of society. These 'industriels' were not 'workers' in the modern and socialist sense of the term; they included *all* those who were engaged in productive activity, not merely labourers and artisans but also and especially managers, entrepreneurs and bankers, and captains of industry. His basic idea was that modern society should shake off the last vestigates of feudal practices in government and social organization and gear itself to production. Administration, urged Saint-Simon, is itself a technique and requires technically competent personnel for its proper execution; society should be run by those who best understand its true and modern purpose, the engineer and economic organizer. In his last work, *The New Christianity* (1825) Saint-Simon described the function of the new technocratic élite as that of managing society 'in order to ameliorate the moral and physical lot of the poorest class; society must be organized in the way best suited to the attainment of this goal.[4]

But Saint-Simon's ideas were not simply a rationalization of the political domination of the community by a new business class – indeed part of the implications of his work was that politics were merely trivial and that the social framework should be constructed solely with reference to the organizational requirements of the economy. His new social order was to be a kind of gigantic workshop in which functions would be determined by aptitude and efficiency, not by class membership. In stressing the fundamental social significance of work, the prior right to social consideration which participation in the productive process confers, the importance of economic organization and the identification of the equitable distribution of output as one of the main purposes of society, Saint-Simon expounded themes which were to be central to socialist doctrine. Engels picked out as Saint-Simon's key insight the statement that 'politics is the science of production' and his prediction of the complete absorption of policies by economics.[5]

Fourier

Saint-Simon himself had little to say about property rights and it was only after his death that his disciples developed his ideas into an extended attack on private property and advocated the collectivism that had been implicit in Saint-Simon's work. François-Marie-Charles Fourier (1772–1837), however, conflated the issues of ownership and organization and stated that 'the first problem for the economist to solve is to discover some way of transforming the wage-earner into a cooperative owner'.[6] Fourier's instrument for this transformation was the '*phalanstère*', an association for cooperative production and consumption. His programme was for the establishment of communes, composed of some 40 families or 1500 people, who could all live under the same roof and benefit from the cheapness and efficiency which the joint-purchasing of articles of consumption and the common provision of services would make possible. The commune members were also to engage in the cooperative production of food and industrial goods for their own consumption. The commune was not to be a rigidly organized institution; there was to be great freedom of choice in accommodation and employment, and even eating at the common tables was to be optional. Members were to include both rich and poor, and were to be drawn from all classes of society. Fourier believed deeply in the influence of environment on character and he intended the *phalanstère* as a social device which would change its members from competitors to cooperators.

Fourier is, perhaps most famous among socialist writers for his hopelessly comic flights of fancy about the coming world epoch of harmony in which the oceans would become sweet and drinkable and evolution would produce new animals like 'anti-lions' who would, unlike their contemporary counterparts, have pacific dispositions. He was also fiercely opposed to industrialization; in the *phalanstère*, manufacturing activity was to be kept to the lowest practicable level and the principal occupation of commune members was to be horticulture. It is, therefore, all the more striking that his ideas about the establishment and operation of the *phalanstères* should have been firmly rooted in modern commercial practice. The communes were to be joint-stock companies and part of the income of members was to be related to their capital contribution. Nor were members to be paid equally in other respects – wages were to depend on the skill employed and the responsibility undertaken. The services within the commune were also to be differentially priced – more elaborate food and better living quarters would cost more. Fourier hoped that this originally inegalitarian arrangement would, through monetary incentive and financial commitment to the success of the enterprise, generate a sense of common responsibility and ultimately a state of essential equality. Fourier's Utopia was constructed on the basis of a belief that the institutions of commercial society could be used for the regeneration of mankind.

Owen

The third of Marx's socialist forerunners was an Englishman, Robert Owen (1771–1858). Owen was one of the most successful businessmen of his day, and it was for his practical efforts to provide better working conditions for his employees and for his social experiments rather than for his theoretical contributions that he became famous. In 1800 he bought the New Lanark cotton mills and, over the succeeding quarter of a century, proved that humane management was compatible with the making of profits. He provided improved housing and education, appointed welfare officers and ensured steady employment whatever the state of trade. Starting out as nothing more than an energetic and enlightened industrialist, Owen's experiences as a manufacturer convinced him that industry, properly organized, not only would ensure the material welfare of the people but could also provide the basis for a new moral community.

The end of the Napoleonic Wars created severe economic dislocation and the resulting unemployment led Owen to press for the introduction of 'villages of cooperation' to provide useful occupation for those thrown out of work. These were basically collective farms, not dissimilar from the *phalanstères*. The profits from these undertakings would provide finance for the expansion of the system so as to transform the whole economy. Like Fourier, Owen attached great importance to the part played by environment in determining behaviour, and consequently believed that his cooperative enterprises, in which the profit motive and the division of labour were to be abolished, would produce workers who were physically, mentally and morally superior to those employed in the unreformed factory system.

His failure to get government support for his ideas and his inability to persuade his fellow industrialists of the cogency of his schemes of labour management led Owen to adopt more radical attitudes. He supported his attack on property with a labour theory of value and attempted to give it practical expression through the establishment of 'labour exchanges' which issued 'labour notes' as a replacement for money. In 1834 he was briefly the president of the short-lived Grand National Consolidated Trades Union. Owen's attempt to abolish profit was also the inspiration of the British cooperative movement, which was formed to eliminate the capitalist middleman in the retailing of consumer goods.

Although Owen's ideas were always tinged with paternalism and were essentially reformist and counter-revolutionary, this was never so marked as to affect the widespread popularity that his ideas enjoyed among radicals; for them he was a man identified with a vision of a society in which industrialization was the key to progressive social organization.

Proudhon

The most important French socialist theorist of the nineteenth century was, perhaps, Pierre-Joseph Proudhon (1809–65). Proudhon found fame with a book called *What is Property?* (1840) which Marx described as 'the scientific manifesto of the French proletariat'.[7] 'Property', declared Proudhon, 'is theft', and it is because a critique of property rights lies at the centre of his ideas that Proudhon, in spite of his own protestations to the contrary, is to be classified as a socialist. Proudhon distinguished himself from other socialist writers by his contempt for the construction of Utopias and his fear that their systems would endanger the value he held most dear, liberty, and strengthen the institution he most fiercely hated, the State. And it is his failure to show how liberty could be maintained without some sort of policing institution that deprive his writings of practical relevance.

Proudhon is the most explicitly economic of socialist writers after Marx and Engels and although, after a personal disagreement with him over political tactics, Marx viciously attacked Proudhon's *Economic Contradictions (1846)* in *The Poverty of Philosophy* (1847), the book was, in fact, an endeavour very like that of Marx himself – a critique of political economy employing concepts derived from Hegel. Indeed, Marx claimed to have introduced Proudhon to the work of Hegel, and was never on the same intimate terms with any other non-German socialist thinker until much later in his life.

The principal difficulty in Proudhon's ideas was the distinction he made between 'property' and 'possession'. Property was the ownership of assets, like land and capital, which generated 'unearned' incomes in the form of rent and interest, which he designated 'theft'. 'Possession' was, according to Proudhon, the result of the legitimate acquisition of goods as the fruit of personal labour. At the same time he was convinced that the market offered the best guarantee of freedom and welfare: 'Division of labour, collective force, competition, exchange, credit, property and even liberty – these are the true economic forces, the raw materials of all wealth, which without actually making men the slaves of one another, give entire freedom to the producer ease his toil, arouse his enthusiasm and double his produce.'[8] Proudhon's distinction between 'property' and 'possession' is, of course, incoherent, and the obscurity which it generates permeates all his work. He valued the liberty which he explicitly identified as the basic principle of political economy, but criticized the political economists, as Marx did, for not seeing that the system they expounded meant the subjugation of men by men. This dilemma is nowhere resolved. He apparently relied on the ability of men to see that society needed to be organized in terms of 'commutative justice', by which he apparently meant a system which would be free from the exploitative element that arises in relations between unequals, and in which contracts would be fulfilled without any coercive institution to enforce them. Like other socialists, Proudhon could neither offer a substantive theory of socialist organization nor could he free himself from the idea that commercial practices offered the key to the social arrangement that would cure men's ills: 'Commutative justice, sovereignty of contract, economic or industrial regime . . . these are just synonyms for the idea which, by its advent, will abolish the old systems of distributive justice, or the sovereignty of law, in more concrete terms, the feudal, governmental or military regime: the future of humanity lies in this substitution.'[9]

Marx's adoption of socialism

Marx's political convictions were initially classically democratic. As late as 1842, while still editor of the *Rheinische Zeitung*, he wrote that his paper could not allow that communist ideas had even 'theoretical reality', although he thought that they needed careful study.[10] Up to that point he still thought, as Hegel thought, in terms of the emancipation of the individual. But in 1843 his reading of political economy, with its explanation of income distribution in terms of social groups, and of historical accounts of the French Revolution, with their stress on the importance of the role played by the proletariat, provided him with the material for a *class* analysis of society.

Following Moses Hess, who was the first of the Young Hegelians to identify Hegel's notion of 'alienation' with the legal concept of alienation – buying and selling – Marx came to see the whole of commercial society as the generator of this new psycho-economic 'alienation'. Commercialization alienates man from himself by catching him up in a web of institutions, relationships and functions, the connexion of which with the rest of society is obscure to him and in which even the significance of his physical participation in production is rendered entirely opaque by the division of labour and the cash nexus. Marx came to believe that this alienation, which affected all those caught up in the hideousness of cash-relationships, applied especially to a social group which was uniquely deprived and exploited – the propertyless working class. Marx then connected this idea of alienation with the category of 'labour', basic, as he thought, to both Hegel and political economy. The commercialization of society produced an impoverished working class so poor that all it had to offer in exchange for the means of subsistence was the toil of the bodies of its members; the workers were reduced, in neo-Hegelian terms, to the alienation of their own labour. Thus the two principles of the Hegelian world, alienation and the dialectical interaction between mind and matter, were rediscovered in propertylessness and work.

Because the proletariat was propertyless it was *totally* alienated, and because it was totally alienated it was, paradoxically, able to see clearly the reality of its own position; there was no benefit which it drew from society which might serve as an incentive for blindness, or act as a veil between it and reality. Thus, the proletariat, the victim of society, would be the instrument of its own salvation, for, as the consciousness of its position grew, as it surely would with increased poverty, it would itself develop into a revolutionary principle.

When the proletariat proclaims the dissolution of the hitherto existing world order, it merely declares the secret of its own existence, since it is in fact the dissolution of this order. When it demands the negation of private property it is only laying down as a principle for the proletariat, what has already been incorporated in itself without its consent as the negative result of society.[11]

It was this identification of the proletariat, a politically active agent, with the economically defined labouring class of political economy's social analysis that enabled Marx to complete the fusion of Hegel, Adam Smith and socialism.

Marx and 'utopian socialism'

While adopting the ideas of earlier socialists and joining in the attack on distributive justice, Marx was anxious to distinguish his own theories from those of his predecessors. The most important point of difference, and it was a genuine one, lay in Marx's notions of social dynamism, the idea that social development was impelled and controlled by certain natural laws of development. What Marx claimed to find wanting in the socialist writers whom he encountered in the 1840s was a systematic account of how a better order of society was to be brought into existence.

Central to Marx's own theory of social change was the proposition that progress derived from the struggle between the classes. According to Marx, it was essential to grasp the revolutionary nature of the proletariat and to see that it would transform society by its own violent political activity. Earlier thinkers, claimed Marx and Engels in the *Communist Manifesto*, were prevented from developing their theories properly because they were historically premature and had been expounded at a time when the fight between proletariat and bourgeoisie had not advanced beyond preliminary skirmishing: 'The undeveloped state of the class struggle . . . causes Socialists of this kind to consider themselves far superior to all class antagonism.'[12] Because their historical circumstances provide them with no firm basis on which to develop a proper social theory, they are reduced to fantasizing and to the belief that individuals, without reference to the social realities of the world in which they find themselves, can change things by simple cuts of will: they misguidedly believe that 'Historical action is to yield to their personal inventive action, historically created conditions of emancipation to fantastic ones, and the gradual, spontaneous class-organization of the proletariat to an organization of society specially contrived by these inventors.'[13] This insufficient awareness of the true nature of the social process vitiated the value of their schemes for social reorganization which Marx dismisses, unfairly in view of his own debt to them, as 'duodecimo editions of the New Jerusalem'.[14] Although their projects are significant, 'attack every principle of existing society' and are 'full of the most valuable material for the enlightenment of the working class', their failure to recognize the centrality of class antagonisms meant that their proposals were purely 'Utopian'.[15]

But Marx's objection was not an objection to the portrayal of a new free world; he himself thought that history would eventuate in an ideal state where 'In place of the old bourgeois society, with its classes and class antagonisms, we shall have an association, in which the free development of each is the condition for the free development of all.'[16] Marx's reservations were on theoretical grounds; the force of describing Owen, Saint-Simon and Fourier as 'Utopian' is to be found in his assertion that they were not 'scientific' – in the vocabulary of Marx and Engels the two terms were antonyms. As the brief section of early socialist ideas given in this chapter shows, the Utopian socialists were not as far removed from reality as Marx maintains, although, to be fair, Proudhon is omitted from his list. Nonetheless, what is implied by Marx's attack is that his own was a theoretical and scientific account of the transition to socialism as distinct from what he was later contemptuously to describe as 'recipes for the cookshops of the future'.[17]

References and Notes

1. 'Preface to the first German edition' (1867) in *Capital*, vol. I, p. 10.
2. Frederick Engels, 'Karl Marx', in Marx Engels, *Selected Works*, p. 142.
3. This first appeared as a series of articles in 1877, and then as part of his *Anti-Dühring. Herr Eugen Dühring's Revolution in Science* (1878), which, Engels states, had Marx's approval: Moscow edition (1969), pp. 13–14.
4. 'New Christianity' in *Henri Comte de Saint-Simon, Selected Writings*, ed. F. M. H. Markham (Oxford 1952), p. 85.
5. Frederick Engels, 'Socialism: Utopian and scientific' in Marx Engels, op. cit., vol. II, p. 113.
6. François-Marie-Charles Fourier, *Association Domestique*, vol. I, p. 466. Quoted in Charles Gide and Charles Rist, *A History of Economic Doctrines*, 2nd English edn (London 1948), p. 259.
7. Karl Marx, *The Holy Family, MEW*, vol. II, p. 43.
8. P.-J. Proudhon, *Idée générale de la Révolution au XIX siècle*, p. 95. Quoted in Gide and Rist, op. cit., p. 304.

9. P.-J. Proudhon, *Idée générale de la Révolution au XIX siècle*, p. 115. Quoted in John Plamenatz, *Man and Society*, vol. II, p. 52, n. 1.

10. *Early Texts*, pp. 47–8. At this period the terms 'communism' and 'socialism' were synonymous, covering all teaching of the kind dealt with in the early pages of this chapter.

11. Karl Marx, 'Towards a critique of Hegel's "Philosophy of Right" ' in *Early Texts,* p. 115.

12. Marx Engels, op. cit., vol. I, p. 62.

13. Ibid.

14. Ibid., vol. I, p. 64.

15. Ibid., vol. I, p. 63.

16. Ibid., vol. I, p. 54.

17. *Capital*, vol. I, p. 17.

Chapter 8

Marx's social theory

The earlier chapters of this book have outlined the main elements in intellectual history taken up by Marx and absorbed into his own theories. Before moving to the more purely economic aspects of his ideas to which the bulk of his work was devoted, it is important to be clear about the way in which Marx's political economy was situated within a deeper and more general, though never comprehensively stated or developed, theoretical purpose. This purpose was the exposition of a general theory of social change which would provide an account of the way in which all aspects of society were being steadily revolutionized and transformed so as to bring in the socialist era. The nature of Marx's theoretical ambition gives rise to a number of difficulties in his work generally and also to some of the idiosyncrasies of his political economy; this chapter is devoted to the examination of them.

Marx and science

Marx claimed that his social theory was a scientific theory like the theories of natural science. The German word, *Wissenschaft*, has a wider meaning than the English word 'science' which it is used to translate; it denotes learning in general as well as the stricter disciplines of the laboratory. Marx, like other Germans, used the word, for example, to refer to the philosophical efforts of Hegel. This sometimes gives translations of Marx's work an odd sound to English ears and one must bear this in mind when considering Marx's claim to have a 'scientific' theory.

In the preface to the first German edition of *Capital*, he speaks of his approach as being like that of the physicist. He stresses that, although his theory is illustrated with English examples, because England is the 'classic ground' of capitalism, what it states as being *now* true of England *will* be true of Germany. It is not even, he writes, a question of certain tendencies exhibiting themselves in varying strength in different countries as a result of the 'natural laws of capitalist production'[1] but of 'these laws themselves ... working with iron necessity towards inevitable results. The country that is more developed industrially only shows, to the less developed, the image of its own future.'[2] In the afterword to the second German edition he quoted with approval a review of his work by Professor Kaufman of St Petersburg University who wrote that 'Marx only troubles himself about one thing: to show by rigid scientific investigation, the necessity of successive determinate orders of social conditions. . . . Marx treats the social movement as a process of natural history, governed by laws.'[3] Marx seems to have intended, or wanted it to be thought he intended, to produce a social theory which was scientific in the same sense that the theories of physicists or chemists were scientific.

Marx straddled two intellectual worlds. He began his intellectual development in the idealism of German philosophy where truth, even truth about the natural world, was pursued, essentially, by introspection. By the time he reached the fullness of his intellectual maturity and was embarked on the writing of *Capital* in the 1850s, experimental science in the sense which we now understand, not only was it established but an associated and simplified materialism had become the rage in popular philosophy. Feuerbach provided Marx with the bridge between these two worlds but it was one across which Marx never transferred the whole of his intellectual apparatus. In his approach to 'science', as in so much else, there remained an ambiguous tension which owes its origin to his essential Hegelian understanding of the world as being at once an objective reality and a subjective creation.

It is clear from what Marx himself writes, that he understood science and the nature of theory differently from the way in which they are now customarily conceived. For example, in the preface to *The Economic and Philosophic Manuscripts of 1844* Marx writes: 'It is hardly necessary to assure the reader conversant with political economy that my results have been attained by means of a wholly empirical analysis based on a conscientious critical study of political economy.'[4] A modern reader who knows nothing of 'transformational criticism' finds it odd that 'results' can be obtained not by testing a theory but by 'studying' it as Marx does in the *Manuscripts*. Again, in *The German Ideology*, the first of Marx's writings to contain an account of his general theory, Marx writes: 'The premises from which we begin are not arbitrary ones. . . . They are the real individuals, their activity and the material conditions under which they live, both those which they find already existing and those produced by their activity. These premises can thus be verified in a purely empirical way.'[5] But in saying that his premises are 'real individuals' Marx does not mean that his theory is based on the study of actual individuals known to him. Rather the force of what he has to say is that he is not being 'metaphysical' in the sense that the German idealist philosophers were when they declared that the primary force in the world was spiritual and explained the relationships between men in terms of something which had no material existence. By 'real' and 'empirical' Marx apparently means what Feuerbach meant: a *point of view* which takes as a basic assumption a vision of emancipated man and the primary importance of his freedom and development as the governing principle of social organization. However, this is still only a 'point of view' and points of view cannot, of course, be proved or scientifically demonstrated.

Nonetheless, Marx is making the familiar distinction between fact and theory when he differentiates between 'real history'and 'ideal history';[6] *Capital* contains long descriptions of working conditions and some statistical material from the most authoritative sources available to Marx, indicating that he felt that his analysis needed to be sustained by extensive factual references; we know that Marx read very widely in modern social history, especially the history of the French Revolution, and that while working on his transformational critique of Hegel in 1843 he studied American and continental history; and his very insistence on the 'empirical' nature of his work would seem to indicate that he knew some such claim had to be made for any work to be described as 'scientific'. The logical distinction between 'data' drawn from the observable world, and the theoretical generalizations about such data is basic to scientific method. The scientist proceeds by distinguishing between particular phenomena which are taken as empirically given, and then developing theories which assert causal relationships in such a way that the truth of these theories may be tested against the facts; Marx appears to accept this when he claims to have established casual relationships between certain social phenomena in such a way as to amount to a prediction of a particular social result – the collapse of capitalism and the establishment of socialism.

It might be argued that Marx's ambiguous use of the term 'empirical' should be attributed to a careless use of terms. But behind his approach to the study of society there are difficulties greater than those which arise from mere carelessness.

Let us revert for a moment to Hume. The distinction between fact and theory is, of course, on the strictest reading of Hume's epistemological analysis, a very uncertain one, for the criteria we use for designating something as a 'fact' are complex intellectual constructions which do not differ in kind from 'theories' themselves. On the other hand, Hume did not conclude from his speculations about the difficulty of establishing criteria for 'truth' or 'objectivity' that investigation of the world was a fruitless task. On the contrary, he felt that the difficulty of being certain of the truth of observations and the need to be sceptical provided a spur for the constant acquisition of new information in order to check the conclusions presently accepted as accurate accounts of the world. And, even as a matter of logic, few people would deny the usefulness of the distinction between facts and theories, while as a matter of commonsense few people would act on theories, the truth of which was vital to their own interests, without seeking confirmation of their truth with reference to 'facts'.[7] But we have Marx's own word that he had originally been attracted to Hegel's work precisely because it offered an answer to Hume or, as he put it, because it was free from 'the . . . opposition "is" and "ought" which is the hallmark of idealism'.[8] Again, although Marx was deeply impressed by Feuerbach's revelatory inversion of Hegel's philosophy, he criticized him for his failure to transcend theory. Feuerbach's achievement, Marx felt, had only been a revolution in *understanding*; he had done nothing to change reality. This is already an odd thing to ask of a philosopher, as opposed to a political activist, but, as we noted in Chapter 6, the problem with which the Left Hegelians felt they were faced was that of putting Hegel's conservative doctrines to radical use. Marx, along with other Young Hegelians, was at first excited by what seemed the startling consequences of reading Hegel as a 'mystified' account of an atheistic world in which man was supreme, but then saw that this was merely a reinterpretation of the universe, not a project for its reconstruction. In his *Theses on Feuerbach*, Marx struggles to give expression to the idea of something which is simultaneously theory and practice. Marx charges Feuerbach with regarding 'the theoretical attitude as the only genuinely human attitude' so failing to grasp the significance 'of "revolutionary", of "practical-critical", activity'.[9] Truth, declares Marx, is not a question of logic: 'The question whether objective truth can be attributed to human thinking is not a question of theory but is a *practical* question. Man must prove the truth in practice . . .'[10] and again 'Feuerbach, not satisfied with *abstract thought*, appeals to cognitive perception; but he does not perceive cognition as *practical*, human-cognitive activity.'[11] As Marx declares in the most famous of the *Theses*, the Eleventh, 'The philosophers have only interpreted the world in various ways; the point, however, is to *change* it.'[12]

In view of the nature of the problem of cognition it is not surprising that so far nobody has been able to offer a comprehensible account of what something which is both theory and practice might be – but central to the whole of Marx's problem as a social theorist was an attempt to arrive at such concept – if 'concept' is the right word for such a thing. This is what lies behind Marx's notion of the proletariat as the leading and inevitably triumphant protagonist in the class struggle. It acquires this role by *being* the union of philosophical understanding and social action which brings society forward; 'As philosophy finds in the proletariat its material weapons so the proletariat finds in philosophy its intellectual weapons and as soon as the lightning of thought has struck deep into the virgin soil of the people the emancipation of the Germans into men will be completed.'[13] The proletariat, because it embodies total alienation, because it is deprived of all that it has created and is surrounded by a hostile world *is itself*, Marx seems to assert, the principle of social emancipation, and therefore the actual, corporal embodiment of theory. Once the proletariat has found in philosophy (i.e. as expounded by Marx) its intellectual weapons, then there will no longer be any need for theorizing or comprehension as distinct from the actual activities in which men engage; the proletariat, by embodying the theory, will transform the world: 'Philosophy cannot realize itself without transcending the proletariat, the proletariat cannot transcend itself without realizing philosophy.'[14] The relationship of Marxism to Hegelianism is, in this respect, a symmetrical one. Hegel's answer to

Hume's dilemma of an empirical and *dualistic* world had been to assert that it was, on the contrary, idealist and *monistic* – – its apparent contradictions were resolved within the total embrace of Spirit. Marx's version is a *materialist* monism. All things, including ideas, theories, notions, are material. Marx accepted the materialism of Feuerbach; there is no God, the world as we actually see it and experience it is all there is to know, and our mental impressions of it are indistinguishable from and produced by it. Man acts upon the world, but he is the product of it, and his behaviour can be explained in terms of the world's material structure and nature. But Marx tried to improve on Feuerbach, who, to Marx's way of thinking, had reintroduced pre-Hegelian dualism by allowing a difference between 'objects of perception' and 'objects of thought'.[15] Marx wanted to show that the construction we put upon our experience of the world is not to be distinguished from that experience. Once this could be shown, then philosophy would itself be redundant: 'When reality is depicted, philosophy as an independent branch of knowledge loses its medium of existence. At best its place can only be taken by a summing-up of the most general results, abstractions which arise from the observation of the historical development of men. Viewed apart from real history, these abstractions have in themselves no value whatsoever.'[16]

Marx's monism is not consistently held – he does distinguish between what men think and what men do, as indeed he is obliged to do, if he is to communicate with readers who themselves habitually make such distinctions. Nonetheless Marx's general social and philosophical theory, as developed after his acceptance of Feuerbach's transformation of Hegel, is an exposition of the belief that notions which we customarily regard as being imputed or mentally constructed, like 'dependence', 'exploitation' and 'freedom', are in fact embedded in and inherently inseparable from the material nature of the world. Later disciples of Marx have been accused of hypostasizing Marx – that is to say they are criticized for the belief that the categories which Marx employed in the theories like 'class', 'surplus value', 'capital' or 'labour' exist naturally and independently of Marx's own analysis. They have been charged with distorting the description of social and economic situations by trying to force all their data into Marxist boxes, even when the societies they study exhibit characteristics quite different from those which Marx has in mind. But it is just such an approach which Marx's own theoretical position invited.

Marx's general theory

Thus Marx's notion of what constitutes a scientific theory was a very special one, and his use of the word 'scientific' different from modern usage. In view of the difficulties which such a position immediately creates for anyone holding it, it is not surprising that Marx never offered a full-scale exposition of his general theory of social development. In the 1840s Marx wrote two books, *The German Ideology* (1845), and *The Poverty of Philosophy* (1847), which contain important statements about and political accounts of his views, but neither is directly concerned with the elaboration of the theory. The first is primarily an attack on the views of other German thinkers, and the second, which Marx recommended as an introduction to the reading of *Capital*, is the polemical attack on Proudhon's critique of political economy referred to earlier. The *Communist Manifesto* (1848) also has a brief account of Marx's developmental ideas which has been discussed in part in Chapter 2. The preface to the first German edition of *Capital* is surprisingly unhelpful and simply announces that *Capital*, Marx's *chef d'oeuvre*, 'forms the continuation of . . . A Contribution to the Critique of Political Economy* published in 1859'. This is a comparatively short book dealing with the subjects covered in the first three chapters of *Capital*, and its preface contains a brief account of Marx's ideas. Marx states, however, that 'A general introduction, which I had drafted, is omitted, since on further consideration it seems to me confusing to anticipate results which still have to be substantiated, and the reader who really wishes to follow me will have to decide to advance from the particular to the general.'[17]

This introduction has been preserved, along with the notes compiled in the 1850s which Marx used for the writing of *Capital*. But the introduction, like the notes, usually known by their German title of *Grundrisse*, was not published during Marx's lifetime.[18] We cannot, therefore, say with certainty how Marx would have resolved the logical difficulties with which his general theory is infested because we do not know what alterations Marx would have made to the unpublished 'introduction', or any other part of the *Grundrisse*, if he had decided to publish it. Even the fact that these documents have survived is no direct help because they are themselves less than absolutely clear. What they do show is that Marx, while writing *Capital*, was still grappling with the task of providing a post-Feuerbachian but still neo-Hegelian interpretation of the world.

Bearing this in mind, let us turn to the best of the various fragmentary accounts of his general theory left for us by Marx – that offered in the preface of *A Contribution to the Critique of Political Economy*.[19] There Marx says that 'the economic structure of society, is the real foundation, on which rises a legal and political superstructure and to which correspond definite forms of social consciousness'. This is the heart of Marx's general analysis. This 'economic structure', or social base, is the 'sum total of the relations of production'. The economic structure changes from time to time, and, as such, constitutes, in any particular period, 'a mode of production' of which Marx distinguishes four, Asiatic, primitive, feudal and bourgeois. The material productive forces are embodied in different forms of organization, different 'relations of production'. Marx's base is thus made up of a systematic organization of labour, arranged in a fashion functional for the kind of economic activity being carried on and with an appropriate distribution of the instruments of production. The superstructure of social, political and legal institutions reflects the substructure. In particular, the relations of production find in the superstructure 'what is but a legal expression for the same thing . . . property relations', or what we would now call a set of property rights. The transition from mode to mode, from social stage to social stage, is caused by changes in the economic structure. The changes in the base are at odds with existing property rights, and in the resulting conflict the whole of the legal and political superstructure is transformed. Marx's idea is that every mode of production produces a particular disposition of property. The development of a new base produces demands for a new distribution of property which, in the medium to long run, are irresistible but which, in the short run, are fiercely fought by those in possession (feudal landowners or bourgeois capitalists), whose opposition is overcome in the course of a political struggle culminating in revolution. The opposing parties in this fight are social classes, defined both by their property rights and with reference to the extent to which they dispose of the means of production, be it land, livestock, or other men's labour. Thus, man's consciousness, his politics, his laws, the very categories which he uses to view the world are themselves determined by the 'real' material base of society. Such is Marx's general theory of 'historical materialism' within which his political economy, an analysis of one of the 'modes of production', capitalism, is contained.

The historical explanation

So far we have examined the 'genetic' elements in Marx's ideas, the notions and analyses which were suggested to him by Hegel, Feuerbach, political economists and early socialists. In particular, we have tried to show how uncertain is the status of empirical data in Marx's theoretical approach, as a result of his adoption of 'transformational criticism'. This and other difficulties were, in part, already inherent in the ideas which Marx took from others. But Marx's difficulties are not, as it were, just an inherited disease. They stem in part from the nature of what he was trying to do and would have arisen whether he had read Hegel or not. In this sense some of his problems can be represented as being parallel to those experienced by those from whom he had learnt so much, rather than derived from them.

Marx was, as we have said, more than an economist. He was a political economist and, as such, also a sociologist who sought to subsume economic activity into a broader and more comprehensive account and theory of the development of mankind. We have already noted that in setting out to study political economy he had meant his examination of the subject as just one of a series of essays in transformational criticism which were to culminate in 'a special work' which would 'present them again as a connected whole showing the interrelationship of the separate parts (see page 80). His ambition, in short, was to provide a 'demystified' theory of the world which would supplant that of Hegel. He never achieved his aims as we have seen, of his general theory we have only an outline sketch – and his essay in political economy, itself incomplete, was to form only a part of it. Nonetheless, this general framework is the basis of his political economy, which is not comprehensible without a recognition of its subordinate part in Marx's more general ideas.

Certain consequences follow from Marx's determination to provide a comprehensive explanation for the whole world. The first of these is self-evident and tautological – it could not be a partial explanation. That is to say, it could not be an explanation which took as given any of the things it was trying to demonstrate. Since for Marx the world was an anthropocentric one and had meaning only in so far as it represented the creative efforts of and relationships between men, the world was essentially, as for Hegel, social. A total explanation of society requires that no one part of society be taken as given in order to explain the rest.

This is the logical reason for resorting to an historical explanation. If partial explanations are logically excluded then some account of society must be given in terms of chronologically prior causes. Given that Marx, like Hegel, believed that society evolves through a series of stages the crucial question then becomes that of explaining how the transition from stage to stage comes about. Hegel's answer was metaphysical and, significantly enough, hardly adequate as an answer; the development of society, he declared, is the manifestation of the development of the Spirit, but he left unanswered *how* it was that the Spirit progressed from stage to stage; he could only declare it to be analogous to the psychological development of the individual. Smith did better in relying on the division of labour and the rational calculation to which it gave rise, i.e. the operation of the market as the explanation of progress. But Marx denied himself the market as the vehicle of social change. His argument that changes in the economic base of society cause changes in the superstructure is an interesting one – certainly the most influential of his ideas – but the question of what brings about the changes in the economic base remains unsatisfactorily answered. How and when the socialist revolution is to come is the most vexed issue in his theories.

The technological explanation rejected

One account of Marx's social theory should be dismissed: it is not a technological theory of history. According to this view of Marx it is simply changes in the kind of tools used in production which determine the kind of society in which these tools are used.

Support for this interpretation is based on the identification of 'productive forces' with particular productive techniques. It is an approach which some passages in Marx certainly seem to support. In his attack on Proudhon, Marx writes: 'In acquiring new productive forces men change their mode of production; and in changing their mode of production, in changing the way of earning their living, they change all their social relations. The hand-mill gives you society with the feudal lord; the steam-mill society with the industrial capitalist.'[20] In the *Communist Manifesto* Marx is even more explicit: 'The bourgeois cannot exist without constantly revolutionizing the instruments of production, and thereby the relations of production, and with them the whole relations of society.'[21] and in *Capital* he asserts that: 'The starting-point of Modern Industry is, as we have shown, the revolution in the instruments of labour, and this revolution attains its most highly developed form in the organized system of machinery in a factory.'[22] But to explain social change by changes in tools would leave Marx's theory hanging in the air: what is it, after all, that explains the changes in tools? Whether these references are the result of carelessness in composition, they are massively contradicted by other of his assertions.

Elsewhere technology is treated in a variety of different ways. Marx suggests that it is an index, rather than the cause of social change: 'Technology discloses man's mode of dealing with Nature, the process of production by which he sustains his life, and thereby also lays bare the mode of formation of his social relations.'[23] In 1846, he was explicit in arguing, as Smith had argued, that machinery is a *derivative* of the division of labour. Not, it is true, 'from the division of labour in general' but from the way in which labour is organized in each economic epoch: 'Each kind of division of labour had its specific instruments of production.' In the same letter Marx further suggests that the extension of mechanization was a response to pressures in the markets for goods and labour:

up to 1825 . . . the development of machinery was a necessary consequence of the needs of the market. Since 1825, the invention and application of machinery has been simply the result of the war between workers and employers. But this is only true of England. As for the European nations, they were driven to adopt machinery owing to English competition with other countries and to lack of hands, that is, to the disproportion between the population of North America and its industrial needs.[24]

In various places Marx stresses that technology is dependent on social change. The application of inventions, he declares, is only possible in a suitable environment: 'The inventions of Vaucanson, Arkwright, Watt and others were, however, practicable only because those inventors found, ready to hand, a considerable number of skilled mechanical workmen, placed at their disposal by the manufacturing period.'[25] And in *The German Ideology* Marx actually makes technology indistinguishable from sociology: 'By social we understand the cooperation of several individuals, no matter under what conditions, in what manner and to what end. It follows from this that a certain mode of production, or industrial stage, is always combined with a certain mode of cooperation, or social stage, and this mode of cooperation is itself a "productive force".[26] Again, in the same letter to Annenkov from which we have already quoted, he writes: 'Machinery is no more an economic category than the ox which draws the plough. The application of machinery in the present day is one of the relations of our present economic system, but the way in which machinery is utilized is totally distinct from the machinery itself.'[27] *A Contribution to the Critique of Political Economy* does not mention machinery, and in its unpublished preface Marx observes that 'political economy . . . is not technology'.[28]

Morals and politics

Marx denied a causal role to technology; he had similarly to deny free effective action to individuals. He could not allow free will to those whose activity was to be explained and predicted by his theory. Morality, according to Marx, was, along with the most of the ideological superstructure, simply the expression of man's material interests: 'The phantoms formed in the human brain are also, necessarily, sublimates of their material life-process, which is empirically verifiable and bound to material premises. Morality, religion, metaphysics, all the rest of ideology and their corresponding forms of consciousness, thus no longer retain the semblance of independence.'[29] and, albeit with some hedging, Marx states that the behaviour of individuals in capitalist society, even when they have overcome their alienation and can see the world for what it is, is value free:

I paint the capitalist and the landlord in no sense couleur de rose. *But here individuals are dealt with only in so far as they are the personifications of economic categories, embodiments of particular class-relations and class-interests. My standpoint, from which the evolution of the economic formation of society is viewed as a process of natural history, can less than any other make the individual responsible for relating whose creature he socially remains, however much he may subjectively raise himself above them.*[30]

The elimination of morality as an independent category of human activity necessarily entails the relegation of politics to the status of a residual in the social process. If human behaviour is determined, it follows that the notions of both the government and the struggle for power which constitutes politics are themselves a result of deeper social causes and are not independent and determining factors. Even the understanding of the laws which govern social development will not help men to avert the necessary consequences of the inexorable development which makes society what it is. As Marx emphasizes, 'even when a society has got upon the right track for the discovery of the natural laws of its movement . . . it can neither clear by bold leaps, nor remove by legal enactments, the obstacles offered by the successive phases of its normal development'.[31] Government is simply the institutionalization of the interests of the ruling class. 'The executive of the modern state is but a committee for managing the common affairs of the whole bourgeoisie.'[32] Since the ruling class is the possessing class this provides Marx with an explanation of *laissez-faire* in commercial society; non-intervention by the government in economic processes is identical with a lack of self-restraint on the part of the capitalists in their accumulation of wealth.

Individuals and commodities

As we have seen, the social theorists of the seventeenth and eighteenth centuries, both political and economic, took as basic postulates that men, as men, are much the same, have similar needs and appetites, calculate their advantages in more or less the same way, and assumed, therefore, that given certain stimuli, their behaviour could be more or less accurately predicted. Marx objected to the elevation of these assumptions into doctrines of individual rights and liberties. Apart from what he felt to be their deceptive nature, he complained that such an attitude towards individuals does not exalt but degrades them because it is a false representation of men's true nature. Such assumptions provide a rationale for substituting market relations and the cash norms for the face-to-face relationships of familial affection, respect for human achievement, and the honour due to virtue. Marx seeks to show that individuals are not self-evidently comprehensible independently of their social context. Sociologically, Marx asserts, man only knows himself for what he is by virtue of his relationships with his fellows. A man's behaviour is conditioned, his values formed and his understanding shaped by his social environment; at the same time he is part of the social environment of others exerting a reciprocal influence on them. Indeed, this social environment is entirely composed of human relationships and to fail to see this is to be 'alienated' from society, to see it as an entity outside and oppressive of the personality, instead of as a web of interactions of which each individual is a part and from which he derives his own significance and meaning and through which he contributes to the significance and meaning of the existence of others. As Marx writes, 'The individual is the social being. His life . . . is . . . an expression and confirmation of *social life*.'[33]

There is in this, of course, an important truth. A knowledge of the physical appearance of a man is of little help in making a personal assessment of him; we need to know what he does for a living, where he comes from, how old he is, his ambitions, his experience, his achievements, his failures, his marital status and so on: a whole series of items of information are required to enable us to develop an idea of the man in terms of what is essentially a bundle of social relationships. To regard men as market units, as 'homines economici', Marx would say, is to see the human race in a 'mystified' form, it is to fail to see it for what it really is, both the producer and the product of social inter-dependence.

Similarly, Marx maintains that the unit in which the wealth of capitalist societies is reckoned up, the commodity, is also a mystification, or, to use Marx's own word, a 'fetishization' obscuring the reality which stands behind the manufactured article. In thinking of wealth in terms of so many yards of cloth or tons of iron and regarding those as the objective reality of the economic world we fail to see that these are merely the material representation of social relations, of the living connexions between human beings. According to Marx, '. . . from the moment that men in any way work for one another, their labour assumes a social form'.[34] But men actually fail to comprehend, or are alienated from, their own products: 'a commodity is therefore a mysterious thing, simply because in it the social character of men's labour appears to them as an objective character stamped upon the product of that labour; because the relation of the producers to the sum total of their own labour is presented to them as a social relation, existing not between themselves, but between products.'[35] In a passage which clearly owes much to Feuerbach, Marx writes that 'in order . . . to find an analogy, we must have recourse to the mist-enveloped regions of the religious world. In that world the productions of the human brain appear as independent beings endowed with life, and entering into relations both with one another and the human race. So it is in the world of commodities with the products of mens' hands.'[36] Just as men are peculiar, incommensurate, incomparable and individually unique, so too, at the bedrock of reality, are commodities, precisely because they are the products of these unique and individual human beings. Fundamentally, Marx is saying, neither men nor commodities can be irreducible categories of analysis – as such they only prevent us from seeing the real 'empirical' nature of effective relations between creatures of flesh and blood.

By taking *relationships* as the centre of his analysis Marx frees himself from the need to adopt any particular object or factor, which would itself need, in turn, to be explained, as a datum point. He makes the concrete manifestations of society and economics – individuals, machinery, and manufactured products – dependent for their meaning on the complex of social interactions which produces them. Society itself is organized so that its dynamism derives from the changing relationship between base and superstructure. Changes in the base are explained, however inadequately, historically. Thus, first causes are pushed back into the mists of antiquity and Marx's social theory is as complete as any social theory can hope to be.

Base and superstructure

But Marx's very ambition to provide a *total* explanation contains the seeds of serious logical difficulties. According to him, the 'economic structure of society' is 'the sum total' of the 'relations of production which correspond to a definite state of development of the material productive forces'.[37] The 'relations of production' are, because they are part of the economic base, something anterior to the property rights in the superstructure which are their 'legal expression'. Now, in Marx's scheme, for these relations of production to be basic, or causal, they must be something other than 'phantoms formed in the human brain ... sublimates of their material life-process'.[38] The relations of production must be part of the environment, they must be real and material. But that is precisely, as we have seen, what relationships are not – relationships, as Hume showed, are *imputed*, they are constructions put upon things by men – they might, perhaps, be called real, but they are not, in the sense that Marx means, material.

However, Marx maintains that the relations into which men enter in production are 'independent of their will', implying again that these relationships do have the material status which he claims for them. What does Marx mean? He cannot mean that social relations are independent of the will in the sense that a slave finds himself in a relationship to his owner which is unwilled, for, if that was all it meant, it would simply be a redundant expression. Nor can he mean that the relations into which we immediately enter are independent of our consciousness – if we did not realize that in taking employment we had entered into a contractual relationship in which we performed certain tasks for reward, it is difficult to see how it would be possible to take employment at all. Almost certainly what Marx has in mind is that it is perfectly possible to enter into certain relationships without being aware of the wider implications of those relationships. A worker may think of himself as simply working for money. But in fact his work issues in commodities which are then marketed and which generate the flow of cash from which he is paid. That cash in turn must have been earned by somebody else engaged in the supply of goods and services and so on in an endless chain. In effect the labour of the workman is exchanged, without his being aware of it, through the medium of money, against the labour of others. The way in which a whole set of economic transactions work together in a market to form uniform sets of prices although it was no single person's intention to create such a uniform set of prices is another example of the kind of indirect relationships which Marx had in mind. It is this possibility which constitutes Adam Smith's 'invisible hand'. But the fact that such orderly systems may arise independently of the volition of any particular individual still does not make them 'material', nor does it mean that they exist except as derivatives of the relationships of which people are conscious.

However well we do or do not understand the rules of behaviour which constitute our relationships with other people, it does not alter the fact that they are rules and depend for their validity on being followed and enforced by men. Rules are simply a manifestation of the agreement, voluntary or involuntary, among men, about suitable behaviour. What men will agree upon as suitable behaviour in particular circumstances cannot be deduced by even the most minute and careful study of the circumstances themselves. The way in which men behave in a given set of material circumstances depends as much on the way in which they calculate and on their appetites as it does on the circumstances. The sets of rules they adopt are devised by men, not by their environment.

It might be argued that the set of rules adopted will in fact be determined by the situation. If some men decide to work individually and others to cooperate in a situation where team-work is vital for success or survival, then a process of natural selection will tend to eliminate the more poorly adopted sets of relationships. But it is rare for there to be a situation in which only one method of organization will be successful and it will still be necessary to establish some criteria for success or functionality and such criteria can only be invented by men with respect to some purpose which they themselves choose. It would, for example, be difficult to find anyone today who would claim that in all circumstances profitability is the best yardstick by which to judge all actions relevent to economic processes, or that self-preservation is the ultimate test of moral actions; nor would it be easy to establish general agreement on just precisely what detailed criteria should be used for economic or moral behaviour. Most philosophers would agree that, in general, morality is best understood as the calculation of interest, but the goals which constitute the content of 'interest' – self, family, flag, God, humanity – have still to be supplied, and they can only be supplied by man, not nature. Thus the base, being an 'economic structure' composed of relationships cannot therefore *determine* man's behaviour: it is a product of man's behaviour or, perhaps better still, it *is* man's behaviour.

Marx and Hegel: logical difficulties

Marx was thus caught in a logical trap of his own making; he could not explain the world in terms of itself and hope to get beyond tautologies. It is instructive to see how Hegel's realistic monism gets Hegel into very much the same quagmire as Marx's materialistic monism gets him; to draw attention to this is to underline the ineluctual nature of the logical problem as much as it is to remind us of Marx's intellectual filiation to Hegel. At the opening of *The Science of Logic,* Hegel writes,

Philosophy misses an advantage enjoyed by the other sciences. It

*cannot like them rest the existence of its objects on the natural
admissions of consciousness, nor can it assume that its method of
cognition, either for starting or for continuing, is one already accepted
. . . it soon becomes evident that thought will be satisfied with nothing
short of showing the necessity of its facts, of demonstrating the
existence of its objects, as well as their nature and qualities. Our original
acquaintance with them is thus discovered to be inadequate. We can
assume nothing, and assert nothing dogmatically; nor can we accept the
assertions and assumptions of others. And yet we must make a
beginning: and a beginning, as primary and underived, makes an
assumption, or rather is an assumption. It seems as if it were impossible
to make a beginning at all.*[39]

Later, he concludes that philosophy is circular:

*It may seem as if philosophy, in order to start on its course, had, like the
rest of the sciences, to begin with a subjective presupposition. . . . But
. . . it is by the free act of thought that it occupies a point of view, in
which it is for its own self, and thus gives itself an object of its own
production. . . . The very point of view, which originally is taken on its
own evidence only, must in the course of the science be converted to a
result, – the ultimate result in which philosophy returns into itself and
reaches the point with which it began. In this manner philosophy
exhibits the appearance of a circle which closes with itself, and has no
beginning in the same way as the other sciences have.*[40]

There are signs that Marx was uneasily aware that his theory was
beset with similar difficulties which were less than satisfactorily
resolved, and this may help to explain why he never gave any extended
explanation of his general theory and why, at his death, he had still only
published the first volume of *Capital*. Like Hegel, Marx, too, was
troubled by what he sensed was the circular reasoning behind his
theory; in discussing the origins of capitalism he writes,

*the accumulation of capital pre-supposes surplus-value; surplus-value
pre-supposes capitalistic production; capitalist production pre-supposes the pre-existence of considerable masses of capital and labour-
power in the hands of producers of commodities. The whole movement,
therefore, seems to turn in a vicious circle, out of which we can only get
by supposing a primitive accumulation (previous accumulation of
Adam Smith) . . .*[41]

At one point in the unpublished introduction to the *Critique of
Political Economy* Marx discusses the connection between production
and consumption. Clearly, he has in mind the distinction that Smith so
ingeniously makes (see page 39) between productive consumption
and unproductive consumption in order to demonstrate that both
investment and consumption are simultaneous flows of resources.
Marx is apparently fascinated by Smith's idea but confuses it with a

notion in which production and consumption are chronologically sequential. This is a result of his search for a causal relationship between the two and it leads him into conclusions hard to reconcile with the general theory as outlined above:

Production is determined by general laws of nature; distribution by random social factors, it may therefore exert a more or less beneficial influence on production; exchange, a formal social movement, lies between these two; and consumption, as the concluding act, which is regarded not only as the final aim but as the ultimate purpose, falls properly outside the sphere of economics, except in so far as it in turn exerts a reciprocal action on the point of departure thus once again initiating the whole process.[42]

Marx, in following this line of reasoning is later forced to abandon the notion of a mechanistic causal chain and resorts to an account which is descriptive rather than analytical, declaring that it is not the case

that production, distribution, exchange and consumption are identical, but that they are links of a single whole, different aspects of one unit. . . . A distinct mode of production thus determines the specific mode of consumption, distribution, exchange and the specific relations of these different phases to one another. *Production in the narrow sense, however, is in its turn also determined by the other aspects. . . . There is an interaction between the various aspects. Such interaction takes place in any organic entity.*[43]

Hegel was careful to deny that his theory had any predictive power; the historian can only explain why and how things happen after the event – the owl of Minerva flies only in the twilight – and he deserves credit for his realization that his work was descriptive and not predictive.[44] Marx, forced by the inexorable requirements of logic into 'organicism' and circular explanations, does not seem fully to have grasped the extent and a nature of his dilemma and never unequivocally withdrew his claim that his political economy, at least with respect to capitalist society, was a predictive science.

Marx's commitment to political economy

It has been argued that the apparent contrast between *The Economic and Philosophic Manuscripts of 1844*, with their concern for the emancipation of man from the shadowy constructions of his own mind, and *Capital*, with its deterministic exposition of the 'iron laws' of political economy, indicates that Marx abandoned, in his maturer years, the optimism and humanism of youth for a dogged and masochistic demand for the submission of mankind to the inexorable processes of history. But it is the same Marx who writes both; the difference between the 'young' and the 'old' Marx stems from a need to deploy different approaches in dealing with different subjects. Writing in a phenomenological and Hegelian tradition, Marx could emphasize the degree to which institutions owe their force to nothing but the men of whose activities they are composed. Turning to political economy for an explanation of material happenings in a quantifiable world Marx was obliged to make determinist assumptions; and he never seems to have been clear about the extent to which these views conflicted.

Marx sets out to write a 'critique' of political economy but, instead of confining himself to analysing in terms of some deeper reality what it is that political economists say, he himself, searching for a 'scientific' account of society, adopted the analyses and many of the most important assumptions of the political economists. Given his ambitions as a social theorist, he had no real alternative. Marx's transformational critique of liberal political and economic theory in 1843 and 1844 still makes stimulating reading – the brilliant insights of Marx in the full vigour of youth shine through the opacity of his prose with a luminous freshness. But to offer an explanation of the way in which men construct their world intellectually is not the same thing as offering an alternative explanation of the world itself. To be a social scientist it is necessary to take up the deterministic and predictive tools of social science.

Thus, Marx's 'Critical analysis of capitalist production' proves to be a new version of Smith and Ricardo, not a demolition of their assumptions. It is this which explains why Marx's criticisms of the political economists in his published works relate only to their failure to see that capitalism, as an economic system, is time-bound, that it was preceded historically by quite different economic arrangements and that it will be succeeded by a revolutionary socialist system: 'Economists express the relations of bourgeois production, the division of labour, credit, money, etc., as fixed immutable external categories. . . . Economists explain how production takes place in the above mentioned relations, but what they do not explain is how these relations themselves are produced, that is the historical movement which gave them birth.'[45]

But Marx is emphatic that the political economists' understanding of the economy is 'real'; 'The economists' material is the active, energetic life of man . . . but . . . the moment we want to see in the [political economists'] categories no more than ideas, spontaneous thoughts, independent of real relations, we are forced to attribute the origin of these thoughts to the movement of pure reason.'[46] To do that would be to deprive Marx's socialism of its basis in the real world and to put it on the same level with the Utopias which he derided. Imperceptibly, and uncertainly, from being the object of a critique, political economy became the *premise* of radical social theory; 'modern socialism', Engels writes in the preface of the first German edition of *The Poverty of Philosophy*, 'no matter of what tendency, starts out from bourgeois political economy'.[47]

Appendix

... a guiding thread for my studies, can be briefly formulated as follows: In the social production of their lives men enter into definite relations that are indispensable and independent of their will, relations of production which correspond to a definite stage of development of their material productive forces. The sum total of these relations of production constitutes the economic structure of society, the real foundation, on which rises a legal and political superstructure and to which correspond definite forms of social consciousness. The mode of production of material life conditions the social, political and intellectual life process in general. It is not the consciousness of men that determines their being, but, on the contrary, their social being that determines their consciousness. At a certain stage of their development, the material productive forces of society come in conflict with the existing relations of production, or – what is but a legal expression for the same thing – with the property relations within which they have been at work hitherto. From forms of development of the productive forces these relations turn into their fetters. Then begins an epoch of social revolution. With the change of the economic foundation the entire immense superstructure is more or less rapidly transformed. In considering such transformations a distinction should always be made between the material transformation of the economic conditions of production, which can be determined with the precision of natural science, and the legal, political, religious, aesthetic or philosophic – in short, ideological forms in which men become conscious of this conflict and fight it out. Just as our opinion of an individual is not based on what he thinks of himself, so can we not judge of such a period of transformation by its own consciousness; on the contrary, this consciousness must be explained rather from the contradictions of material life, from the existing conflict between the social productive forces and the relations of production. No social order ever perishes before all the productive forces for which there is room in it have developed; and new, higher relations of production never appear before the material conditions of their existence have matured in the womb of the old society itself. Therefore mankind always sets itself only such tasks as it can solve; since, looking at the matter more closely, it will always be found that the task itself arises only when the material conditions for its solution already exist or are at least in the process of formation. In broad outline Asiatic, ancient, feudal, and modern bourgeois modes of production can be designated as progressive epochs in the economic formation of society. The bourgeois relations of production are the last antagonistic form of the social process of production – antagonistic not in the sense of individual antagonism, but of one arising from the social conditions of life of the individuals; at the same time the productive forces developing in the womb of bourgeois

society create the material conditions for the solution of that antagonism. This social formation brings, therefore, the prehistory of human society to a close.[48]

References and Notes

1. *Capital*, vol. I, p. 3.
2. Ibid., vol. I, pp. 8–9.
3. Ibid., vol. I, p. 18.
4. *The Economic and Philosophic Manuscripts of 1844*, p. 65. Nor did he ever think it necessary, for example, to demonstrate the empirical nature of 'classes', a category that still awaits definitive elucidation. Although it played such an important part in his theory, Marx hardly went beyond declaring that 'no credit is due to me for discovering the existence of classes in modern society, nor yet the struggle between them. Long before me the bourgeois historians had described the historical development of this struggle of the classes and bourgeois economists "the economic anatomy of the classes"' – Marx to J. Weydemeyer, 5 March 1852, in Marx Engels, *Selected Works*, vol. II, p. 410. Chapter lviii of *Capital* vol. III, which is promisingly entitled 'Classes', breaks off, unfinished, after some 400 words.
5. Karl Marx and Frederick Engels, *The German Ideology* (Moscow 1968), p. 31.
6. *Early Texts*, p. 121.
7. This was obviously the view shared by Marx and Engels when they wrote in the preface to *The German Ideology* (p. 24) 'Once upon a time a valiant fellow had the idea that men were drowned in water only because they were possessed with the *idea of gravity*. If they were to knock this notion out of their heads, say by stating it to be a superstition, a religious concept, they would be sublimely proof against any danger from water. His whole life long he fought against the illusion of gravity, of whose harmful results all statistics brought him new and manifold evidence.'
8. *Early Texts*, p. 3. 'Idealist' is now customarily used to refer to all the German philosophers of the period from Kant to Hegel. Marx excludes Hegel from the category of idealist thinkers because he had, as Marx felt when he wrote the letter from which the situation is taken, reconciled 'reality' with the 'ideal'.
9. Karl Marx, 'Theses on Feuerbach' in Marx Engels, *Selected Works*, vol. II, p. 365; *MEW*, vol. III, p. 533.
10. Marx Engels, *Selected Works*, vol. II, p. 365.
11. Ibid., vol. II, p. 366.
12. Ibid., vol. II, p. 367.
13. Karl Marx, 'Introduction to a critique of Hegel's "Philosophy of

Right" ' in *Early Texts*, p. 128.
14. Ibid., p. 129.
15. Karl Marx, 'Theses on Feuerbach' in Marx Engels, *Selected Works*, vol. II, p. 585.
16. Marx Engels, *The German Ideology*, p. 38.
17. Karl Marx, *A Contribution to the Critique of Political Economy* (London 1971), p. 19.
18. Karl Marx, *Grundisse, Foundations of the Critique of Political Economy* (Penguin Books, Harmondsworth and Baltimore 1973).
19. The following references, except where stated otherwise, are to the quotation from Marx printed in the Appendix to this chapter.
20. Karl Marx, *The Poverty of Philosophy* (Moscow 1955), Progress Publishing, p. 95.
21. Marx Engels, *Selected Works*, vol. I, p. 37.
22. *Capital*, vol. I, p. 394.
23. *The Poverty of Philosophy*, p. 95.
24. Ibid., pp. 159–60. It is not clear why Marx here distinguishes between the market and 'the war between workers and employers'.
25. *Capital*, vol. I, p. 382.
26. Marx Engels, *The German Ideology*, p. 41.
27. Marx to Annenkov, 23 December 1846, in *The Poverty of Philosophy*, p. 160.
28. Ibid., p. 191.
29. Marx Engels, *The German Ideology*, p. 38.
30. *Capital*, vol. I, p. 10.
31. Ibid.
32. 'Manifesto of the Communist Party' in Marx Engels, *Selected Works*, vol. I, p. 36.
33. *The Economic and Philosophic Manuscripts of 1844*, pp. 137–8.
34. *Capital*, vol. I, Ch. i, Sect. 4, p. 71.
35. Ibid., vol. I, Ch. i, Sect. 4, p. 72.
36. Ibid.
37. The following references, except where otherwise stated, are again to the passage quoted in the Appendix to this chapter.
38. Marx Engels, *The German Ideology*, p. 38.
39. *The Logic of Hegel*, pp. 3–4.
40. Ibid., pp. 27–8.
41. *Capital*, vol. I, p. 713.
42. *A Contribution to the Critique of Political Economy*, p. 194.
43. Ibid., pp. 204–5.
44. Hegel, *The Philosophy of Right*, p. 13.
45. *The Poverty of Philosophy*, p. 91.
46. Ibid., pp. 91–2.
47. Ibid., p. 6.
48. 'Preface to "A Contribution to the Critique of Political Economy" ' in Marx Engels, *Selected Works*, vol. I, pp. 362–3.

Chapter 9

The labour theory
of value: price

In the next five chapters we shall be dealing with Marx's political economy proper – his economic ideas as set out in *Capital*. *Capital* is a long work of three volumes and 2,000 pages and was, as we know from the masses of notes left by Marx, intended to be much longer. But Marx's economics are primarily devoted to the explanation of two things:

(a) why prices are as they are,
(b) a theory of economic growth.

(a) is the concern of Marx's labour theory of value which simultaneously shows how prices are determined and how the worker is exploited; (b) takes the form of Marx's theory of the declining rate of profit which, at the same time, predicts the collapse of capitalism and the advent of a new socialist mode or production. Labour theories of value and theories of the declining rate of profit were, of course, common to all the political economists.

The next three chapters will deal with the labour theory of value. This is the most difficult of Marx's theoretical ideas and some patience and application is needed for its understanding. A grasp of the labour theory of value is vital, however, in order to appreciate the nature of Marx's main speculative effort, that of 'transforming' the market and revealing its true and esoteric nature *à la* Feuerbach. But the difficulties should not be exaggerated; the reader will perhaps need to go a little more slowly than usual.

Value: objective and subjective

Value has had such a vexed history in economic thought, that it is important to be secure in one's own mind about the meaning of the word before immersing oneself in the complexities and confusions to which misunderstandings about its nature have given rise in the past. It will be much easier to follow the arguments offered by Marx and his predecessors if a logically impregnable understanding of value is established independently of the historical texts.

We are accustomed to think of value in terms of the objective criteria which we use to identify it. That is to say, when we say that something is valuable, we tend to mean that it has a particular price, is beautiful or obviously useful. But value is, of course, as we know from our reading of Hume, not a material thing, something physically inherent in the things of which the world is composed, but something which men impute to things. Like Hume's causality, value is a relationship and, as such, external to the objects to which it is attributed. Beauty, as the proverb rightly has it, lies in the eye of the beholder. Similarly, neither an understanding that diamonds are crystallized carbon nor the realization that water is a combination of hydrogen and oxygen will help to establish in what relationship water and diamonds either do, or should, exchange against one another.

The impossibility of deciding value independently of human and therefore subjective preferences tends to be obscured by the fact that we are not accustomed, in well-established commercial societies, to bargaining; we are used to regarding market prices as fixed and 'objective'. But suppose that someone offers to take another person in their car to a place to which there is in any case ready access by public transport. What is the value of this offer? Should the passenger pay the cost of the journey by the alternative and public means of transport? Or should what the passenger pays be related to the cost of the journey to the owner of the car – half the value of the petrol consumed perhaps? Again, it could be argued that since the driver is making the journey in any case, then the cost to him of conveying his passenger is nothing since it involves him in no extra measurable expense, and that therefore he should take the passenger free. There is no necessarily acceptable way of deciding whether anything should be paid for the journey; everything depends upon the kinds of factors taken into account, and which factors are actually considered depends entirely upon the individuals concerned. Again, the prices demanded for goods and services in every-day life rarely correspond to the value which we ourselves put upon them, if this were not the case we would not so frequently refer to some things as 'overpriced' or to others as 'bargains'.

All concepts like value are subjective, but agreement on the criteria for identifying most of them are usually reached without too much difficulty. Some, like 'beauty', remain the object of academic as well as popular dispute. In the ordinary course of events this is no vital matter because the practical consequences of giving a very precise meaning to 'beauty' are not great. With respect to value, however, the issue is much more urgent, because the whole structure of modern industrialized societies depends crucially on the nature of the value systems which are used to distribute goods and services among people and functions. In an important sense, both political economy and modern economics are concerned with the examination and elaboration of these systems. And the crucial difference between political economy and its modern successor lies in their respective theories of value.

Political economy: 'objective' value

The political economists were not greatly interested in the pricing of individual commodities. For them the economic world was made up of three great lumps which constituted the factors of production: labour, agricultural land or food, and capital. Although in eighteenth-century and early nineteenth-century England capital was scarce, by the same token, there was, *with respect to the relatively scarce capital*, labour and food in abundance. Malthus's theory of population gave to the idea of a large and persistent surplus of working hands a compelling force. Ricardo, it is true, was preoccupied with the problem of the constraints on the supply of food, but was convinced that these stemmed from the perversity of politicians and that, although the supply of land in the world was, in principle, limited, the point at which the wheatlands of eastern Europe and North America would be unable to meet the demand of an expanding population might be consigned to a point in the future so distant that it could, for practical purposes, be disregarded.

Consequently, not only were labour and food, at least theoretically, cheap, so that their long run price could be thought of as relatively unchanging and low, but they were thought of as being, together with capital, relatively undifferentiated. In the political economists' coarse-grained world, land can only be used to grow a very limited variety of food, which has one purpose, that of keeping the labourers alive; labourers can only engage in very similar kinds of work; capital only provides work for labourers and incomes for entrepreneurs; the economy was composed of large and virtually homogeneous aggregates. This is a model of the world in which there is very little in the way of alternatives; the overriding need is obvious – to create more capital to provide more employment for a growing population and incidentally to provide a solid base for the fiscal needs of government. The problem was not how to ration resources between individuals or purposes but how best to mobilize them. In this economy choice was not important; labourers living at subsistence level were obliged to spend their incomes on securing the bare necessities of life; entrepreneurs and landlords could, admittedly, spend their money on luxuries, but this was felt to be both wasteful and irrational, diverting resources from the real and productive activities of society which were the true source of wealth; investment decisions were not thought to be complex – Smith was concerned only to establish the priority of agriculture over industry, Ricardo had little or no interest in the subject, and Marx never seems to have given much thought to the nature of investment decisions by capitalists, being content to visualize them as impelled by blind unreasoning greed, sometimes in despite of their own more enlightened interests.

The political economists thus ironed out individual preferences from their analysis. Although Smith's theory rested on a powerful insight into the working of the market as an allocative device, it was only an insight, and the rationality and effectiveness of the market were assumed rather than studied. Political economy was much more interested in the way to which, given the generation of prices by an efficiently operating market, incomes were distributed among the various groups of which society is made up. Once they had provided a convincing account of this process they were concerned only to urge that no institutional barriers should be opposed to its free development – their conviction that only through free competition could employment, efficiency and growth be achieved was virtually *a priori*. They failed to integrate value-in-use with value-in-exchange, while the difference between values to individuals, and values to individuals aggregated into a society, was not analysed or discussed and it seems likely that they thought that it was trivial. They also failed to analyse the way in which prices move from their position at any given moment in the market to their long run position; that they do so is not much more than an act of faith required by the logic of their arguments. This leaves prices as the reflection of the conditions of production – hence the predominance of labour in their theories of value and their description as 'cost-of-production' theories. Given demand, the cost of supplying a commodity might well be said to be objectively determined.

Modern economics: 'subjective' value

In the 1860s and 1970s, working independently of each other, Jevons (1835–82), Karl Menger (1840–1921) and Walras (1834–1910), arrived at a new theory of value which was to shift the centre of gravity of economic studies. It was an analytical refinement which greatly increased the power of economic theory and changed, some would say sharply narrowed, the field which economics took as its own. Their key assumption was the reverse of that made by the political economists; it was that resources are *not*, in principle, unlimited. Because the diversion of any resource to an alternative use takes time, in the shortest of short runs everything is absolutely limited. Moreover, in any situation abundance is only relative as between factors and each possible combination of resources excludes every other possible combination. This meant that the crucial problem in the economy was the allocation of resources between conflicting ends. In the new theory, choice was the central concern and its aim was to offer an explanation both of the way in which goods and services were accorded their places in an array of preference and also of the way in which choice itself was structured at different levels of satisfaction. This new approach, which underlies all modern economic thinking, was known as 'the subjective theory of value', or 'the theory of marginal utility'.

Where the political economists had explained long run price exclusively in terms of the 'objective' costs of production, the new economics now showed how prices were also derived from the subjective preferences of those participating in the market. Political economy is concerned almost exclusively with the conditions under which goods will be *supplied*: the new theory showed how these were to be integrated with the circumstances which determine *demand*. The essence of the 'subjectivist' idea is simply stated – price is a function of the intensity of subjective demand and the relative abundance of supply. In one sense, of course, this is Adam Smith's position, more demand, price goes up, more supply, price goes down. But the new theory set out to give a much more elaborate account of the nature of demand. It was now accepted that demand was not simply given for any individual, but would vary for a number of factors, and especially and significantly with regard to the degree to which his subjective needs had already been satisfied. In other words, having had no food and being hungry, an individual's demand for food, i.e. his subjective estimate of its *utility* to him, will be very intense and he will be prepared to give a lot for something to eat. As the amount of food he obtains nears the level at which he is perfectly satisfied, the intensity of his demand will diminish until it is extinguished altogether. The more of some commodity that anyone obtains, according to this theory, the less intense will be at their demand for any more of it; its marginal utility declines. The theory went on to assume that the relationship between the subjective intensity of demand and the degree of satisfaction could be established by examining market behaviour and could be expressed numerically. On this basis it was possible to represent graphically a schedule of prices correlated with demand in such a way as to show *mathematically* how the quantity of goods demanded by an individual would vary with the price *and* with the intensity of his demand. By aggregating a number of individual 'demand curves' of this kind, a demand curve for a whole market or economy could be developed. Similarly, a schedule could be drawn showing how the quantities of goods which manufacturers would supply were related to the prices which they would fetch in the market.

In general, by contrast with political economy, this new kind of analysis, although embracing both supply and demand, saw consumer preferences as prior to production possibilities. In particular, its novel assumptions enabled it to concentrate on the small, marginal changes in supply and demand and to provide a persuasive account of how anyone of such changes, however small, would bring about a new set of prices. Whereas the numerical examples of Ricardo and Marx were confined to the simple arithmetic of averages, the new economics was able to employ the more powerful and complex analytical procedures of marginal calculus; the study of economics became at once more specialized, more technical, more rigorous and much more powerfully predictive. Subsequently, the 'subjectivist' notion was extended to generate theories not only of the price of finished goods but also of interest, the price of capital, and wages, the price of labour. Although the central interest of economists is no longer that of the price formation of 'microeconomics', the general analytical framework on which the modern discipline rests is still derived directly from the innovations of the 'marginalists' and their subjectivist theory of value; it is this account of price formation which is still taught to undergraduate students of economics.

The weakness of 'subjectivist' theory

In spite of the elegance and power of the theoretical constructions of the 'neo-classical' school of Marshall, Jevons and Walras, and in spite of the fact that no theory of price determination in the market surpasses it in coherence and persuasiveness there was a number of good reasons for doubt about the 'realism' of marginal and subjectivist economic analysis over and above the standard objections that markets are never perfect and resources are not in fact substitutable.

The predictions of marginal analysis are based on certain questionable assumptions about the way in which the market adjusts to changes in supply or demand. It is supposed that this comes about because the functions which relate price and quantity are convergent. In non-mathematical terms this simply means that in order for the market to reach equilibrium it must be the case that, as economic operations of any kind are repeated, the pay-off or gain from them gradually dwindles to nothing; as consumers get more, the price they are prepared to pay gets less; as suppliers produce more their costs of production per unit of output after a certain point increase; as quantities available in the market increase, then, for any given set of consumer preferences and production possibilities, both consumer benefits and profits decline and finally are extinguished. When the price consumers are prepared to pay for one more item of a commodity is equal to the price which makes it just worthwhile for the manufacturer to produce one more item, the system reaches equilibrium.

Unfortunately for the theory of marginal utility, it was never possible to demonstrate empirically, except trivially, that the intensity of demand varies significantly with the degree to which desire is satisfied. There appear to be goods for which demand actually increases when their price is raised; it would seem that the value placed by consumers on some kinds of clothing and perfume and similar 'luxury goods' is actually a positive function of the price charged. It is also probably true that there are services, the supply of which decreases when their price rises. A man may be willing to labour at an unpleasant job if he has no alternative and only for so long as is necessary to secure him an income sufficient for a quite restricted set of wants. When paid more per hour he is only willing to work for a shorter period of time – some such explanation has been offered for the behaviour of the labour force in underdeveloped countries as well as for absenteeism, for example, among miners in industrialized countries. Clearly, the behaviour of our putative consumers of luxury goods is at odds with the basic idea of diminishing marginal utility: the more the manufacturer charges the more he sells. Similarly, in the case of the 'perverse' behaviour of labour, the more the cane-cutter is paid, the less he works. Although they must give pause for thought, these are not very serious exceptions, for there are obvious commonsense limits to both relationships; consumers will not spend an infinite amount on fur coats and there is a minimum income which even the most uncommercial of plantation workers must have. The theory can still be patched up to hold in the long run of the short run as it were. Much more difficult to accommodate to the theory is the observation that there seems to be no limit, in principle, to the advantages of producing on a large scale. That is to say, over long periods of time it seems to be the case that the more the manufacturer produces the less it costs him to produce every additional unit. This means that the manufacturer is not in general constrained by the onset of a point of marginal discouragement – i.e. that point at which the cost of producing an extra item is more than the price it will command in the market. This means, that in the long run, there is no point at which the market provides anything other than an incentive to go on and therefore there is no long run equilibrium point. It is still true that for the analysis of the short run, 'marginalism' and 'subjectivism' remain indispensable tools, but the hope that these theories once seemed to support, of providing a framework for a full-scale account of modern society and a prescription for its efficient organization have looked very threadbare for sometime. Certainly they can now pretend to offer nothing to those, Marxist or otherwise, who are concerned with our social destiny.

The Marxist attack on 'subjectivism'

In the nineteenth century, non-Marxist socialists accepted the subjectivist account of value without much difficulty. The Fabian socialists in England in the 1880s adopted the marginal theory of value without feeling that it invalidated their own ideas about the need for income redistribution. But the Marxists[1], oddly enough, chose to attack the theory, not on empirical, but on metaphysical grounds. They complained that the theory of marginal utility revealed a failure to understand that commodities are *social* products, that they owe their value not primarily to the estimation of their utility by consumers, but to the existence of the social relations which constitute the fabric of society and which make the production of the commodity possible in the first place. They complained that this absorption in price formation diverted attention from the inequities generated by the maldistribution of property which characterized 'capitalist' society, and concealed the exploitative relationships which underlie all economic activity in the bourgeois mode of production. They argued too, against the contention that the primacy of the consumer was a demonstration of the democratic nature of market allocation; they asserted that to allow production to be organized as a residual of subjective ideas of value was to admit that the mainspring of capitalism was the chaos of individual whim and fantasy. These are sensible and important criticisms although not as powerful as the empirical objections referred to in the previous section of this chapter. But the Marxist contention that the subjective theory of value was a less adequate account of price determination than was their own labour cost of production theory is clearly false. Both theories are *only* theories, but, as an analytical account of short run price formation, whatever its other shortcomings, marginalism is infinitely superior to cost-of-production theories and no modern Marxist economic theorist with any pretensions to analytical rigour would pretend that the labour theory of value offers him much help in formulating policy recommendations for economic management, socialist or otherwise.

The real reason for the Marxists' objection to subjectivist theory lay not in what it explained but what it appeared to justify. The labour theory of value as deployed by Marx is, as we shall see, a protracted attempt to deny the economic usefulness of allowing or imputing any income to capital. Marginalist theory not only accounted for this income but also suggested that it played a vital role in ensuring that consumer preferences were accurately reflected in the nature and timing of output.

The impossibility of a labour theory of value

Before moving to an examination of Marx's labour theory let us finally consider why a theory of price determination based on labour cost of production alone must always be inadequate.

An explanation of the income to capital, similar to that adopted by the marginalists, although theoretically unintegrated, was advanced by Marx's English contemporary, Nassau Senior (1790–1864), in terms of a reward for abstaining from consumption; and this explanation of capitalist wealth as a form of asceticism provoked Marx to one of his most entertaining flights of vituperation.[2] In spite of Marx's contempt, Senior had in fact hit upon the reason why there must be some return to capital over and above its original cost; it lies in the need to provide an index of the time taken for a productive process to be carried out.

Let us assume that, in a given productive process, the land on which the activity takes place costs nothing and that none of the materials used in production have any element of rent in their prices. The only resources used in this activity will then be labour and capital. Now the labour theory of value argues that the capital employed can be reduced to the value of the labour employed in manufacturing it. The capital used in the manufacture of capital can itself be reduced to its labour costs and so on backwards in an historical regression to the first man who engaged in the manufacture of capital. In this way, by adding up all the labour, measured in, say, hours of work, the whole price of output can be reduced to its labour value. Now, even if it were possible to make such a calculation, this would not account for the market price. Let us imagine the first man to produce a capital good, a tool. Let us suppose that there is a market for capital goods. What price must be paid to the tool-maker in order to induce him to part with his product? The utility of the tool rests in the fact that it enables its maker to produce more in a given period of time than he could before he made the tool. In order to recompense him for parting with the tool he will need to receive not only the equivalent of the labour-time he spent in making the tool, but *also* a sum of money or commodity which will compensate him for the extra time it will now take him to carry on production. Not only will he have to spend time in producing a new tool but he will also have to forego, meanwhile, the advantages which the actual possession of the tool conferred upon him in terms of increased output for a given effort. Every theory of value which purports to explain market prices must account for subjective preferences in terms of the point in time at which produce is made available as well as in terms of its cost of production in any physical sense. That is only to repeat that economics is concerned not only with the costs of production but also with the question of how products are distributed among individuals and purposes and in space and over time. Even if we assume, unrealistically, that price need provide no indication of the relative scarcity of a commodity, and even if we assume, more reasonably, that transport costs can be reduced to labour costs, any theory of price which ignores the cost of accumulating capital, i.e. *time*, is certain to be deficient in explanatory value when applied to a market situation.

References and Notes

1. This refers to those who subscribed to Marxism after Marx's death in 1883, not to Marx himself. Although Marx at one time studied calculus and exponential functions, he is not known to have taken any interest in the work of the marginalists, and his very unsatisfactory and brief reference to the marginal costs of production (*Capital*, vol. III. Part II, Ch. x, p. 179) shows no awareness of the relevance of his mathematical interests to his economic analysis. Engels refers to George Bernard Shaw's 'plausible vulgar socialism' as being 'built . . . on the foundation of Jevon's and Menger's theory of use-value and marginal utility' in the preface to his edition of vol. III of *Capital* (p. 10).
2. Ibid., vol. I, Part VII, Ch. xxiv, Sect. 5, pp. 596–8.

Chapter 10

The labour theory of value: market transformation

Why should anyone be interested in Marx's labour theory of value? As we have seen, prices can never be reduced to labour costs of production unless time is valueless. No modern economist, Marxist or non-Marxist, has been able to show how it might be used to show how prices are determined. Marx's effort has often been written off, quietly by Marxists, and derisively by non-Marxists, as something which looks like a wrong-headed attempt to meddle in an area of technical analysis which he did not fully understand. To dismiss it in this way is to fail to do justice to Marx's purpose. While nothing can make a success of a theory which has logical shortcomings, it remains the case that intellectual history is littered with such notions; Aristotle and Hobbes are still read and studied even though the claims they made for their work have not been justified. Their failures are instructive. There is no reason to approach Marx differently. The labour theory may be inadequate in terms of the results which Marx thought could be achieved with it; it is nonetheless of great interest as the central effort of the most influential thinker in the history of social thought.

It will be recalled that Marx conceived his theoretical task as that of writing a transformational critique of the world and that, with respect to economics, he proposed to do this by analysing the work of the political economists. Marx castigated them, with the honourable but only partial exceptions of Smith, Ricardo and John Stuart Mill, for being preoccupied with the *superficial appearance* of things, i.e. with the explanation of market phenomena in terms of themselves, with vacuous accounts of prices in terms of prices. Marx wanted to go deeper, to show how the pattern of market relations had its origins in the real actions of real human beings. The labour theory of value – an explanation of prices in terms of human effort – is central to this intention.[1]

The peculiarity of labour

Marx began his approach to the question of prices by considering the problem of the origins of profit. Profits cannot come, thought Marx, from exchange; buying cheap and selling dear is only a short term policy because in a well-developed market the buying and the selling of a commodity take place at the same price. Market imperfections and swindling mean that 'commodities may be sold at prices deviating from their values, but these deviations are to be considered as infractions of the laws of the exchange of commodities, which in its normal state is an exchange of equivalents, consequently, no method for increasing value'.[2] Thus, profit, the means by which capital is accumulated, 'cannot be created by circulation, and therefore . . . in its formation, something must take place in the background, which is not apparent in the circulation itself'.[3] On the other hand, Marx writes that 'The circulation of commodities is the starting-point of capital. The production of commodities, their circulation, and that more developed form of their circulation called commerce, these form the historical ground-work from which it arises. The modern history of capital dates from the creation in the 16th century of a world-embracing commerce and a world-embracing market.'[4] Marx faces the contradiction squarely and asserts that capital 'must have its origin both in circulation and yet not in circulation'.[5] The labour theory of value offers an answer to this conundrum.

Marx's difficulty with profits stems from his acceptance of the political economists' tautological price theory which stated that commodities were sold at the cost of their production. Interest or profit is simply the price to be paid for the capital or stock employed in production. But, Marx was asking, if commodities are sold for the price given for their acquisition, how does anybody grow rich? Marx's answer was that this was because of the peculiar characteristics of labour. Labour, Marx insisted, was a commodity like anything else, and was sold, like everything else, as the political economists thought, at the price of its cost of production. This is simply the subsistence theory of wages as modified by Adam Smith to include in 'subsistence' a provision for supporting a wife and rearing children – wages are, as it were, the cost of reproduction. But labour has the unique property of producing commodities the value of which is greater than the labourer's cost of reproduction. The capitalist buys the *labourer* for a day, at a rate calculated with reference to his subsistence costs, but in so doing acquires, Marx affirmed, his *labour-power* for a day, so securing an output which exceeds in value the value of the labourer's wages. In labour, the capitalist finds a use value which exceeds its exchange value. This means that the capitalist can buy the necessary ingredients of a commodity – raw materials, tools and labour – at their exchange value, but then sell the commodity at a higher price because the labourer adds, as a free gift to his capitalist, by the application of his labour power, extra value to the other ingredients, which the capitalist is able to realize on the sale of the commodity. The increase in value, profit, thus takes place not in the market, but in the production process, as a result of the activity of labour. In this way Marx was able to claim that the exchange of equivalents was compatible with the generation of profits. He was half-way to 'transforming' the market – profits are only *apparently* the result of exchange, in *reality* they are produced by workers.

The three great ratios: exploitation, mechanization and profits

In order to elaborate the theory based on this notion Marx employed some simple algebra. Marx declares that price is made up of three elements; constant capital, c; variable capital, v; and surplus value, s. In short, price $= c + v + s$.

The first of the two parts into which Marx divides the capitalist's outlay, constant capital, denotes the wear and tear on machinery and the raw materials employed in the productive process. These resources are 'constant' capital, because, unlike labour, they add no value to the final product other than the value which they themselves embody by being the products of historical labour.

The spinning machine which produces cotton thread partly wears out in the process; this depreciation is conceived as a transfer from the machine to the cotton – the cotton is increased in value by an amount exactly equal to the value of the wear and tear on the spinning machine.

The cotton which is worth sixpence before it is worked up into cloth is still worth sixpence as part of the finished product. Constant capital is embodied but dead labour and is simply a passive participant in output.

The second part of the capitalist's investment is variable capital, which represents wages, the cost of labour. This part of his capital is 'variable' because the extent to which he exploits it determines the amount of his profits. Labour is the only source of added value in the commercial system.

The third part of price, surplus value, is, quite simply, profit.

Marx uses the symbols to express three ratios. The first of these is $s : v$, the amount of profit per man employed. It follows from the fact that profits are produced exclusively by labour that this is the key relationship in the capitalist system; Marx calls this the rate of exploitation. Marx always assumes, in his illustration of his theory, that the rate of exploitation is 100 per cent.[6]

The second ratio is that which obtains between the two parts of capital, $c : v$, the amount of capital employed per man. Marx calls this the 'organic composition of capital'; the more of the capitalist's outlay devoted to constant capital, the higher the organic composition, i.e. the higher the ratio of capital to labour.

The third and final ratio $s : (c + v)$, the ratio of surplus value to the total outlay of capital, is more familiar – it is the rate of profit.

The value of these algebraic formulae is that they show succinctly the anatomy of Marx's concept of capitalism and indicate the three relationships crucial to his theory (i) the degree to which the worker is exploited by the capitalist s/v, (ii) the degree to which the economy has progressed as shown by the extent to which industry is mechanized and the amount of plant and raw materials operated and worked up by each worker, c/v, and (iii) the amount of value extracted by the capitalist in relation to his total outlay, $s/(c + v)$.

The great contradiction

Marx's labour theory of value states that 'The value of one commodity is to the value of any other, as the labour-time necessary for the production of the one is to that necessary for the production of the other.'[7] This is very straightforward but leads immediately to complications the nature of which can be most readily seen by reference to the two tables given here which are adaptations of those used to illustrate his argument by Marx himself.[8] They are offered without apology because they involve nothing more than some very simple arithmetic and, in combination with the definitions given above, make the understanding of Marx's problem much easier.

Table 10.1 shows what would happen in five different industries (numbered I to V) if Marx's theory of value were true and the relative prices of commodities were determined by their relative labour costs. The industries have different 'organic' compositions of capital (column 1) and the workers are equally exploited in each industry (column 2). Since the rate of exploitation is 100 per cent the surplus value is, it so happens, equal in each case to the cost of the labour employed (column 3). This need not be the case, of course, but it makes the working easier. In order to give his model some 'realism' Marx supposes that not all the c in column 1 is used up – after a production process is completed all the raw materials would be consumed but the depreciated machinery would remain – and the amount of c transferred to the finished article is given in column 4. Column 5 gives the final price, arrived at by adding up the expended c, together with v and the s which it produces.

Table 10.1

Col no.	1 Capital outlay	2 Exploitation rate	3 Surplus value	4 Constant capital expended	5 Value of commodities expended
	$c + v$	s/v (in per cent)	s	c	$c + v + s$
I	80 + 20	100	20	50	90
II	70 + 30	100	30	51	111
III	60 + 40	100	40	51	131
IV	85 + 15	100	15	40	70
V	95 + 5	100	5	10	20
	—		—	—	—
Totals	390 + 110		110	202	422

When commodities are sold at their labour values (column 5) the rate of profit $(s/c + v)$, (columns 3 and 1) varies from industry to industry. For the system as a whole the rate of profit is given by $\left[\dfrac{110}{(390 + 110)}\right] \times 100$ (total columns 3 and 1) = 22 per cent.

But, and this is both the crux of Marx's theory and the rock on which it finally shatters, such a state of affairs could not last for long. Manufacturers invest in the branch of activity where the rate of profit is highest. In Table 10.1, the rate of profit (column 1 divided by column 3) varies from 40 per cent in industry III to 5 per cent in industry V. Manufacturers in less profitable industries will start to invest in industry III and then, as competition brings down profits in that industry, in the others until the rates of profit throughout the system are brought to the same level. Marx acknowledged this, writing that 'these different rates of profit are equalized by competition to a single general rate of profit'.[9] These rates of profit are equalized by a competitive reduction in prices. But a change in prices, given this rate of exploitation and these ratios of capital to labour, would mean that prices no longer reflected relative labour costs. Marx is quite explicit about the difficulty; 'It would seem, therefore, that here the theory of value is incompatible with the actual process, incompatible with the real phenomena of production, and that for this reason any attempt to understand these phenomena should be given up.'[10] In short, relative prices are *not* determined by relative labour costs.

When Marx died in 1883 volumes II and III of *Capital* had not yet been published. In spite of the sixteen years that had passed since the publication of volume I in 1867 Marx had not been able to get his text into order. Engels undertook the posthumous publication of these texts and the appearance of volume III in 1894 was especially eagerly awaited because it was known to contain the answer to the problem of how labour costs determined prices in industries with different organic compositions of capital. When it appeared it proved to be a great disappointment, and the disillusionment it earned gave a powerful impulse to those tendencies, especially in the German Marxist Social Democratic Party, which sought to revise and adapt Marx's economic ideas.

In volume III Marx abandons the attempt to explain relative prices as promised in volume I. Instead, he offers as the 'law of value' the assertion that labour inputs in *the economy as a whole* determine prices in *the economy as a whole*. From Table 10.1 Marx derives a rate of profit for the whole economy by treating it as if it were one firm and the various industries were simply sub-departments.[11] Total profits at 110 (total column 3) set against total outlay of capital at 390 + 110 (total column 1) give a profit rate of 22 per cent. Applying this profit rate and using the same rate of exploitation the situation produced by the equilibrating action of market competition is shown in Table 10.2. This shows that although the prices of individual commodities differ from their labour-determined values, all the deviations when added (column 9) cancel each other out. Moreover, total profits in market prices (column 5) equal total surplus value in labour values (column 6) and total market prices (column 7) equal total output in labour values (column 8). In other words, Marx argues, although *individual* prices

Table 10.2

	1	2	3		4	5	6	7	8	9
	Capital outlay	Constant capital expended	Wages	=	cost price	Average profit	s	Market price	Labour value price expended	Deviation of market price from labour value price
	c+v	c +	v			%		expended c+v +av. profit	c+v+s	col. 7–col. 8
I	80+ 20	50	20	=	70	22	20	92	90	+2
II	70+ 30	51	30	=	81	22	30	103	111	−8
III	60+ 40	51	40	=	91	22	40	113	131	−18
IV	85+ 15	40	15	=	55	22	15	77	70	+7
V	95+ 5	10	5	=	15	22	5	37	20	+17
	390+110	202	110	=	312	110	110	422	422	0

When commodities are sold at market prices;

a. The deviation of market prices from labour value for the whole system is zero (total column 9)

b. Total profits in market prices = total surplus value (total columns 5 and 6)

c. Total market prices = total labour values (total columns 7 and 8) deviate from labour values, in the economy *as a whole* the relationship between profits and wages is determined by the rate of exploitation of labour. Marx is emphatic about the importance of his discovery; 'this intrinsic connection is here revealed for the first time,' he writes, and equates this version of the labour theory with the 'scientific approach'.[12]

On verbal grounds alone it is hard to see how Marx thought that his version of the labour theory of value as given in volume III is compatible with the theory as set out in volume I – an explanation of the division of output between capitalists and workers *is* a different thing from an explanation of the relative prices attached to the commodities of which output is composed.[13] Even so, this solution is vacuous. The symmetries of Table 10.2 are achieved by begging the central question; how does Marx know what the rate of exploitation s/v is in any industry? Quite apart from the fact that Marx himself does not pretend that Tables 10.1 and 10.2 are based on empirical evidence or are anything more than an arithmetical exercise composed in the privacy of his own study, he himself admits that entrepreneurs never think about the rate of exploitation and are indeed ignorant of it: 'The distinction between variable and constant capital escapes the capitalist.'[14] Capitalists are guided in investment by the rate of profit and not by the rate of exploitation. Marx offers no way of *knowing* how much profit is derived from labour as opposed to constant capital. He declares that the equalization of the rate of exploitation between industries 'is the actual premise of the capitalist mode of production'[15] and that this is brought about by 'competition among labourers and equalization through their continual migration from one sphere of production to another'.[16] But the labourers cannot identify the rate of exploitation any more certainly than can their employers and their changes of employment are prompted by wage-differentials, which have no necessary connexion with the supposed rate of exploitation. Marx himself comes near to admitting the insubstantiality of his theory when he writes, 'The general law of value acts as the prevailing tendency only in a very complicated and approximate manner, as a never ascertainable average of ceaseless fluctuations.'[17]

Once the unascertainable rate of exploitation had been *assumed*, all the tricks of Table 10.2 are easy to turn. Marx arrived at the average profit by adding up the surplus value in each industry and dividing by the number of industries. Total profits *must* equal total surplus value because Marx derived the one from the other. Similarly total market price *must* equal total labour value price because the same elements comprise both. Finally, the sum of the derivations of market price from labour value price in each industry *must* equal zero because of the way in which those two quantities are constructed.

But even these tautologies are less than Marx requires to support his own assertions. It can be seen from Table 10.2 that, although Marx has transmuted the labour values of inputs into the market values of outputs, he has not completed the task. The capitalists buy each other's outputs in order to provide themselves with inputs, and they do this, of course, not at labour values, but at 'transformed' market prices. In order to provide a complete solution to the transformation problem, a set of prices has to be found to cover commodities both as inputs *and* outputs which is consistent with Marx's propositions about the relationship between profits and exploitation. Marx's model has only five industries and nothing is said about the destination of outputs, but the problem can be reformulated and solved on the more realistic assumptions of an *n*-industry economy in which outputs can be used as inputs in any industry. The solution shows, however, that while it is possible for 'the sum of the profits in all spheres of production to . . . equal the sum of the surplus-values', or 'the sum of the prices of production to equal the sum of its value', it is not possible, as Marx thought necessary for the truth of his theory, for both to obtain at once.[18]

Let us recapitulate the point of taking the reader on this pilgrimage through Marx's algebra. Marx sought, as part of his main analytical interest, to find a real and objective criterion by which to measure the price phenomena of the market – to penetrate to the real world behind the veil of prices. He thought that he had found this in labour. He was then forced to concede that relative prices are not determined by relative labour inputs because another factor, constant capital, is involved, and prices are determined by a general rate of profit applied to all the capitalist's investment. The transformation tables are meant to show, how, in spite of this, profits in general are derived from labour alone. But even here it can be shown that the prices of labour inputs will not account for all prices and all profits. The labour theory of value is, on logical grounds, a complete failure.

Marx and subjective value

Having dealt with its logical structure and shown how its short-comings are entailed by Marx's purpose we must now look at a number of other criticisms of Marx's theory of value. The first of these is quickly disposed of – this is the complaint that Marx failed to evolve a theory of subjective value.

Marx assumes that it is no part of the function of labour theory of value to explain why non-produced goods like water and diamonds are priced the way they are. This undoubtedly detracts from the explanatory power of his theory but it is not, in context, an important deficiency. Marx thought of non-produced goods as gifts of nature and felt that to demand any price for them was illegitimate. This idea is not well integrated with his main theory but in confining himself to an explanation of the price of manufactured goods Marx was being very orthodox. It will be recalled that Smith distinguished between use values and exchange values but only offered an explanation of the latter. Marx proceeds similarly and contends that commodities 'as exchange-values . . . do not contain an atom of use-values'.[19] Marx was explicit about the source of his categories and correctly claims that his market price is 'really what Adam Smith calls *natural price*, Ricardo calls *price of production . . .* and the physiocrats call *prix nécessaire*'.[20] Marx was directly in the tradition of the political economists – it was, after all, their results which he was trying to explain. To complain that Marx failed to evolve a theory of subjective value is to fail to grasp the historical coherence of political economy and is rather like criticizing an eighteenth-century naturalist for failing to anticipate Darwin.

Market 'transformation'

Much more serious is the charge that Marx is disingenuous in his claim to have 'transformed' the market; at many points his explanation of what he contends is 'really' going on 'behind' the market is crucially dependent on market relationships. For example, Marx suggests that there are historical situations in which commodities *do* exchange at their labour 'values'. 'It is quite appropriate to regard the values of commodities as not only theoretically but also historically *prius* to the prices of production. This applies to conditions in which the labourer owns his means of production.'[21] Marx asserts that, in this case, 'these commodities would not be products of capital'.[22] Here he seems to think that, because the labourer *owns* his own tools, they cease to affect calculations about relative values. But tools, whoever owns them, are the result of accumulation and their presence must be taken into account in any economic analysis – failure to do so creates a weakness in the argument.

According to Marx, in a pre-capitalist society, i.e. one in which the means of production are owned by the producers, goods *will* exchange at prices determined exclusively by relative labour costs. This will be true even though the amounts devoted to supporting himself (the pre-capitalist equivalent of wages, v) and to the fixed means of production (the pre-capitalist equivalent of constant capital c) vary from producer to producer. In such a situation prices would be as in Table 10.1

'In these circumstances' writes Marx, 'a difference in the rates of profit would be immaterial'.[23] Now, it is of course possible to imagine a very primitive society in which production is carried on at a very low level of technique, and to suppose that in such an economy a few poorly differentiated goods are exchanged in some sort of ritual fashion (although it is hard to see how such a ritual exchange would establish relative values by labour cost of production). But Marx insists that the economic circumstances of the situation he has in mind are highly commercialized. In order that commodities should be sold at labour value prices, i.e. in a *money* economy, it is necessary

(1)... for the exchange of commodities to cease being purely accidental or only occasional: (2) ... for commodities to be produced ... in approximately sufficient quantities to meet mutual requirements something learned from mutual experience in trading and therefore a natural outgrowth of continued trading; and (3) ... for no natural or artificial monopoly to enable either of the contracting sides to sell commodities above their value or to compel them to undersell.[24]

In a society in which there is an established market for output it is difficult to believe that some of the means of production are not traded. If that is so, and given that the time over which labour inputs are spread is what lies at the heart of the notion of an income to capital, it is even harder to believe that 'a difference in the rates of profit would be immaterial'. If they were not immaterial, the situation could not be stable; the advent of the situation set out in Table 10.2 could not be delayed for long, if at all. But Marx is insisting that there *is* a market; and he must do so, because without it, it would not be possible to be sure that commodities embodying equal amounts of labour exchanged with each other. Marx is trying to give substance to Adam Smith's idea that, in a very primitive society, deer are exchanged against beaver at ratios determined by the relative amounts of time taken to trap them. But he has changed Smith's precommercial situation into a commercial society. The 'real' situation, generating labour determined prices, proves to be indistinguishable from the market which it is supposed to anticipate.

The measurement of labour

Marx's difficulty can be reduced to a measurement problem; how is the value of commodities to be measured? The answer is again unequivocal and straightforward: 'Plainly, by the quantity of the value-creating substance, the labour, contained in the article. The quantity of labour, however, is measured by its duration, and labour-time in its turn finds its standard in weeks, days, and hours.'[25] If labour-time were homogeneous, if, that is to say, it were the case that the labour of any man for one hour were of exactly the same value as the labour of any other man for one hour, there would be no further problem. But, of course, in the market this is not so. The work of a highly skilled craftsman, of great experience and intelligence, is worth more than that of a new apprentice still learning the basic processes of his trade – he will produce more and of a better quality in a given time. The value added by an engineering fitter to his raw materials per unit of time is greater than the value added by a collector of driftwood. But even as between watchmakers of *equal* experience and training, some men's work will be more highly prized than others and they will command higher wages. Marx deals with all this by writing that skilled labour *counts only as simple labour intensified, or rather as multiplied simple labour, given quantity of skilled being considered equal to a greater quantity of simple labour. Experience shows that this reduction is constantly being made. A commodity may be the product of the most skilled labour, but its value, by equating it to the product of simple unskilled labour, represents a definite quantity of the latter labour alone. The different proportions in which different sorts of labour are reduced to unskilled labour as their standard, are established by a social process which goes on behind the backs of the producers, and, consequently appear to be fixed by custom.*[26]

Nowhere does Marx pretend that some authorized body of time-keepers and work assessors is establishing the physical norms for unskilled labour, and the multiples to be applied in order to arrive at the various degrees of skilled labour: instead, he writes that 'experience shows this reduction is constantly being made' and labour standards 'are established by a social process which goes on behind the backs of the producers'.

But, by his 'social process which goes on behind the backs of the producers' Marx can only mean the market. The price of labour is deduced from the price offered for its output. In other words, the very standard which Marx has seized upon in order to 'transform' market prices, turns out to have its relative value established by the market and, if the price of labour is determined by the market, then to say that relative prices are determined by labour is only to say that all prices are interdependent – and it is precisely this circularity from which Marx has been trying to escape.

Supply and demand

Nowhere in his work does Marx devote very much space to the study of how market adjustments actually take place. This is not surprising; although it was a commonplace of political economy that price was determined by supply and demand – what Adam Smith called 'the higgling and bargaining of the market' – the political economists' interest was centred on the long run where the constraints were those of production costs. At one point, however, Marx does turn explicitly to the examination of supply and demand, and in his determination to tear aside the veil of the market, finally concludes that the basic assumption of political economy – that the economic system owes both its coherence and its dynamism to continuously self-adjusting market relationships – is false. Although this is a disastrous result it is worth dwelling on briefly, as it illustrates Marx's stubbornly determined search for the 'real' foundation of commercial exchange.

The relevant passage is to be found in Chapter X of volume III of *Capital*. Significantly the context is Marx's discussion of how labour values are transmuted into market prices. Marx first discusses, in orthodox fashion, how market price and market value deviate from each other in response to fluctuations in supply and demand until their 'mutual proportions are such that the mass of commodities of a definite line of production can be sold at their market value, neither above or below it'.[27] But then he goes on to assert that 'if supply and demand balance one another, they cease to explain anything, do not affect market values, and therefore leave us so much more in the dark about the reasons why the market-value is expressed in just this sum of money and no other,'[28] and that 'supply and demand never coincide, or, if they do, it is by mere accident, hence scientifically = 0, and to be regarded as not having occurred'.[29]

Marx here is either being disingenuous or speaking so loosely and thinking so incoherently as to have misled *himself*. When supply is said to exceed demand, what is meant is that supply is excessive at a given price. To speak of deficiency or excess of demand is to refer to the need to raise or lower price if, in a given situation, the market is to be cleared. Given that, as Marx assumes, markets are never absolutely perfect but only nearly or approximately so, demand and supply will necessarily and often equilibrate at price levels which differ from Marx's market labour values. At these prices demand *does* equal supply, i.e. no supplier is left with goods on his hands and there are no queues. It is difficult to see, therefore, what Marx means by maintaining that the situation where market price equals market value is the only point at which supply equals demand and yet that this is, at the same time, the point at which 'they cease to explain anything'.

This conclusion is, in fact, subversive of much of Marx's own analysis because, as we have seen, the measuring and ordering effects of the market are fundamental to Marx's theory of history as well as to many of his economic propositions. The whole of his theory of value with its elaborate account of how the law of labour value 'ultimately' determines the apparently divergent market prices is firmly based on the assumption that the market provides a mechanism of adjustment.

What is Marx getting at? Underlying this perhaps wilful confusion are two important points. In the course of his attack on the orthodox account of price formation he declares that 'the real inner laws of capitalist production cannot be explained by the interaction of supply and demand'[30] in the terms described above but then adds '(quite aside from a deeper analysis of these two social motive forces, which would be out of place here)'. In fact there are several references to ways in which such a deeper analysis might proceed, and it is not clear why Marx thought that they would be 'out of place'.

The first line of inquiry which may have been on the verge of formulation by Marx could have been the consideration of the way in which social structure and relative competitive ability affect market outcomes. He writes that

*'social demand', i. e. the factor which regulates the principle of demand,
is essentially subject to the mutual relationship of the different classes
and their respective economic position, notably therefore to, firstly, the
ratio of total surplus-value to wages, and, secondly to the relationship
of the various parts into which surplus-value is split up (profit, interest,
ground-rent, taxes, etc.).*[31]

In other words, the structure of demand as a whole is itself a function of
the degree to which capitalists exploit workers. Or, to put it in yet
another way, is the result of the way in which output is shared between
capitalists and their employees and how the capitalists' share is broken
up to meet the costs of government, investment and capitalists'
consumption. Although this does nothing to detract from the
importance of demand in determining price, as Marx seems to think,
Marx's insistence that *demand itself* is the result of the disposition of
resources within society is both unexceptionable and worthwhile.

Secondly, Marx may have been trying to suggest, or perhaps already
believed, that the level of demand can be established independently of
the market. The argument is not clear, but if this were Marx's aim it
would help to explain some of his difficulty. For Marx, as for Adam
Smith, demand and utility were social categories. Need and utility were
considered with reference not to individuals but to society. Hence the
lack of interest in the problem of the value of diamonds; however great
their value to a *duchess* as an indispensable means of signalling her
status, their value to *society* at large is negligible. Food and clothing, on
the other hand, the wheat and cotton to which Marx constantly refers,
are self-evidently vital. It might be argued that the demand for the staple
items of consumption in a comparatively poor society, i.e. for food and
clothing, is a given which can be ascertained independently of the
market. A man can only eat and wear so much, and the quantity he eats
and the thickness of the clothes he wears are obviously directly related,
in primitive circumstances, to the work he does and the climate in which
he lives. It may be a notion of this kind which is hovering at the back of
Marx's mind when he writes, 'One of the first promises of selling was
that a commodity should have a use-value and therefore satisfy a social
need. The other premise was that . . . its individual value (and, what
amounts to the same . . . its selling price) should coincide with its social
value',[32] and again 'The limits within which the need for commodities in
the market, the demand, differs quantitatively from the *actual social
need*, naturally vary considerably for different commodities; what I
mean is the difference between the demanded quantity of commodities
and the quantity which would have been in demand at other money or
living conditions of the buyers.'[33]

It is as if, even under capitalism, Marx felt that justice was more
nearly being done when market prices are identical to labour 'values'
because at that point the prices paid represent most accurately the
exchange of social labour for social need. But nothing can really make

this coherent, and speculation about what Marx really meant begins to take us away from the text.

Conclusion

There is no way of rescuing Marx's theory, and even the hints about avenues of fruitful exploration which he throws up in the course of his exposition are drowned out by the immense noise of his unrelenting pursuit of a logical impossibility – an absolute measure of value. At times, it must be admitted, Marx is reduced to fatuities, as when he writes that 'Whatever the manner in which the prices of various commodities are firstly mutually fixed or regulated, their movements are always governed by the law of value. If the labour time required for their production happens to shrink, prices fall; if it increases, prices rise, provided other conditions remain the same.'[34] But his purpose and its connexion with his original inspiration, is clear. He wanted to show that others had 'fetishized' the market, and that when they claimed that it was 'natural' and, as such, ensured the best possible disposition of wealth and allocation of employment, they were showing themselves to be deceived by spurious and superficial appearances. But his attempt to unveil the truth failed because he confused the *logic* of market relationships with the examination of institutional arrangements and physical conditions. What lies 'behind' the market, if anything can be said to do so, is not a perverted logic, but sets of phenomena which are the subject of anthropology, sociology and psychology. Economics cannot be criticized from within itself – it is its premises which must be scrutinized. In confusing logic with the establishment of what is empirically the case Marx was again falling foul of the deliberate conflation of the 'real' and the 'ideal' which, along with Feuerbach, he had inherited from Hegel. It is a sad failure: the hypocrisies and insensitivity which he sought to expose were not the creatures of his imagination: they and the suffering they caused were real enough – but Marx's inability to free himself from the political economists' straitjacket, which for all his determination to 'transform' it proved too powerful for him, meant that the promise of the 1844 *Manuscripts* was unfulfilled and the nineteenth century was the poorer for it.

Appendix: Marx, Smith, Ricardo and Labour

Marx, Smith and Ricardo were united in a common endeavour – the search for an invariable standard for measuring value independently of prices; all three find this in labour. But, while Marx is engaged in this pursuit for what are really philosophical reasons, Smith and Ricardo are trying to solve a technical problem, the problem of measuring economic change over time.

The problem arises out of the limitations on the market's aggregating function. It is because price provides a mathematical expression of imputed values that we can add up and compare unlike things. Price enables us to compare a given number of hawks and handsaws with a given quantity of buckwheat and bedspreads. But this is only possible in a particular market at a particular time. If any *one* of the commodities offered for sale is altered in quality or quantity this will effect *all* relative values. All prices are interdependent and an alteration in the evaluation of one good means an alteration of its value in terms of all other goods offered for sale at the same time. A change in the market will tend to produce changes in the relative *prices* of goods whose relative *quantities* are unchanged. When the market array of prices is altered in this way, we cannot compare the new aggregate of hawks, handsaws, buckwheat and bedspreads with the old ones because they are based on different relative values.

As Smith puts it, 'At the same time and place . . . money is the exact measure of the real exchangeable value of all commodities. It is so, however, at the same time and place only.'[35] But, given that Smith was trying to account for the history of economic growth, he needed to be able 'to compare the different real values of a particular commodity at different times and places'.[36] He chose labour as the measure of 'real value' because he assumed that work is something of which all men have experience and something which they are all concerned to minimize for themselves and that, therefore, 'What everything is really worth to the man who has acquired it, and who wants to dispose of it or exchange it for something else, is the toil and trouble which it can save to himself, and which it can impose on other people.'[37] He then argued that, in the long run, whatever the money price of wages, i.e. whatever their *relative* value, the *real* value of labour is determined by the quantity of wheat wages purchase. Since the subsistence theory of wages suggests that labour incomes are fairly constant in terms of physical quantities of food, and since Smith believed that the technology of agriculture, on balance, showed no similar tendency to advance, he could then claim that over long periods, labour measured in wheat provides a reasonably invariable standard of value.

This, it should be noted, is distinct from a labour cost theory of price. Ricardo misunderstood Smith and thought that Smith had contradicted himself by speaking of 'the quantity of labour bestowed on the production of any object . . . and . . . the quantity which it can command in the market . . . as if those were two equivalent expressions'.[38] Marx followed Ricardo in this error.[39] But obviously the labour commanded by a commodity in the market necessarily exceeds its labour cost of production because its price includes, in addition, elements for profit and rent.

Like Smith, Ricardo has to find some way of comparing values in different market situations: 'When commodities varied in relative value, it would be desirable to have the means of ascertaining which of them fell and which rose in real value, and this could be effected only by comparing them one after another with some invariable standard of value, which should itself be subject to none of the fluctuations to which other commodities are exposed.'[40] Specifically, Ricardo wanted to show how incomes to capital, labour and land change with the growth of population. He could not do this by using prices, because relative market values are constantly changing. His explanation of the generation of rent (see pages 44–45) depends on using labour but in a rather more circuitous fashion than Smith. Unlike Smith, Ricardo was tempted to use labour simultaneously both as a determinant of price and as an invariable standard of value, as Marx did, but was held back by his superior logical sense. Like Marx, Ricardo saw that market prices were affected by the ratio of capital to labour employed; unlike Marx he realized that, therefore, labour could never be more than an approximate determinant of price. He assumed, however, that an invariable standard of value could be provided by a commodity produced with a capital labour ratio which was equal to the average for the economy as a whole. He thought that gold was such a commodity. He thought too, that wheat was similarly produced, so that gold and wheat had a constant relative value over time. Then, as for Smith, the trick is turned by the subsistence theory of wages so that labour and wheat also have a constant relative value, and labour, via wheat and gold, is the invariable measure of value.

The structural affinity of this theory with Marx's analysis is very clear. In Marx's economy, as portrayed in Table 10.2, a commodity produced with the average organic composition or capital will sell at a market price which exactly corresponds to its relative labour value.

But, to repeat, Ricardo and Smith used labour to measure changes independently of market values over time and neither claimed to show that labour uniquely determined prices; Marx uses labour in an attempt to prove that labour is not only the only source of value but is also the only *true* measure of value even within a given market situation.

References and Notes

1. The exposition of Marx's theory given here is simplified in the text of *Capital*; for example, Marx did not consistently distinguish between capital as a stock and capital as a flow. A more detailed analysis can be found in the commentaries cited in the Bibliography.
2. *Capital*, vol. I, Part II, Ch. iv, p. 159.
3. Ibid., vol. I, Part II, Ch. iv, p. 165.
4. Ibid., vol. I, Part II, Ch. iv, p. 146.
5. Ibid., vol. I, Part II, Ch. iv, p. 166.
6. Marx believed that the rate could be less than 100 per cent but

thought that it had an upper limit and appears to have considered 100 per cent as the maximum rate of exploitation. The reasons for and consequences of this arbitrary assumption will be discussed in Chapter 11.

7. *Capital*, vol. I, Part I, Ch. i, Sect. 1, pp. 39–40.
8. See ibid., vol. III, Ch. ix, pp. 155-7.
9. Ibid., vol. III, Ch. ix, p. 158.
10. Ibid., vol. III, Ch. viii, p. 153.
11. Ibid., vol. III, Ch. ix, p. 158.
12. Ibid., vol. III, Ch. ix, p. 168.
13. But the fact remains that Marx had drafted vols. II and III of *Capital* before the publication of vol. I and had arrived at the solution of the 'great contradiction' by 1862. (See Marx to Engels, 2 August 1862, in *MEW*, vol. XXX, p. 263-7.) Marxists have argued that vols. I and III are not contradictory; Marx's failure to get vol. III out before his death may mean that he himself was less certain.
14. *Capital*, vol. III, Ch. viii, p. 155.
15. Ibid., vol. III, Ch. x, p. 175.
16. Ibid., vol. III, Ch. ix, p. 161.
17. Ibid.
18. Ibid., vol. III, Ch. x, p. 175.
19. Ibid., vol. I, Ch. i, p. 38.
20. Ibid., vol. II, Ch. viii, p. 198.
21. Ibid., vol. III, Ch. x, p. 177.
22. Ibid., vol. III, Ch. x, pp. 175-6.
23. Ibid., vol. III, Ch. x, p. 177.
24. Ibid., vol. III, Ch. x, p. 178.
25. Ibid., vol. I, Ch. i, Sect. 1, p. 38.
26. Ibid., vol. I, Ch. i, Sect. 1, p. 44.
27. Ibid., vol. III, Ch. x, p. 189.
28. Ibid.
29. Ibid.
30. Ibid., vol. III, Ch. x, p. 189.
31. Ibid., vol. III, Ch. x, p. 181.
32. Ibid., vol. III, Ch. x, p. 182.
33. Ibid., vol. III, Ch. x, p. 189.
34. Ibid., vol. III, Ch. x, p. 177.
35. *The Wealth of Nations*, Book I, Ch. v, vol. I, p. 55.
36. Ibid.
37. Ibid., Book I, Ch. v, vol. I, p. 47.
38. Ricardo, *Works*, Ch. i, vol. I, Sect. 1, p. 14.
39. *Capital*, vol. I, p. 46, n. 1.
40. Ricardo, op. cit., Ch. i, vol. I, Sect 6, p. 43.

Chapter 11

The labour theory of value: exploitation and property rights

We have seen that, as a device for achieving its stated purpose, the explanation of prices in the capitalist mode of production, Marx's labour theory of value is very unsatisfactory. We have seen, too, how this failure is related to Marx's intention to write a transformational critique of political economy. But this does not exhaust the interest of his theory of value. In its exposition, Marx was, as we have noted, trying to show the necessary and scandalous connexion between the egalitarian and libertarian assumptions of the market on the one hand and its inequitable and repressive outcome on the other. The structure of the argument which Marx deploys can be shown to be strikingly similar to that employed by Locke in his teaching on the origin of property and incidentally again serves to underline the extent to which Marx's general social analysis was deeply rooted in market concepts.

Property rights: allocation and distribution

Before going on to examine the connexion, in Marx, between price and property, it is necessary first to make an analytical point about the distinction between two functions of the market: allocation and distribution. In the generation of prices the market performs a number of tasks. First, it measures and provides a way of comparing values. Consequent to, and dependent on, this main activity, are the functions of allocation and distribution. By indicating relative scarcities, market prices direct productive effort in terms both of the combination of inputs employed and of the output the inputs are designed to produce. This *allocative* function is, as it were, a technical one; the relative price of coal and wood decide which shall be used to fuel steam-engines; the relative price of labour and machinery decide whether a more or less mechanized productive process should be adopted. Decisions of this kind are made without regard to the pattern of income *distribution* which they also produce.

The *distribution* effect of prices refers to the way in which total output is divided up among the owners of the factors of production i.e. between capitalists and labourers.

The distributive function arises out of the allocative function. The prices of the various factors of production are not only indicators to their users but are also incomes to the owners of these factors. The way in which the market distributes income is obviously vital in deciding on the relative wealth of social classes but the distinction between *allocation* and *distribution* should be borne in mind. It may be a help to remember that, even in the heyday of nineteenth-century *laissez-faire* the market was not the only factor determining the distribution of property. It is true that the market rules which regulate the transfer of property are themselves embodied in the law and policed by the State – but, by the same token, these are not the only rules for the alienation or acquisition of property rights. There were then, as there are now, many other legally enforceable rules defining claims to the possession of certain goods and the enjoyment of certain benefits; property could be inherited, found, won, received as a gift or even created, as well as exchanged for other goods and services. Even in Victorian England, the State levied taxes and paid subsidies, and provided police, parks, education, and a variety of cultural institutions indiscriminately, so transferring resources within the community without any reference to the market.

Socialism and property rights

Marx's labour theory of value is essentially a dislocated theory of property rights. Early nineteenth-century socialism is a critique of the distribution of property. Marx first became interested in political economy partly because he thought that it would help in the discussion of 'material interests' and the disposition of wealth. In Engels's anticipation of Marx, his 'Critique of Political Economy' he concluded that 'The only *positive* advance which liberal economics has made is the unfolding of the laws of private property.'[1]

It is *ownership* that is the critical issue in all Marx's different social formations. The classes of society are identified not even by how much they own, but by what they own. The very index of social change is the way in which the workers' property is wrested from them: 'The essential difference between the various economic forms of society, between, for instance, a society based on slave-labour and one based on wage-labour, lies only in the mode in which this surplus-labour is in each case extracted from the actual producer, the labourer;'[2] and 'the capitalist mode of production and accumulation, and therefore capitalist private property, have for their fundamental condition the annihilation of self-earned private property; in other words, the expropriation of the labourer'.[3] Capitalism owes its origins to acts of expropriation and is superseded by socialism when 'the exproprietors are expropriated'. The very notion of expropriation is meaningless unless it refers to the violation of a property right.

Marx was not the first to propound a labour theory of value with radical intent and he made no secret of his debt to earlier socialist critics of political economy who had done the same. In *The Poverty of*

Philosophy, Marx cites Thompson (d. 1855), Hodgskin (1785–1869) and Bray (1809–95), the last at great length, as part of his demonstration that Proudhon was not the first to claim that labour, considered as an economic category, offered the key to the future organization of society. In *Labour's Wrongs and Labour's Remedy* (1839), Bray claims that Ricardo had shown that 'it is not to any one commodity or set of commodities, but to some given *quantity* of labour, that we must refer for an unvarying standard of real value. Here is a recognition of the principle that real value is dependent upon labour; and the only inference we can draw from it is that all men who perform an equal quantity of labour ought to receive an equal remuneration'.[4] Marx was much taken with Bray's pamphlet, while Hodgskin's *Labour defended against the Claims of Capital* (1825) has a similar argument and also contains striking passages on the worship of capital as a God which are interesting anticipations of Marx at his most Feuerbachian. Significantly, although Marx identifies their work as 'the equalitarian application of the Ricardian theory'[5] and although they emphasized the extent of the value added to the final product by labour, they were not concerned to explain prices, but to establish their claim that labour was in equity entitled to a much larger share of output; i.e. that the property rights of labour were being frustrated.

But these early proponents of the right of labour to its product were merely the occasion of Marx's interest in the labour theory of value. His interest was wider, more exact and more *theoretical* than theirs. In his search for a reductionist explanation of the origins of wealth and poverty he overlooked again the distinction to be made between the *effects* of market rules and property rights, which are essentially political imputations, and the *reasons* for these political imputations which are socially rather than economically determined. Marx confined his attention to the logic of the market and sought to find the empirical world in these analytical rules. He confused the allocative and distributive functions of the market and then made the distributive function the sole determinant of wealth. Such was the result of Marx's overwhelming desire to drive his theory through, in spite of a clear analytical objection which had been put by John Stuart Mill in 1848 and with which Marx was undoubtedly familiar.

In his *Principles of Political Economy* (1848) Mill, whose book is also notable for its moderately socialistic sympathies, was quite categorical about humanity's freedom, in principle, from the iron laws of the market, writing that 'the distribution of wealth . . . is a matter of human institution solely. The things once there, mankind, individually or collectively, can do with them as they like. They can place them at the disposal of whomsoever they please, and on whatever terms.'[6] This Marx refused to recognize. We can see why. To separate allocation and the techniques of production from the distribution of property is to sever the base from the superstructure. If men can do what they like with output then the existence of poverty is a function of human wickedness and ceases to be *necessary*. Over a quarter of a century after Mill, Marx was still writing that

Any distribution whatever of the means of consumption is only a consequence of the distribution of the conditions of production themselves. The latter distribution, however, is a feature of the mode of production itself . . . Vulgar Socialism . . . has taken over from the bourgeois economists the consideration and treatment of distribution as independent of the mode of production and hence the presentation of Socialism as turning principally on distribution. After the real relation has long been made clear, why retrogress again?[7]

To repeat, Marx tries to identify what is imputed with what can be observed empirically. All output, claims Marx, is produced by labour and therefore self-evidently its property. But it is clear that labour is not the only factor of production and, even if it were, property is a matter of human institution and not economic fact. Marx nonetheless thought that he had nailed property rights to their material foundations and so could demonstrate that the capitalist mode of production was implicitly a systematic infraction of the property rights of the workers to their own product. The labour theory of value is a 'scientific' demonstration of a moral evil.

Hobbes, Locke and Marx

Thomas Hobbes (1589–1679) and John Locke (1632–1784) are the most important figures in the early articulation of modern political theory, and the 'prehistory' of economic thought. Their work consisted of the establishment of different but closely related individualistic theories of political obligation which proved to be highly functional for the operation of an extensive market. According to their ideas, political authority was contractual in origin and derived from mutual agreement, as in the conclusion of a market bargain. They account for the necessity and desirability of individual subordination to a sovereign in terms of the advantages – peace, security and the enforcement of justice – which the sovereign provides in return. For the first time, a fully developed theory of government was provided in terms which were individualistic, rationalistic and utilitarian. Marx observed that Locke's philosophy 'served as the basis for the whole of subsequent English political economy'.[8]

Hobbes's theory, set out in *Leviathan* (1651), deals with the institutions needed to secure order in the 'state of nature'. This is a situation in which men are atomized individuals, owing allegiance to nobody, and in which each is seeking only to secure himself against the depredations of his fellows, who, like himself, are impelled solely by a desire to compete with all other men in the appropriation to themselves of as much of other men's possessions and as many of other men's persons as possible. In this state of nature, in Hobbes's famous phrase, 'the life of man is solitary, poore, nasty, brutish and short'.[9] Hobbes lived through the Civil War in England and grew up in an era of protracted and bloody political chaos in Europe. His consequent belief' that man was an aggressive, acquisitive, and dangerous but rational animal, made him stress the vital importance and logical necessity of establishing a powerful sovereign endowed with an exclusive licence for the use of force in society. Hobbes was notorious rather than popular among his contemporaries because, in his anxiety to establish utilitarian grounds for government, he used arguments which could readily be reduced to the proposition that 'might is right' and employed to legitimize any government so long as it preserved order. At a time when political theorists were principally concerned to find some justification for a political mechanism which would allow for greater participation in government and provide for the alteration, if necessary, of its personnel, Hobbes's views were regarded with great distaste. But in the light of the subsequent development of political economy, and especially in view of the Marxist account of this development, what is striking is that Hobbes's 'Commonwealth', once established, is not one which obviates or suppresses the self-seeking appetites of natural men, but rather one which channels and facilitates them. The state of nature is an 'Inference, made from the Passions'[10] and the institution of civil society is a change in man's social environment, not a change in man's nature. The establishment of a sovereign simply limits the extent to which men can prey upon each other; by guaranteeing man's physical security and enforcing contracts, the State actually enables men to compete with each other more effectively, laying down the rules of the competition and securing for the winners the fruits of their success. Hobbes's argument implies a society in which social organization is coextensive with commercial institutions and which portrays with disturbing clarity, what socialists of a later century felt were the true and unlovely features of market man.

Locke, who published his *Second Treatise of Government* in 1698, after, that is, the Restoration of 1660 and the 'Glorious Revolution' of 1688 which displaced James II, had a milder view of human nature. Locke was anxious to dissociate himself from Hobbes's unpleasant account of the human disposition and the unqualified absolution of sovereignty which that seemed to entail, but structurally his ideas were very similar. Like Hobbes, he suggested the existence of a state of nature from which man was emancipated by the creation of a political system. But his more confident approach to the question of social stability enabled him to take a less anxious view of the state of nature and a more expansive interpretation of the purpose of the political order. Hobbes had stressed the importance of civil society to the preservation of life itself; Locke conceived its function as the guarantor of a more general concept of 'property' within which he included the person.

The inwardness of Locke's arguments derives from the fact that his purpose was to establish that citizens had rights in the disposal of their persons and in the acquisition of property which were anterior to the establishment of society. This was part of an attempt to provide a justification for limiting the absolute power of government over the individual. But in deploying his reasoning he touched on the basic logic of the commercial situation. Chapter v of his *Second Treatise* is devoted to an explanation of how the inequalities of society are explained and legitimized by the equalities of the state of nature. He set out to show 'how men might come to have a property in several parts of that which God gave to mankind in common, and that without any express compact of all the commoners'.[11]

Just as the assumption of individualism implies philosophically an interest in how man apprehends things mentally, so economically, individualism directs attention to the question of how man acquires things physically. According to Locke, the source of property is labour, because 'every man has a property in his own person. The labour of his body and the work of his hands we may say are properly his. Whatsoever, then, he removes out of the state and left it in, he hath mixed his labour with, and joined it to something which is his own, and thereby makes it his own property'.[12] To this fundamental proposition Locke adds an auxiliary argument: 'It is labour ... that puts the difference of value on everything ... it will be but a very modest computation to say that of the products of the earth useful to the life of man nine-tenths are the offsets of labour.'[13] The state of nature is egalitarian because accumulation is restricted. According to Locke, in the state of nature property rights did not extend to the appropriation of land which a man could not himself till nor to the amassing of perishable commodities which he was incapable of consuming; if he did so 'he offended against the common law of nature, and was liable to be punished; he invaded his neighbour's share'.[14]

The transition from this peaceable, uncompetitive and egalitarian idyll to civil society comes about with the invention of money and the appearance of market. These make it possible to store up value beyond the demands of immediate consumption and also confer a value on things hitherto valueless;

And thus came in the use of money – some lasting thing that man might keep without spoiling, and that, by mutual consent, man would take in exchange for the truly useful but perishable supports of life. And as different degrees of industry were apt to give men possessions in different proportions, so this invention of money gave them the opportunity to continue and enlarge them; for supposing an island, separate from all possible commerce with the rest of the world . . . what reason could any one have there to enlarge his possessions beyond the use of his family and a plentiful supply to his consumption.[15]

Locke's not altogether logically coherent view seems to be that while property is an exercise of 'natural' i.e. pre-social, right, money is the expression of a social convention and since it 'has its value only from the consent of men . . . it is plain that the consent of men have agreed to a disproportionate and unequal possession of the earth'.[16] Locke's argument is that to will the means, money and the market, is to will the end, inequality. Locke has an interesting subsidiary and basically economic argument for property, according to which 'he who appropriates land to himself by his labour does not lessen but increases the common stock of mankind'.[17] This is because appropriation and enclosure increases productivity and so lessens the demand for land; 'the encloser has a greater plenty of the conveniences of life from ten acres than he could have from a hundred left to nature [and] may truly be said to give ninety acres to mankind.'[18]

The similarity of the general structure of Locke's reasoning with Marx's exposition of the way in which the worker's labour, exchanged for its market equivalent, is at the same time the source of the capitalist's accumulation of wealth, scarcely needs emphasizing.

As Marx writes:

At first the rights of property seemed to us to be based on a man's own labour . . . now, however, property turns out to be the right, on the part of the capitalist, to appropriate the unpaid labour of others . . . and to be the impossibility, on the part of the labourer, of appropriating his own product. The separation of property from labour has become the necessary consequence of a law that apparently originated in their identity.[19]

Although Marx read Locke there is no reason to suppose that his account of the way in which egalitarian assumptions give rise to inegalitarian outcomes was consciously derived from him – or anybody else. Rather it is an interesting example of the way in which the contemplation of market logic leads to similarly organized attempts to render it coherent, albeit for very different purposes. Both Hobbes and Locke, in works which are not explicitly economic, prefigure the problem of market coherence and individual autonomy which Smith resolves by 'the invisible hand'. Locke attempts to resolve the fundamental market paradox – that while the justification of the market is the liberty and equality of opportunity which it affords, it lays itself open to the charge that those are only the preconditions for inequality in property and a consequent system, not of liberty, but of dependence. Modern State intervention through taxes and welfare payments, it could be argued, does no more than offer botched remedies for the social disequilibration by the market. In the labour theory of value Marx wrongly thought that he had found a philosopher's stone that would turn all facts into value judgements. But the deficiencies and confusions of Marx's exposition of his discovery should not be allowed to obscure the fact that his real concern was with the central and unresolved moral dilemma of commercial society; how is equality of opportunity to be reconciled with the unequal distribution of advantage which it produces?

References

1. Frederick Engels, 'Outlines of a critique of political economy' in *The Economic and Philosophic Manuscripts of 1844*, p. 288.
2. *Capital*, vol. I, Ch. ix, p. 217.
3. Ibid., vol. I, Ch. xxxiii, p. 774.
4. J. F. Bray, *Labour's Wrongs and Labour's Remedies* (1839), p. 199. Quoted in M. B. Foxwell, 'Introduction' in Anton Menger, *The Right to the Whole Produce of Labour* (1899) (reprinted Frank Cass & Co. Ltd, London 1962), p. lxviii.
5. *The Poverty of Philosophy*, p. 60.
6. Mill, *Principles of Political Economy*, Book II, Ch. i, p. 200.
7. Karl Marx, 'Critique of the Gotha Programme' in Marx Engels, *Selected Works*, vol. II, pp. 23-4.
8. Karl Marx, *Theories of Surplus Value* (Moscow 1969), Part I, p. 367.
9. Thomas Hobbes, *Leviathan*, Everyman edn (London 1914), Part I, Ch. xiii, p. 65.
10. Ibid., Part I, Ch. xiii, p. 65.
11. John Locke, *The Second Treatise of Government*, ed. J. W. Gough (Oxford 1946), Ch. v, para. 25, p. 15.
12. Ibid., Ch. v, para. 27, p. 15.
13. Ibid., Ch. v, para. 40, pp. 21-2.
14. Ibid., Ch. v, para. 37, p. 20.
15. Ibid., Ch. v, paras. 47-8, p. 25.
16. Ibid., Ch. v, para. 50, p. 26.
17. Ibid., Ch. v, para. 37, p. 20.
18. Ibid.
19. *Capital*, vol. I, Ch. xxiv, Sect. 1, pp. 583-4.

Chapter 12

The declining rate of profit: poverty and immiseration

The last three chapters have dealt with the first of the two basic elements in Marx's political economy – his theory of value. The next three chapters are devoted to the examination of his theory of the declining rate of profit and the propositions clustered round it.[1] The theory of the declining rate of profit is Marx's theory of economic growth or, it would perhaps be better to say, his theory of economic decline, for it is meant to provide an economic and 'scientific' explanation of the inevitability of capitalist collapse and revolution.

Marx's belief that the rate of profit was declining was based, of course, not on the study of contemporaneous statistics but on the assertions of the political economists. These all argued that the extension of markets would eventually diminish the very motive that induces the entrepreneur to expand change and production – the rate of profit – and that, therefore, there was an imminent tendency for society to 'run down'. Ironically, neither the political economists nor Marx could know whether the rate of profit was falling or not; the statistics available to them did not make this possible.[2]

Rather, Smith and the other political economists assumed that profits tended to decline, partly because of a widely disseminated belief that this was in fact the case, and partly because a falling profit rate was logically entailed by the nature of their own assumptions about the economy. Nothing more clearly shows the extent to which Marx was a victim of the political economists' strait-jacket than the way in which his own analysis of the collapse of capitalism was rooted in their unjustified fears about the future of the commercial system.

All Marx's predecessors thought that the falling rate of profit would eventually lead to a stagnant society. They viewed this prospect with varying degrees of disquiet. According to Smith, workers' incomes would then be at their lowest possible level (see page 37). Ricardo, who, to be fair, was much more interested in the technical and analytical problems of political economy than in its sociological aspects, was less categorical and less consistent. He was sure that, in his contemporaneous world, the rate of profit was being brought down by the Corn Laws, but declared, in his contribution to the 1820 edition of the *Encyclopaedia Britannica*, that once the impediments to the import of food had been removed, there was, in principle, no limit to the expansion of industry. In the *Principles*, however, he shows that he is aware that, in the very long run, his assumptions implied a steady deceleration in the course of progress.[3] John Stuart Mill supported his own prognosis of social stasis by an insistence that it was implicit in the whole of political economy: 'The doctrine that, to however distant a time incessant struggling may put off our doom, the progress of society must "end in shallows and in miseries", far from being, as many people still believe, a wicked invention of Mr. Malthus, was either expressly or tacitly affirmed by his most distinguished predecessors.'[4] For Mill this prospect was rendered palatable by his conviction that Malthus's predictions would be falsified by the voluntary limitation of population increase.

Marx thought that once the concentration of capital had depressed the rate of profit sufficiently 'the vital flame of production would be altogether extinguished. It would die out. The rate of profit is the motive power of capitalist production. Things are produced only so long as they can be produced with a profit. Hence the concern of the English economists over the decline of the rate of profit.'[5] He regards his own explanation of the falling profit rate as one of his greatest theoretical achievements:

Simple as this law appears from the foregoing statements, all of political economy has so far tried in vain to discover it . . . The economists saw the problem and cudgelled their brains in tortuous attempts to interpret it. Since this law is of great importance for capitalist production, it may be said to be that mystery whose solution has been the goal of the entire political economy since Adam Smith. The difference between the various schools since Adam Smith consists in their different attempts to solve this riddle.[6]

For Marx, the political economists' declining rate of profit offered an economic explanation of the revolution which was to bring in socialism, that post-capitalist mode of production in which mankind would at last be emancipated.

The algebra of the declining rate of profit

It will help if we again rehearse Marx's elementary algebra in order to make clear the simplicity of Marx's falling rate of profit and to show how it is connected with a number of other propositions which we shall examine in this and the next two chapters.

There are, it will be remembered, three elements in the bourgeois mode of production:

c = fixed capital
v = variable capital or wages
s = surplus of profits

Marx asserts that the progress of capitalism is synonymous with the substitution of fixed capital for labour in the manufacturing process. This simply means increasing mechanization in factories, i.e. the use of more machinery per man. This can be expressed by saying that, in the expression c/v Marx's algebraic representation of the 'organic composition of capital', c grows larger relative to v and that therefore the value of c/v tends to increase.

Marx also asserts that the exploitation of the worker, the amount of profit s which each produces as compared with his wages v, tends upward to a limit. In other words the value of s/v grows until it reaches a certain point and then stops.

The capitalist arrives at his rate of profit by comparing his profits s with his outlay on fixed capital c and wages v so that the rate of profit can be expressed as $s/(c + v)$.

Thus, when exploitation s/v has reached its maximum value and mechanization, c/v continues to increase then, necessarily, by the rules of arithmetic, the value of the expression $s/(c + v)$ must fall. This is the 'law' of the declining rate of profit.

In this and the next three chapters we shall examine Marx's theory of the falling profit rate under three headings:

1. The theory of the immiseration and exploitation of the working class – the tendency of v to be minimized and of s/v to be maximized.
2. The theory of capital and technological change – the tendency of c/v to increase.
3. The theory of capitalist breakdown or revolution – the ambiguity inherent in the tendency of $s/(c + v)$ to decline.

Population and poverty

Marx's theory of poverty is an abortive attempt to 'transform' Malthus's theory of population. The political economists' long run theory of workers' incomes was, as we have seen, based on this theory; the population tends to expand more rapidly than the food supply can be increased and therefore there is always a tendency for there to be more workers than there are resources to employ them, which in turn implies chronic unemployment, while the wages of those with jobs will tend to be very low. Moreover, the agricultural possibilities of Eastern Europe and North America mean that there will be a long run increase in the supply of food so that the labour supply will continue to grow. As long as labour is abundant, capital can go on growing as a result of the increasing division of labour which an increasing work force makes possible. Capital accumulation is thus dependent on a Malthusian profusion of poorly paid working hands.

Marx, however, tried to deny that there was any 'natural' tendency for labour to outrun the means of employment and wrote that 'if tomorrow morning labour generally were reduced to a rational amount, and proportioned to the different sections of the working-class according to age and sex, the working population to hand would be absolutely insufficient for the carrying on of national production on its present scale'.[7] This again suggests that Marx supposed that mid-nineteenth-century capitalism had already achieved its task of providing material abundance; the fact that there is more than enough capital to provide full employment organized humanely implies that there are more than enough goods to meet human needs, and that, as Mill suggested and against what Marx says elsewhere, the remaining social problem is one of distribution, not of production. But Marx now has to explain why, if there is really a *shortage* of workers, unemployment should be endemic in the capitalist system.

The answer to this paradox Marx found in the belief that Malthus's law of population was a 'pretended law of nature' which represented, in a distorted form, the true law of capitalist accumulation according to which 'The labouring population ... produces, along with the accumulation of capital produced by it, the means by which itself is made relatively superfluous, is turned into a relative surplus-population.'[8] It is not man's sexual drive that creates over-population but the process of capital accumulation.

Marx discusses the effect which economic growth has on population on two separate assumptions. The first is that capital accumulation takes place without technical progress. This is what is called 'extensive' growth, i.e the expansion of the economy simply by amassing more plant and more workers to produce more of the same output in the same way. This is an expository device used elsewhere by Marx to clarify the way in which the elements in his model of the economy are connected before going on to discuss the second, more complex and more realistic case of 'intensive' growth. Intensive growth is the result of improved techniques of production and, in Marx, entails more output and a higher ratio of capital to labour in investment.

In the first case, Marx argues, 'sooner or later a point must be reached, at which the requirements of accumulation begin to surpass the customary supply of labour, and, therefore, a rise of wages takes place'.[9] Then, either the wage rate continues to go up, at least for a while, 'because its rise does not interfere with the progress of accumulation' or 'accumulation slackens in consequence of the rise in the price of labour, because the stimulus of gain is blunted'.[10] When this happens the demand for labour falls off until wages again reach a level at which it again becomes profitable to employ workers. Marx maintains that these two possible outcomes show that 'the rate of accumulation is the independent, not the dependent variable; the rate of wages, the dependent, not the independent variable'.[11] The logic of this is unsatisfactory. On the one hand, Marx says that capital accumulation determines wages, but on the other, that 'the rise in the price of labour' reduces profits which are 'the stimulus of gain' – from which it follows that wages determine capital accumulation.

Marx's discussion of the effect of intensive economic growth on population is also less than perfectly coherent. According to Marx capitalist accumulation is always accompanied by an increase in the organic composition of capital, i.e. a decline in the proportion of investment embodied in labour. This steady increase in the capital intensity of production, argues Marx, means that capitalism 'constantly produces, and produces in the direct ratio of its own energy and extent, a relatively redundant population of labourers'.[12]

But, as Marx himself says, the increase in the organic composition of capital does not of itself mean that the demand for labour decreases absolutely, only that it is increasing at an ever-diminishing rate. Marx's contention is perhaps more comprehensible in the light of the observation that 'the old capital, periodically reproduced with a change of composition, repels more and more of the labourers formerly employed by it'.[13] But again, this 'constant metamorphosis of old capital' cannot take place without growth, and growth, by however small an amount, does increase the absolute demand for labour. The text betrays uncertainty. Marx was perhaps trying to find a theoretical formulation which would both account for the unemployment which he felt to be endemic in the capitalist mode of production and would not run counter to the fact that industrialization, in spite of its apparent labour-saving tendency, employed far more workers at the time Marx was writing than it had done even twenty years before when he first became interested in political economy.[14]

The point here is that, however shaky his logic, Marx's theory of wages and poverty is not fundamentally different and indeed is derived from the political economists. In spite of his effort to rework Malthus, Marx's world is still one in which the number of workers exceeds the number of employment opportunities and it is this brute fact which keeps down wages.

Immiseration: relative and absolute

Marx quotes Adam Smith in support of his belief that the oppression of the working class does not arise simply out of the low level of their wages: the division of labour is itself stultifying.

The understanding of the greater part of men are necessarily formed by their ordinary employments. The man whose whole life is spent in performing a few simple operations . . . has no occasion to exert his understanding . . . He generally becomes as stupid and ignorant as it is possible for a human creature to become . . . The uniformity of his stationary life naturally corrupts the courage of his mind . . . It corrupts even the activity of his body and renders him incapable of exerting his strength with vigour and perseverance in any other employments than that to which he had been bred. His dexterity at his own particular trade

seems in this manner to be acquired at the expense of his intellectual,
social, and maritial virtues. But in every improved and civilised society,
this is the state into which the labouring poor, that, the great body of the
people, must necessarily fall.[15]

He stresses Smith's debt to Adam Ferguson's *Essay on the History of*
Civil Society, and in so doing, incidentally underlines the affinity of this
element in his own thinking with the social ideas of his eighteenth-
century German predecessors who also thought that 'progress' could
fragment and dissolve societal bonds (see p. 64). These and other
passages in Marx have been used to argue that Marx's theory was one of
relative not *absolute* impoverishment, and that his critique of the social
effects of capital accumulation is compatible with rising real incomes
for the population as a whole.

In 1847, for example, Marx wrote that

The rapid growth of productive capital brings about an equally rapid
growth of wealth, luxury, social wants, social enjoyments. Thus,
although the enjoyments of the workers have risen, the social
satisfaction that they give has fallen in comparison with the increased
enjoyments of the capitalist, which are inaccessible to the worker, in
comparison with the state of development of society in general.[16]

And in *Capital*, he writes that, when capital accumulation outruns the
labour supply, workers are able to 'extend the circle of their
enjoyments', buying clothes and furniture and even saving.[17] Although
Marx contends that increased consumption only disguises and cannot
dissolve the bonds of dependence which are still embedded in the cash
nexus, he does so in terms which can be read as implying that a rise in
living standards might be permanent: 'A rise in the price of labour . . .
only means . . . that the length and weight of the golden chain the wage-
worker has already forged for himself, allow of a relaxation of the
tension of it.'[18] But if these references are taken as meaning that the long
run trend of wages is anything other than downwards the force of
Marx's theory is very much diminished.

In fact, in considering the possibility of rising incomes for workers,
Marx was reflecting a nuance of the political economists' ideas. Smith
and Ricardo, in spite of subscribing to a long run theory of subsistence
wages, did not think that at any given moment wages were necessarily at
their lowest level. Smith thought that 'the liberal reward of labour . . . is
the natural symptom of increasing national wealth'.[19] Ricardo, at one
point in his work, qualifies his subsistence theory of wages, by
suggesting that what constitutes 'subsistence' wages is determined by
social rather than economic norms, stating that for the labourer the
'natural rate' of wages is 'the quantity of food, necessaries, and
convenience become essential to him from habit' and that this would
afford moderate comforts[20]: Smith thought that 'liberal wages' were a
function of the rate at which the economy was growing: 'It is not the

actual greatness of national wealth, but its continual increase, which occasions a rise in the wages of labour', and, conversely, 'though the wealth of a country should be very great, yet if it has long been stationary we must not expect to find the wages of labour very high in it'.[21]

In Ricardo the argument is similar. The reason for the rise of wages above subsistence is that, although these wages will *ultimately* increase the labour force to the level at which wages are again just enough to maintain the marginal worker, in the short run there is a time lag before the immediate effect on the birth rate produces an eventual increase in the supply of adolescent labour.[22] But in both Smith and Ricardo the tendency of wages is towards a minimum – if this were not so there would be no sense in their invariable measure of value.

Marx's references to 'relative' immiseration are to be explained in the same way. He cites Adam Smith in support of the argument that it is not 'the actual extent of social wealth' but 'the degree of rapidity' of economic growth that determines the level of wages.[23] But the long run trend is unambiguous. An increase in social wealth means an increase in the numbers of the unemployed: 'The more extensive . . . the lazarus-layers of the working class, and the industrial reserve army, the greater is official pauperism. *This is the absolute general law of capitalist accumulation.*'[24] Although there is a limit below which wages cannot fall 'the constant tendency of capital is to force the cost of labour back toward . . . zero'.[25]

Writing in 1865 Marx also, following Ricardo, referred to the part which 'historical tradition and social habitude' as well as the 'mere physical element' can play in determining the value of labour, but he is quite clear that this 'historical or social element . . . may be . . . altogether extinguished'.[26] In the same address he suggests that since 'the general tendency of capitalistic production is . . . to sink . . . the average standard of wages . . . the working class ought not to exaggerate to themselves' the effectiveness of the trades unions in attempting to alter wage rates.

They ought not to forget that they are fighting with effects, but not with the causes of those effects; that they are retarding the downward movement, but not changing its direction; that they are applying palliatives, not curing the malady. . . . Instead of the conservative motto, 'A fair day's wage for a fair day's work!' they ought to inscribe on their banner the revolutionary watchword, 'Abolition of the wages system'.[27]

As long as wages are paid, there will be poverty.

The physical limit of exploitation: the working-day

Unless the rate of exploitation, s/v, has a limit, Marx's theory of the declining rate of profit collapses. If there is no limit to the amount of profit which can be extracted per man then there is in principle no limit to the increase in output as capitalism advances. If output goes on rapidly increasing, then since output has only two possible destinations – the worker or the capitalist – either capitalist incomes are rising and the rate of profit may not fall, or workers' incomes have a long run tendency to rise and the working class is not immiserated, or, possibly, both wages and profits rise together.

Marx never fully explains why the rate of exploitation has a limit, and the text suggests that he thought, or hoped that the reader thought, that this was a self-evident fact. He states categorically that 'the compensation of a decrease in the number of labourers employed, or of the amount of variable capital advanced, by a rise in the rate of surplus-value, or by the lengthening of the working-day, has impassable limits'.[28]

We shall suggest, in the next chapter, reasons for supposing that Marx thought that there was some physical limit to the increases in productivity to be derived from technological innovations. But, from the text, it looks as if Marx was also of the opinion that the actual length of the working-day was a constraint on the rate of exploitation. According to Marx the day is divided into two parts; the first is that in which the labourer produces the value of his own wages, the second is that in which the capitalist reaps the surplus benefit from his purchase of the worker's labour power. In order to increase the amount of surplus value extracted from the worker the capitalist must make his employee work for longer hours and more intentensely. The amount of surplus value depends on the number of hours of surplus labour which the capitalist can make the worker embed in the finished product. Once this is accepted it becomes plausible to argue that the 'impassable limits' to exploitation are to be found in 'the absolute limit of the average working-day'.[29] In his discussion of what this 'certain point' is, Marx concludes that 'the working-day contains the full 24 hours, with the deduction of the few hours of repose without which labour-power absolutely refuses its services again'.[30] This is, of course, no real answer, because it fails to deal with labour productivity but imaginatively tends to lend colour to Marx's other attempts to show that the limit on productivity is a physical and insuperable boundary. This, in turn, is intimately connected with Marx's very peculiar approach to machinery, which we shall consider in the next chapter.

References and Notes

1. This makes it particularly unfortunate that the most important parts of Marx's analysis of capitalism's collapse were only published posthumously by Engels in vols. II and III of *Capital* and

by Karl Kautsky, the ideologue of the German Social Democratic Party, in *Theories of Surplus Value*, which was intended by Marx as vol. IV of his great work. None of the manuscripts had been prepared for the printer by Marx and many of them were at a relatively early stage of composition. The texts, therefore, abound with expositional difficulties.

2. And indeed, modern studies have not been able to establish any long term trend in the way in which output is divided between the owners of equity capital and the workers, and the subject remains contentious.

3. Ricardo, *Works*, vol. I, p. 265.

4. Mill, *Principles of Political Economy*, Book IV, Ch. vi, Sect. 1, p. 747.

5. *Capital*, vol. III, Ch. xv, Sect. 3, p. 259.

6. Ibid., vol. III, Ch. xiii, p. 213.

7. Ibid., vol. I, Ch. xxv, Sect. 1, p. 621.

8. Ibid., vol. I, Ch. xxv, Sect. 3, p. 631.

9. Ibid., vol. I, Ch. xxv, Sect. 1, p. 613.

10. Ibid., vol. I, Ch. xxv, Sect. 1, p. 619.

11. Ibid., vol. I, Ch. xxv, Sect. 1, p. 620.

12. Ibid., vol. I, Ch. xxv, Sect. 3, p. 630.

13. Ibid., vol. I, Ch. xxv, Sect. 2, p. 628.

14. See ibid., vol. I, Ch. xxv, Sect. 3, p. 630 n. 1.

15. *The Wealth of Nations*, Book V, Ch. i, pp. 751–82. Quoted in *Capital*, vol. I, Ch. xiv, Sect. 5, p. 358.

16. Karl Marx, 'Wage labour and capital' in Marx Engels, *Selected Works*, vol. I, p. 94.

17. *Capital*, vol. I, Ch. xxv, Sect. 1, p. 618.

18. Ibid.

19. *The Wealth of Nations*, Book I, Ch. viii, p. 65.

20. Ricardo, *Works*, vol. I, Ch. v, pp. 93–4.

21. *The Wealth of Nations*, Book I, Ch. viii, pp. 61–2, 63.

22. This was Malthus's own view and is referred to as such by Marx in *Capital*, vol. I, Ch. xxv, Sect. 3, p. 634.

23. Ibid., vol. I, Ch. xxv, Sect. 2, p. 621.

24. Ibid., vol. I, Ch. xxv, Sect. 4, p. 644.

25. Ibid., vol. I, Ch. xxiv, Sect. 4, p. 600.

26. Karl Marx, 'Price and profit' in Marx Engels, *Selected Works*, vol. I, p. 443.

27. Ibid., vol. I, p. 446.

28. *Capital*, vol. I, Ch. xi, p. 305.

29. Ibid.

30. Ibid., vol. I, Ch. x, Sect. 5, p. 264.

Chapter 13

The declining rate of profit: technology

The most acute weakness in Marx's economic theory is his account of technological change and the part it plays in increasing output. In a sense, this is a corollary of his labour theory of value; having assigned to labour a role as the unique origin and measure of value, Marx's purpose appears to have been to deny that machinery contributes anything to the size of output. Although his arguments are not entirely consistent, the text can only be read as an attempt by Marx to 'make a case' against technology as a factor of production. Paradoxically, therefore, his economic analysis is at its most lamentable when he is dealing with what lies at the centre of his theoretical interest – the technical composition of accumulated capital. Once again, Marx's difficulties can be seen to stem from his 'transformational' ambitions, his desire to reduce technology to its 'real' basis – labour.

In this chapter we shall consider the following:

1. Marx's view of technological advance as labour-saving.
2. Marx's attempt to reduce technology to labour.
3. Marx's interpretation of technological innovation as a device for exploiting workers.
4. The connexion between Marx's ideas about technological advance and those which he could find in the work of the political economists.
5. The connexion between Marx's ideas about technology and the distribution of property.

The increasing organic composition of capital: technology as labour-saving invention

Marx held that the progress of the capitalist mode of production was identical to the introduction of labour-saving devices into the productive process. To say that the 'organic composition of capital' increases is to say that work formerly done by men is increasingly performed by machines. But if, as Marx asserts, only labour can produce value, to economize on labour by mechanization appears irrational. As he writes, 'Some people might think that if the value of a commodity is determined by the quantity of labour spent on it, the more idle and unskilful the labour, the more valuable would his commodity be, because more time would be required in its production.'[1] His answer to this paradox is that the labour value of any commodity is determined by 'the labour-time socially necessary to produce an article under the normal conditions of production, and with the average degree of skill and intensity prevalent at the time'.[2] By *socially* necessary Marx means, of course, *commercially* necessary. In other words, an industrialist cannot, because of competition, use a productive method less mechanized than that prevalent in his industry generally, without eventually losing money. But this still does not explain why the 'labour-time socially necessary' should fall or, in other words, how it is that capitalists ever come to economize on labour, for by increasing the ratio of capital to labour they are causing their rate of profit to fall. As Marx observes 'no capitalist ever voluntarily introduces a new method of production, no matter how much more productive it may be, and how much it may increase the rate of surplus-value, so long as it reduces the rate of profit'.[3]

However, according to Marx, the first capitalist to introduce a labour-saving innovation will reduce his labour costs, while the market price still remains that determined by the 'socially necessary' labour time. Until other capitalists have followed him in numbers large enough to lower labour costs and to reduce the 'socially necessary' labour time he will be able to pocket super-profits. But the reduction of the labour content of the commodity will lower the surplus-value per unit of the commodity 'independent of the will of the capitalist' and thus, led by short-sighted selfishness and competitive greed, the capitalists undermine their own system.

But this is still very unsatisfactory. Even if it is accepted, as Marx suggests, that the capitalists, in some sense, do not fully understand what they are doing, or, in modern terms, are being led by the pursuit of short-term microeconomic gain to wreak their own long term macroeconomic destruction, their behaviour still remains odd. A capitalist taking an investment decision faces, in Marx's economic world, a free market in the means of production, i.e. of capital goods and of labour. The relative price of capital and labour will vary over time. The price of labour tends towards a fixed subsistence minimum but a decline in the profit rate means that, *relative to capital*, the price of labour is rising. As Marx says, the capitalist is indifferent to the organic composition of capital, i.e. he does not care how his capital outlay is divided between wages and constant capital. A rise in the relative cost of labour is what provides the incentive to economize on it. But the introduction of *labour*-saving devices should increase the rate of profit, not lower it. Our capitalist would cease to economize on labour and start to economize on *capital* once the profit rate reached a point at which labour becomes relatively inexpensive, and capital relatively dear. It is true that, once an investment with a particular ratio of capital to labour has been made, the capitalist is locked into it. But he is not locked into it for ever and new entrants to the market, and established capitalists replacing their plant or expanding their enterprises, are continually making free investment decisions in which the organic composition of their outlays will be determined by the relative prices of labour and capital. Marx himself knew that innovation could be capital-saving as well as labour-saving, and that capital-saving investment is a response to the decline in the rate of profit; the whole of Chapter v of Volume iii of *Capital*, entitled 'Economy in the employment of fixed capital' is devoted to this problem.[4] Marx never shows why innovation has to be *labour*-saving only, he simply assumes that it is so.

Moreover, Marx shows signs of uneasiness about the connexion between rising output and the applications of capital, which suggests that he was aware that, analytically, it was reasonable to impute increased output directly to investment. He writes, for example, that the

Productivity of labour may also exert a direct influence on the rate of profit . . . In effect, the value-composition of a capital invested in a branch of industry, that is, a certain proportion between the variable and constant capital, always expresses a definite degree of labour productivity. As soon, therefore, as this proportion is altered by means other than a mere change in the value of the material elements of the constant capital, or a change in wages, the productivity of labour must likewise undergo a corresponding change, and we shall often enough see, for this reason, that changes in the factors, c, v and s also imply changes in the productivity of labour.[5]

Perhaps Marx was himself not altogether convinced that his solution of the transformation problem adequately dealt with the differences in labour productivity from industry to industry and firm to firm. But he never provided any close examination of this issue.

Technology reduced to labour

It should never be forgotten that Marx's prime aim was philosophical rather than economic. He was, as we have seen in examining his use of Feuerbach, always concerned to show that all social phenomena are manifestations of the energies of man. And, just as he tried to reduce the market to the 'real' activities of 'real' people, his approach to technology was based on the assumption that it was of no importance in itself except as the bodying forth of the creative power of mankind. This is not, of course, logically incompatible with an attempt to evolve a theory of technological innovation and establish an index of its contribution to production – but Marx seems to have thought that it was.

Part IV of volume I of *Capital*, 'The concept of relative surplus-value' is an extended discussion of technology, and, in a sense, a sustained attempt to deny it a crucial role in development. The fact that technology is discussed under the heading of 'relative surplus-value' is itself significant. *Absolute* surplus-value, it will be recalled, is derived from the number of hours the worker can be made to labour over and above the time necessary for him to produce the value of his own wages. *Relative* surplus-value is Marx's term of art for the increase in profit arising from the increased productivity of labour – but he sees it as essentially derived from the fact that the worker can now produce his means of subsistence in a shorter time than before and is thus able to devote more of the working-day to the production of surplus-value for the capitalist. In this way, attention is focussed not on what new techniques enable the worker to produce in a given time but rather on the increased contribution the worker is now able to make to the capitalist. As Marx writes 'the object of all development of the productiveness of labour, within the limits of capitalist production, is to shorten that part of the working-day, during which the workmen must labour for his own benefit, and by the very shortening, to lengthen the other part of the day, during which he is at liberty to work gratis for the capitalist'.[6]

Following Adam Smith, Marx sees the origin of the commercial era in the division of labour which he includes under the heading of cooperation. So anxious is Marx to stress that capitalism owes its origins to labour and the distribution of property rather than to technique, that at one point he goes so far as to declare that the bourgeois mode of production is nothing more than a change in property rights: 'At first, capital subordinates labour on the basis of the technical conditions in which it historically finds it. It does not, therefore, change immediately the mode of production.'[7] The advent of capitalism is not the result of any important technological change; 'the workshop of the mediaeval master handicraftman is simply enlarged'.[8] Marx mentions the advantages which larger units of production provide by spreading overheads but again declares in what is obviously a further attempt to minimize the importance of technical change, that for the transition from pre-capitalism physical propinquity alone will suffice because 'mere social contact begets in most industries an emulation and stimulation of the animal spirits that heighten the efficiency of each individual workman',[9] and a new mode of production is established, 'even when the numerous workmen assembled together do not assist one another, but merely work side by side'.[10]

Pre-capitalist civilizations, Marx declares, show how much could be achieved by straightforward 'simple cooperation', i.e. with the minimum of equipment, and its 'colossal effects . . . are to be seen in the gigantic structures of the ancient Asiatics, Egyptians, Etruscans, etc.'.[11] Modern capitalism disguises the fact that its productive power is simply the efforts of its workers; the subordinating and organizing functions of the capitalist give rise to an illusion of creative strength peculiar to capital but 'this power costs capital nothing, and because .... the labourer himself does not develop it before his labour belongs to capital, it appears as a power with which capital is endowed by Nature – a productive power which is imminent in capital.[12]

The Origin of the Species by Charles Darwin (1809–82), published in 1859, fired Marx's imagination. Darwin, who claimed to have been inspired in part by Malthus's *Essay on Population*, produced a theory of evolution which explained the variety of animal life, including man, in terms of the way in which, over time, the struggle for existence eliminated species and varieties which failed to adapt themselves to the environment, while encouraging the development and further functionally efficient adjustment of those who were. Quite apart from the atheistic implications of this idea, Marx was especially impressed by it as a comprehensive and developmental theory of the natural world which readily lent itself in support of his own more purely social theory. In particular, he felt that it provided a basis for an account of technology:

Darwin has interested us in the history of Nature's Technology, i.e. in the formation of the organs of plants and animals, which organs serve as instruments of production for sustaining life. Does not the history of the productive organs of man, or organs that are the material basis of all social organization, deserve equal attention? . . . Technology discloses man's mode of dealing with Nature.[13]

Marx's account of technological development in his Darwinian mood is very peculiar and, although he writes, for example, that 'among the instruments of labour, those of a mechanical nature, we may call the bone and muscle of production, . . . those . . . like pipes, tubs, baskets, jars, etc., . . . we may . . . call the vascular system of production,'[14] elsewhere it is less clear whether he is writing metaphorically or whether he means the reader to take his descriptions literally and not just as analogies. Marx sees the worker emerging from the pre-capitalist era as an 'independent artificer'. But progress decomposes the 'process of production into its various successive steps'[15] so that the craftman 'gradually loses, through want of practice, the ability to carry on, to its full extent, his old handicraft'.[16] The new specialization in some particular part of the manufacturing process turns each worker into part of an organic whole, 'the collective labourer'. This, says Marx, 'is the machinery specially characteristic of the manufacturing period'.[17] Later, mechanical invention and the application of the steam-engine leads to the development of a higher stage of economic organization which Marx again refers to as if it were a natural rather than a man-made phenomenon: 'Here we have, in the place of the isolated machine, a mechanical monster whose body fills whole factories, and whose demon power at first veiled under the slow and measured motions of his giant limbs, at length breaks out into the fast and furious whirl of his countless working organs.'[18] This gives imaginative force to the idea that machinery and factory organization are the results, rather than the cause of capitalism – the organic outcome of which is the appearance and development of the post-feudal Leviathan. And Marx is explicit and unequivocal that industry is developed within the womb of capitalism and is not its progenitor. He divides capitalism into two stages, the first of which, beginning in the sixteenth century, is characterized by the use of tools and the division of labour, while the second is marked by the use of complex machinery. The first stage is manufacture, the second, industry. Cooperation and specialization, as for Adam Smith, are themselves the origin of inventive ingenuity. And in this invention the substitution of mechanical contrivances for operations formerly carried on by hand is of greater causal importance than the application of steam with which the Industrial Revolution is normally associated: 'The steam-engine itself, such as it was at its invention, during the manufacturing period at the close of the 17th century, and such as it continued to be down to 1780, did not give rise to any industrial revolution. It was, on the contrary, the invention of machines that made a revolution in the form of steam-engines necessary.'[19]

Marx stresses that scientific discovery, like the 'natural' forces of the collective labourer, is or ought to be, free, since, like the natural environment, it is a gift of nature. As he writes,

We saw that the productive forces resulting from cooperation and division of labour cost capital nothing. They are natural forces of social labour. So also physical forces, like steam, water, etc., when appropriated to productive process, cost nothing . . . Once discovered, the law of the deviation of the magnetic needle in the field of an electric current, or the law of the magnetisation of iron, around which an electric current circulates, cost never a penny.[20]

But why then does the equipment of modern capitalism cost so much if it is based on a knowledge of ways of exploiting the natural world which is essentially costless? The answer lies in the fact that 'the exploitation of these laws for the purposes of telegraphy, etc. necessitates a costly and extensive apparatus'[21] which can only be constructed by the expenditure of enormous quantities of labour so that,

Although, therefore, it is clear at the first glance, that, by incorporating both stupendous physical forces, and the natural sciences, with the process of production, Modern Industry raises the productiveness of labour to an extraordinary degree, it is by no means equally clear, that this increased productive force is not, on the other hand, purchased by an increased expenditure of labour.[22]

In this way, the most spectacular achievements of technology are firmly placed in a causal chain emphasizing their origins in natural forces and in human labour.

Technology and exploitation

Marx argues that the *real* purpose of technological innovation is to be found in the fact that factory organization and the interdependence of mechanical operations provide a way of enabling the capitalist more effectively to control and discipline workers and so more effectively to exploit them. The inadequacy of hand-production or manufacture is ascribed to its ineffectual management of the work force: 'Since handicraft skill is the foundation of manufacture, and since the mechanism of manufacture as a whole possesses no framework apart from the labourers themselves, capital is constantly compelled to wrestle with the insubordination of the workmen.'[23]

The most developed form of production, the factory system, in which a single prime mover supplies the power for a whole array of machines, is seen by Marx as primarily a system of discipline;

The technical subordination of the workman to the uniform motion of the instruments of labour, and the peculiar composition of the body of workpeople, consisting as it does of individuals of both sexes and of all ages, give rise to a barrack discipline, which is elaborated into a complete system in the factory, ... dividing the workpeople ... into the private soldiers and sergeants of an industrial army.[24]

This system, apparently devised for the accommodation of machinery, makes it possible not only to exploit fit and able-bodied males but also 'becomes a means of employing labourers of slight muscular strength ... women and children';[25] it reduces the value of a man's labour power by 'throwing every member of his family onto the labour-market'.[26] The labourer himself becomes a minor tyrant in a hierarchical system of despots; 'previously, the workman sold his own labour-power, which he disposed of nominally as a free agent. Now he sells wife and child. He has become a slave-dealer.'[27] At the same time machinery 'becomes in the hands of capital the most powerful means, in those industries first invaded by it, for lengthening the working-day beyond all bounds set by human nature'.[28]

The capitalist now has a powerful incentive, because of the expense of his outlay on fixed capital, to keep it employed for as long as possible. Moreover, 'It is self-evident, that in proportion as the use of machinery spreads, and the experience of a special class of workmen habituated to machinery accumulates, the rapidity and intensity of labour increase as a natural consequence.'[29] The function of machinery is to increase the exploitation of labour.

All of this, is, of course, very unsatisfactory because of the way in which normative statements are confused with positive statements, metaphors shade off into empirical description, financial costs are conflated with social costs, and important categories are left inadequately defined. But Marx's rhetorical purpose is obvious – to minimize the importance of technology. The task of the capitalist, even in conditions of continued industrialization is to use mechanization to squeeze the last drop of surplus-value from the already exhausted bodies of the proletariat; machinery and factory organization are only means to end – the exploitation of the worker to the limits of his physical endurance.

Marx, political economy and technical progress

The confusions and inadequacies of Marx's theory of technical innovation are, in part, related to the political economists' ideas about inventions and productive improvements. In this section we shall briefly consider the views of Smith, Ricardo and John Stuart Mill on technical progress and examine their connexion with Marx's own ideas.

In the eighteenth century, technical advance and the annual increase in output, especially agriculture, were very slow. All the political economists before Marx thought that economic growth, even if it could be increased, could not be expanded for ever. At some point, they thought, it would be bound to come to a halt. In their theories the rate of profit declines precisely because, in their view, the technical possibilities of increasing output per worker were limited.

In the twentieth century, the possibility of virtually unlimited compound growth has come to be a fact. In spite of recent fears about the exhaustion of natural resources there seems to be no reason, except in the very long run, to suppose that the possibilities of specialization and invention will do anything except go on producing steadily increasing output per worker and unit of capital, as far ahead as it is possible to guess. This supposition is based on a faith in the ability of mankind continually to devise new and more efficient methods of combining and harnessing the properties and substances of the natural world. It was this faith that Marx, in common with all the other political economists, did not share; they all thought that, in the long run, the economy would stagnate or collapse.

Writing in the mid-nineteenth century, Marx was caught mid-way between the settled and stable agrarian economy of Smith and the violently gyrating industrialized world of today. The theoretical structure devised by Smith was not well adapted to account for the exponential movements in industrial output which were characteristic of advanced economies by the time that all three volumes of *Capital* had been published. The effect of the changes in science and productive organization witnessed by Smith and Ricardo were relatively small. Marx, writing a generation later than the latter and publishing nearly a century later than the former, had seen not only a revolution in economic administration – the factory system – but lived in an age of the first miracles of applied science. Marx's conviction that the economic analyses of Smith and Ricardo were adequate to explain the economic phenomena of a later period made it very difficult for him to find a place for technical progress in his own theory of capitalism.

For Adam Smith, the mainspring of economic growth is the division of labour, of which he says that 'the extent of this division must always be limited . . . by the extent of the market'.[30] A modern economist would extend Smith's notion of specialization, making the point that if, as Smith so acutely suggests, science is itself a function of specialization, then the division of labour and its fruits are limited only by the discoveries of science and the ability of technology to substitute capital for labour where manpower is scarce. Smith did not make this further step but appears to have supposed that the scientific advances which stem from specialization were likely to be no more spectacular in their effects than the series manufacture of pins. For Smith, the market is limited by its geographical compass, the boundaries to growth are set by transport possibilities, and the exhaustion of market opportunities causes the rate of profit ultimately to decline. He thus had a very cautious view of technological possibilities.

Ricardo was an even more pernicious influence in Marx's attempts to discuss the technological element in economic growth. Ricardo, as we have seen, argued that the increasing marginal cost of food production wears down the industrialists' income and confers an uncovenanted benefit on the owners of intra-marginal land. In this situation 'The natural tendency of profits is then to fall; for in the progress of society and wealth, the additional quantity of food required is obtained by more and more labour.'[31] Ricardo's model is unnaturally restricted. He does not give any serious consideration to the possibility of improving agricultural productivity, and he assumes that industrial expansion is fundamentally extensive, i.e. grows without technical progress. His view of the economy was that its key problem was an agrarian one, which could be solved by trade rather than investment, and, apart from the abortive chapter on machinery in the third edition of the *Principles*, he had nothing to say about technology.

John Stuart Mill, to whom Marx was particularly indebted for certain parts of his analysis of capitalist breakdown, was also pessimistic about the chances of technical progress delaying the onset of the stationary state. This applied to industry as well as agriculture; 'Agricultural skill and knowledge are of slow growth and still slower diffusion. Inventions and discoveries, too, occur only occasionally, while the increase of population and capital are continuous agencies.'[32] Thus maturity in an economy, to Mill's mind, makes progress even less, not more, likely:

When a country has long possessed a large production, and a large net income to make saving from, and when, therefore, the means have long existed of making a great annual addition to capital . . . it is one of the characteristics of such a country, that the rate of profit is habitually within, as it were, a hand's breadth of the minimum, and the country therefore on the very verge of the stationary state.[33]

It is thus not hard to see what underlies the political economists' suppositions about the downward trend of profits; it is the belief that returns to any activity have a tendency to diminish. This is the same notion, of course, that underlies the concept of marginal utility and the convergent functions that are necessary for equilibrium in economic analysis. Strictly speaking, the 'law' of diminishing returns in economics is expressed by saying that, if in any combination of factors in production is held constant except for one, then the returns to every extra unit of that factor will, after a certain point, successively decline. At first, extra quantities may bring greater and greater improvements but later they will produce an absolute reduction in efficiency. As the proverbs have it – 'two heads are better than one' but 'too many cooks spoil the broth'. If it is supposed that 'inventions and discoveries occur only occasionally' then all one's hopes must be pinned on doing things on a larger and larger scale – but there is obviously a limit beyond which a farm cannot be extended and it is equally clear that the maximum size of a steam-boiler is physically constrained.

Marx's theory of extensive growth, in spite of its various logical deficiencies, betrays strong family likenesses to this basic idea of his mentors. As we have noted, Marx was aware that innovations could be capital – as well as labour-saving, but he is quite categorical in his assertion that 'the growth of constant capital in relation to variable capital' is 'a law of capitalist production'.[34] Now Marx's account of technology implies that increases in production can be attributed to two discrete jumps in productive methods. The first, manufacture, is a manifestation of the advantages offered by the division of labour. When these are fully exploited there is another jump, an industrial revolution, brought about by the introduction of machines. As we have seen, Marx is at pains to show that machines are not qualitatively different from the division of labour; cooperation forms a machine out of men together with their instruments of production – the development of machinery is simply a process by which the instruments of production gradually come to subordinate men to themselves. What really makes the difference between industry and manufacture is the size of the equipment involved. Every machine, says Marx, is a combination of 'the simple mechanical powers, the lever, the inclined plane, the screw, the wedge, etc.',[35] but it 'supersedes the workman, who handles a single tool, by a mechanism operating with a number of similar tools' and this 'increase in the size of the machine, and in the number of its working tools, calls for a more massive mechanism to drive it'.[36] The final development of technology is the application of machines to the production of machines and even here, he emphasizes, the difference between this and the workman's implements is one of size:

If we now fix our attention on that portion of the machinery employed in the construction of machines, which constitutes the operating tool, we find the manual implements re-appearing, but on a cyclopean scale. The operating part of the boring machine is an immense drill driven by a

*steam-engine; without this machine, on the other hand, the cylinders of
large steam-engines and of hydraulic presses could not be made. The
mechanical lathe is only a cyclopean reproduction of the ordinary foot-
lathe; the planing machine, an iron carpenter, that works on iron with
the same tools that the human carpenter employs on wood; the
instrument that, on the London wharves, cuts the veneers, is a gigantic
razor; the tool of the shearing machine, which shears iron as easily as a
tailor's scissors cut cloth, is a monster pair of scissors; and the steam-
hammer works with an ordinary hammer head, but of such weight that
not Thor himself could wield it.*[37]

The one assumption that makes it possible to believe that both profits
and wages decline together as Marx asserted is that increases in output
are predominantly and ultimately dependent in increases in the physical
scale at which production is carried out. Given that other opportunities
for increasing output have been exhausted, then as the limits set by
physical constraints are approached the extra outlays of capital
required to produce each incremental unit of output will start to rise
very sharply. In these circumstances, even if the rate of exploitation –
the relative share of the capitalist and the worker in output – remains the
same, the absolute levels of both profits and wages could decline.

This provokes a number of interesting reflections. It suggests that
Marx's supposition that the increase in the organic composition of
capital is the root of the tendency of the rate of profit to fall is thus not
simply a confusion of the physical composition of capital with its
composition in terms of value;[38] it is directly related to the classical
economists' apprehension that the productive powers of industry are
limited. But if the productivity of capital is *physically* constrained this
means that in the socialist mode of production output would not
necessarily be any higher. Marx has more to say about post-capitalist
society than is often supposed, but he has almost nothing to suggest
about the technology of the new society. At one point he writes that 'in
the communistic society there would be a very different scope for the
employment of machinery than there can be in a bourgeois society'[39] –
but the limits to the employment of machinery that Marx has in mind
stem from the fact that in some capitalist societies labour is very cheap
and therefore the incentive to substitute capital for labour is either weak
or non-existent. Marx suggests only that labour will be more liberally
rewarded in communism; he says nothing which betrays a belief that the
physical constraint on the limit to which this substitution is possible is
peculiar to capitalism. This again is to emphasize that Marx was at one
with other socialists in the nineteenth century, in spite of his
protestations to the contrary, in believing that socialism would concern
itself with the distribution of output rather than with the task of
increasing it. An instinctive tendency to derate the long run importance
of machinery to society, as opposed to the social freedom which
abundance bestows, would also help to explain the otherwise

extraordinary fact that in Marx's first economic publication, *A Contribution to the Critique of Political Economy* (1859), the prelude to *Capital* itself, contains no reference to machinery, while the unpublished introduction mentions technique only to dismiss it: 'Production is always a *particular* branch of production – e.g. agriculture, cattle-breeding, manufacture – or it is the *totality* of production. Political economy, however, is not technology.'[40]

Monopoly and technology

Marx's proposition that the ownership of capital, with the progress of its accumulation, is concentrated in fewer and fewer hands, is a corollary of the immiseration of the working class. The working class is the only possible source of surplus-value and its poverty is the direct result of the appropriation of its product by the capitalist class – in one sense, capitalism is the institutionalization of robbery. But there are three peculiarities in Marx's idea which should be noted.

First, although capital accumulation is the result of exploitation, Marx also thought that it was connected with the nature of technical change. Capitalist development means that there is an 'increasing minimum of capital required with the increase in productivity for the successful operation of an independent industrial establishment ... Smaller capital can carry on independently in the various spheres of industry only in the infancy of mechanical inventions.'[41] This again illustrates the overwhelming importance to Marx's theory of economies of scale and also reveals the way in which this in turn is intimately connected in his mind with the nature of property rights. This large-scale production constitutes the 'relations of production' which are part of Marx's economic base; they supposedly dictate the concentration of ownership which are part of his legal superstructure.

Secondly, Marx thought that accumulation was not the only, or the most effective, cause of monopolization. This other force, which Marx calls the tendency to 'centralization' covers two phenomena – competition and credit. Competition 'always ends in the ruin of many small capitalists, whose capitals partly pass into the hands of their conquerors, partly vanish'.[42] The struggle for profits drives smaller enterprises to the wall and their assets are either sold off or they are taken over by the more successful firms. In addition, the credit system, by mobilizing savings, enables capitalists to carry out their undertakings on a larger and larger scale, and the whole financial structure 'becomes a new and terrible weapon in the battle of competition and is finally transformed into an enormous social mechanism for the centralisation of capitals'.[43] Marx was quite explicit about his pessimistic view of the rate at which the surplus could be pumped out of the workers, writing that 'accumulation ... is clearly a very slow procedure compared with centralisation'.[44] It is interesting, therefore, that Marx, after devoting most of his analytical effort to an explication of the essentially economic laws of capitalist accumulation, comes to the conclusion that perhaps the most important element in the progress of capitalism is not something inherent in the process of production but the general trend of property transfers. As he writes, 'The world would still be without railways if it had had to wait until accumulation had got a few individual capitals far enough to be adequate for the construction of a railway.'[45] This again demonstrates how cautious are his views about the addition to output which can be attributed to technical progress.

Thirdly, Marx does not allow the establishment of a monopoly position to enable the capitalist to raise prices. There is a logical reason for this, of course; if he could raise prices he would prevent his profit rate from declining. Marx does not cover this point although he realized that monopolies mean a diminution in competition and observed that competition is 'in direct proportion to the number, and in inverse proportion to the magnitudes, of the antagonistic capitals'.[46] This is readily explicable if one again supposes that he was thinking of profits in real terms: if output per unit of input is declining because of physical constraints on technical progress then monopoly will make no difference except in so far as the availability of greater physical resources makes it possible to get nearer to the point at which the diminishing returns to scale actually become negative.

References and Notes

1. *Capital*, vol. I, Ch. i, Sect. 1, p. 39.
2. Ibid.
3. Ibid., vol. III, Ch. xv, Sect. 4, p. 264.
4. Since Marx's day, inventions appear to have betrayed no particular bias – electricity is capital saving, mechanical engineering is labour-saving – and this no doubt helps to explain the difficulty in establishing whether the rate of profit in the modern world exhibits any long term trend.
5. *Capital*, vol. III, Ch. ii, pp. 50–1.
6. Ibid., vol. I, Ch. xii, p. 321.
7. Ibid., vol. I, Ch. xi, p. 310.
8. Ibid., vol. I, Ch. xiii, p. 322.
9. Ibid., vol. I, Ch. xiii, p. 326.
10. Ibid., vol. I, Ch. xiii, p. 325.
11. Ibid., vol. I, Ch. xiii, p. 333.
12. Ibid.
13. Ibid., vol. I, Ch. xv, Sect. 1, p. 372, n. 3.
14. Ibid., vol. I, Ch. vii, Sect. 1, p. 180.
15. Ibid., vol. I, Ch. xiv, Sect. 1, p. 338.

16. Ibid., vol. I, Ch. xiv, Sect. 1, p. 336.
17. Ibid., vol. I, Ch. xiv, Sect. 3, p. 348.
18. Ibid., vol. I, Ch. xv, Sect. 1, pp. 381–2.
19. Ibid., vol. I, Ch. xv, Sect. 1, p. 375.
20. Ibid., vol. I, Ch. xv, Sect. 2, p. 356.
21. Ibid., vol. I, Ch. xv, Sect. 2, pp. 386–7.
22. Ibid., vol. I, Ch. xv, Sect. 2, p. 387. The uncertainty of Marx's thinking is illustrated by his assertion in the passage immediately following this that 'in Modern Industry man succeeded for the first time in making the product of his past labour work on a scale gratuitously, like the forces of nature', ibid., vol. I, Ch. xv, Sect. 2, p. 388. Again, n. 1 of p. 388 suggests that capital adds something to the product over and above the wear and tear incurred in production.
23. Ibid., vol. I, Ch. xiv, Sect. 5, p. 367.
24. Ibid., vol. I, Ch. xv, Sect. 4, pp. 423–4.
25. Ibid., vol. I, Ch. xv, Sect. 3a, p. 394.
26. Ibid., vol. I, Ch. xv, Sect. 3a, p. 395.
27. Ibid., vol. I, Ch. xv, Sect. 3a, p. 396.
28. Ibid., vol. I, Ch. xv, Sect. 3b, p. 403.
29. Ibid., vol. I, Ch. xv, Sect. 3c, p. 409.
30. *The Wealth of Nations*, Book I, Ch. iii, p. 31.
31. Ricardo, *Works*, vol. I, p. 120.
32. Mill, *Principles of Political Economy*, Book IV, Ch. iii, Sect. 5, p. 721.
33. Ibid., Book IV, Ch. iv, Sect. 4, p. 731.
34. *Capital*, vol. III, Ch. xiii, p. 212.
35. Ibid., vol. I, Ch. xv, Sect. 1, pp. 371–2.
36. Ibid., vol. I, Ch. xv, Sect. 1, p. 376.
37. Ibid., vol. I, Ch. xv, Sect. 1, p. 385.
38. Ibid., vol. I, Ch. xxv, Sect. 1, p. 612; ibid., vol. III, Ch. xiv, Sect. 3, p. 236.
39. Ibid., vol. I, Ch. xv, Sect. 2, p. 393, n. 1.
40. Marx, *A Contribution to the Critique of Political economy*, p. 191. Engels, it should be noted, never shared Marx's pessimism about the prospects of technical advance nor does he show any awareness that his optimism was destructive of Marx's theoretical position. See his *Critique of Political Economy*, p. 217, where he writes 'The productive power at mankind's dispersal is immeasurable. The productivity of the soil can be increased *ad infinitum* by the application of capital, labour and science.'
41. *Capital*, vol. III, Ch. xv, Sect. 4, pp. 262–3.
42. Ibid., vol. I, Ch. xxv, Sect. 2, p. 625.
43. Ibid., vol. I, Ch. xxv, Sect. 2, p. 626.
44. Ibid., vol. I, Ch. xxv, Sect. 2, p. 627.
45. Ibid., vol. I, Ch. xxv, Sect. 2, p. 628.
46. Ibid., vol. I, Ch. xxv, Sect. 2, p. 626.

Chapter 14

The declining rate of profit: revolution

So far, we have seen how Marx's theory of the declining rate of profit is connected with immiseration, technological change and monopolization, but nothing has been said about the way in which this is to culminate in the collapse of capitalism and the birth of a new society – socialism. Unfortunately, it is precisely at this point that Marx is most obscure and ambiguous. Nonetheless, the nature of the fundamental ambiguity is both interesting and significant – it turns on the question of whether the transition from capitalism to socialism will be violent or relatively peaceful.

Breakdown: discontinuity

There are unequivocal statements in Marx to the effect that the end of capitalism comes about because of the increasing severity of business cycles. In the *Communist Manifesto* Marx refers to 'the commercial crises that by their periodical return put on its trial, each time more threateningly, the existence of the entire bourgeois society'.[1] Writing in 1847 Marx declared that as the 'capitalists are compelled . . . to exploit the already existing gigantic means of production on a larger scale . . . there is a corresponding increase in industrial earthquakes . . . in a word, *crises* increase'.[2] In the high capitalism of mid-nineteenth-century England, he wrote, 'every fresh development of the productive powers of labour must tend to deepen social contrasts and point social antagonisms' and will be accompanied by 'the quickened return, the widening compass, and the deadlier effects of the social pest called a commercial and industrial crisis'.[3] Not only are crises endemic and increasing but 'their crowning point is the universal crisis'.[4] The increasing amplitude of commercial oscillations will eventually shatter the whole of the capitalist framework.

Marx's theory of crisis is intimately linked with his theory of immiseration. The decline in the rate of profit 'breeds over-production, speculation, crises, and surplus-capital alongside surplus-population'.[5] The connexion between unemployment and crisis is clear. The success of a new labour-saving technique in creating super-profits will lead to its widespread application. This expansion of investment will, in spite of its being labour-saving, increase the demand for labour. This will in turn increase wages. But an increase in the share of workers in output must reduce profits. Thus 'the *real barrier* of capitalist production is *capital itself*'.[6] Crises are engendered by the way in which the system attempts to re-establish the rate of profit and to break through this 'real barrier'. Such efforts are vain, for the only way to escape from the pressure of wages is to introduce yet another labour-saving technique which, with its diffusion, will eventually bring the rate of profit down to a yet lower level.

At the level of employment and technology Marx probably had in mind the effects of the expansion of the textile industry especially after the Napoleonic Wars. On the one hand the spread of mechanization wrought a demographic revolution in the English northern manufacturing towns, sucking workers into the factory system, and on the other hand it rendered hundreds of thousands of handloom weavers redundant and gave rise to the most serious single cause of social unrest in the first half of the nineteenth century. Marx tries to integrate the two phenomena in a vision of an economy in which the entrepreneur continually runs up against labour shortages which induce him to seek labour-saving methods. The innovating capitalist bankrupts his competitors, while creating unemployment in technologically outmoded industries. In this process the adjustments are sudden and discontinuous;

in all spheres, the increase of the variable part of the capital, and therefore of the number of labourers employed by it, is always connected with violent fluctuations and transitory production of surplus-population, whether this takes the more striking form of the repulsion of labourers already employed, or the less evident but not less real form of the more difficult absorption of the additional labouring population through the usual channels.[7]

But the effects of the jerky and fitful development of capital are not confined to or simply buffered by an 'industrial reserve army' of the unemployed; the system itself is constantly racked by the effects of the declining rate of profit on investment because the 'periodical depreciation of existing capital . . . disturbs the given conditions, within which the process of circulation and reproduction of capital takes place, and is therefore accompanied by sudden stoppages and crises in the production process.'[8]

The origins of the recoveries from these periodic crises are to be found in the breakdown itself. In a depression the value of equity shares falls, the value of capital equipment falls, the money supply contracts and the metals which constitute this lie idle, and output can only be cleared by drastic price-cutting. 'This confusion and stagnation paralyses the function of money as a medium of payment . . . the chain of payment obligations due at specific dates is broken in a hundred places' and this in turn leads to 'a real falling off in reproduction'.[9] The rate of profit is reduced by the excessive production of capital; the response of the system is to bring about the destruction and waste of this excess. At the same time the increased number of unemployed workers tends to depress the rate of wages and the conditions for a renewal of the cycle are created.

Breakdown: continuity

But Marx's assertion that crises become more severe with the accumulation of capital is not supported by the implicit logic of his argument; the case is rather the reverse. The fact that the rate of profit not only declines over short periods in order to resolve each crisis but in each successive recovery returns to a level somewhat lower than before implies that the amplitude of the oscillations is not increasing but diminishing. As the rate of profit falls nearer and nearer to the minimum consistent with the survival of the system the boundaries within which it can fluctuate are drawing closer and closer together. This too, rather than deeper slumps and more elevated booms, fits better with the implications for profits of Marx's technological theory, dependent as it is on ever diminishing and increasingly hardly won economies of scale.

This ambiguity, which cannot be resolved satisfactorily from the text, is not a chance result: it stems, in part, from the same cause which gives rise to many of the other theories of Marx – his dependence on the market, an *equilibrating* institution, for the provision of explanations of *instability*. The approach of the profit rate to zero itself is an equilibrating effect, and the analytical structure in which Marx has embedded all the important factors of the process he is studying, technological change, capital accumulation, the employment and redeployment of labour, suggests that the outcome will be, not a social explosion, but the generation of near social and economic entropy in which capital barely reproduces itself in the midst of a stagnant population.

But this curious implication of Marx's theory of revolution has origins which can be even more precisely located. If Marx's understanding of the origins of 'capitalism' is derived from Adam Smith, and his explanation of the labour theory of value taken from Ricardo, then his account of the cause of revolution owes much to John Stuart Mill. A central problem for Mill, given the pessimism about the possibility of scientific advance which he shared with Marx, was that of explaining why 'the great annual savings which take place in this country' had not already depressed 'the rate of profit much nearer to that lowest point to which it is always tending, and which, left to itself, it would so promptly attain'.[10] Marx, in a similar passage, feels that, given 'the enormous development of the productive forces of the labour in the last 30 years' and 'the enormous mass of fixed capital, aside from the actual machinery, which goes into the process of social production', the analytical difficulty is not to explain why the rate of profit falls but 'why this fall is not greater and more rapid'.[11]

The principal reason given by Mill for the failure of the rate of profit to fall more rapidly is identical to that offered by Marx; it is 'the waste of capital in periods of over-trading and rash speculation, and in the commercial revulsions by which such times are always followed'. Moreover, the fact 'that such revulsions are almost periodical is a consequence of the very tendency of profits which we are considering'.[12] Like Marx, Mill believes that crises are the self-correcting result of the declining rate of profit. Both Marx and Mill have distinct passages in which they discuss various other factors which tend to decelerate the decline of the profit rate: they both cite improvements in production which cheapen articles of consumption and hence the cost of labour; foreign trade acts similarly by providing wage goods; and foreign investment assists in the production of such goods by providing capital which foreign countries cannot find from their own resources.[13]

Furthermore, it is easy to see how Mill's own analysis of price movements might be misunderstood, so that insufficiently careful reading might lead one to suppose that Mill was himself guilty of giving two contradictory accounts of the progress of society. For Mill thought that fluctuations in prices were of two types. Apart from the changes connected with commercial crises there were, at a more basic level, 'fluctuation of values and prices arising from variations of supply, or from alteration in real . . . demand'. These were the result of market imperfections and the lack of reserve stocks in a relatively under-developed economy dependent on the harvest. The progress of society, by improving communications and generating entrepreneurial activity to exploit and eliminate market imperfections, would make transitions in value even smoother and more predictable, so that price variations 'may be expected to moderate as society advances'.[14]

On the other hand, commercial crises of the kind which appeared periodically in the British economy in the half century before the publication of Volume I of *Capital*, Mill attributed to 'miscalculation and especially . . . the alternations of undue expansion and excessive contraction of credit which occupy so conspicuous a place among commercial phenomena',[15] Moreover, in contrast to the more basic fluctuations in prices, Mill asserted that 'such vicissitudes, beginning with irrational speculation and ending with a commercial crisis, have not hitherto become either less frequent or less violent with the growth of capital and the extension of industry. Rather they may be said to have become more so.'[16] But the use of the adjective 'irrational' is an indication of the theoretical status which Mill accorded to these phenomena – they were, in some sense, superficial aberrations, which could be moderated by government legislation to control the currency. His assertion that these commercial crises had become more frequent and violent is implicit in his argument for the proper regulation of the currency and is part of his critique of the Bank Charter Act of 1844.

Marx's failure, or refusal, to see that these two acounts of price movements operated at different levels, allowed him, in his borrowing from Mill's *Principles*, to see as essential and fatal, what Mill had regarded as secondary and remediable. Even so, the logical implication, even in Marx's model, that the outcome of economic development is likely to be a peaceful rather than a cataclysmic transition to a new social situation remains. Indeed, Mill's own description of the stationary state is so striking for the similarity it bears to the implications of Marx's own writings as to the nature of socialism that it is worth quoting in full;

It is scarcely necessary to remark that a stationary condition of capital and population implies no stationary state of human improvement. There would be as much scope as ever for all kinds of mental culture, and moral and social progress; as much room for improving the Art of Living, and much more likelihood of its being improved, when minds ceased to be engrossed by the art of getting on. Even the industrial arts might be as earnestly and as successfully cultivated, with this sole difference, that instead of serving no purpose but the increase of wealth, industrial improvements would produce their legitimate effect, that of abridging labour. Hitherto it is questionable if all the mechanical inventions yet made have lightened the day's toil of any human being.[17] They have enabled a greater population to live the same life of drudgery and imprisonment, and an increased number of manufacturers and others to make fortunes. They have increased the comforts of the middle classes. But they have not yet begun to effect those great changes in human destiny, which it is in their nature and in their futurity to accomplish. Only when, in addition to just institutions, the increase in mankind shall be under the deliberate guidance of judicious foresight, can the conquests made from the powers of nature by the intellect and energy of scientific discoverers become the common property of the species, and the means of improving and elevating the universal lot.[18]

Except for Mill's belief that the key to this happy state of affairs lay in inculcation of the need to regulate the birth rate, Marx could have subscribed to all of this, including the belief in the superiority of moral to merely material progress, and the assumption that the true purpose of technical progress is to relieve mankind of the burden of work. As Marx writes,

In fact, the realm of freedom does not commence until the point is passed where labour under the compulsion of necessity and of external utility is required. In the very nature of things it lies beyond the sphere of material production in the strict meaning of the term ... Beyond it begins that development of human power, which is its own end, the true realm of freedom ... The shortening of the working-day is its fundamental premise.[19]

Nor should it be supposed that the possibility of the transition from capitalism to socialism might be a comparatively tranquil process is merely something to be teased out of Marx's work by the Talmudic dissection of the text. Engels himself wrote that Marx was 'a man whose whole theory is the result of a life-long study of the economic history and condition of England, and whom that study led to the conclusion that, at least in Europe, England is the only country where the inevitable social revolution might be effected entirely by peaceful and legal means'.[20] Marx himself acknowledged that the replacement of capitalism by socialism might be less bloody than is usually supposed;

The transformation of scattered private property, arising from individual labour, into capitalist private property is, naturally, a processs, incomparably more protracted, violent and difficult, than the transformation of capitalistic private property already practically resting on socialised production into socialised property. In the former case, we had the expropriation of the mass of the people by a few usurpers; in the latter, we have the expropriation of a few usurpers by the mass of the people.[21]

Capitalism comes in like a lion and goes out like a lamb.

Money and underconsumption

It will be recalled that the early socialists were underconsumptionists and that in this they differed from the orthodox political economists who held that underconsumption was impossible – a position formally expressed in Say's Law: if all incomes are spent then all output must be sold (see p. 49). Underconsumption is a doctrine which asserts that commercial society is doomed by the very nature of its own productive arrangements and constitutes the first economic theory of capitalist collapse. Marx has sometimes been described as an underconsumptionist and sometimes defended against that charge; in this section we shall consider what part underconsumptionism played in his thinking.

The theory of money implied by Say's Law holds that currency is a neutral medium of exchange which does not affect real market activity. John Stuart Mill, however, did believe that the issue of currency needed to be controlled by the State and in this departed from the strictest monetary orthodoxy. He was not alone in this, for Ricardo also believed that the unregulated activity of banks would not necessarily produce the optimal level of currency and credit. They arrived at this position, known as that of the Currency School, in the course of the debates on currency and banking which the Napoleonic upheavals provoked. Their opponents, adherents of the Banking School, held the view advocated by Smith, which became known as the Real Bills doctrine, according to which, provided that banks strictly restricted the issue of credit to the financing of real transactions, i.e. actual contracts for the delivery of goods, then no further control was necessary. Given that all currency was convertible into gold, any attempt to overissue banknotes would simply result in their being returned to the banks. The debate had many complex ramifications, and it is given here in a grossly simplified form, but both Schools were united in a common purpose, to ensure that the currency and credit behaved so as exactly to reflect the economic changes and developments which it existed to facilitate. The Currency School thought that legislation was needed to ensure that this end was achieved; the Banking School had a stronger faith in the automatic equilibrating force of the market system.

Not surprisingly, given his predilection for endogenous explanations, Marx was a supporter of the more traditional and less interventionist Banking School. In strictly orthodox terms he refers to 'the illusion begotten by the intervention of money'[22] in exchange, and observed that 'the currency of money, generally considered, is but a reflex of the circulation of commodities'.[23] Against the Currency School, he specifically rejects any monetary explanation of crises, writing, no doubt with Mill in mind, that 'the superficiality of Political Economy shows itself in the fact that it looks upon the expansion and contraction of credit, which is a mere symptom of the periodic changes of the industrial cycle, as their cause'.[24] Like all the political economists, he thought that the withdrawal of money from circulation or hoarding was in principle irrational as long as there were markets in which capital can be profitably employed: 'Exclusion of money from circulation would also exclude absolutely its self-expansion as capital, while accumulation of a hoard in the shape of commodities would be sheer tomfoolery'.[25] By excluding the possibility of hoarding and denying that monetary phenomena can be the cause of crisis or breakdown Marx would appear, in principle, to have denied himself the grounds which make the underconsumptionism possible. Nonetheless he offers, in various places, an explanation of the cause of crises which sounds very much like Malthus's theory of gluts. The most succinct version of this is his statement that 'the ultimate reason for all real crises always remains the poverty and restricted consumption of the masses as opposed to the drive of capitalist production to develop the productive forces as though only the absolute consuming power of society constituted their limits'.[26] Elsewhere he writes that 'antagonistic conditions of distribution reduce the consumption of the bulk of society to a minimum varying within more or less narrow limits. It is furthermore restricted by the tendency to accumulate, the drive to expand capital and produce surplus-value on an extended scale . . . The market must therefore be continually extended . . .'[27]

It is easy to read this, as many Marxists read it, to indicate that Marx was an underconsumptionist who believed that capitalists were always faced with the problem of disposing of their surplus. There is no doubt that Marx thought that extending the market would help to relieve or delay the onset of the critical difficulties endemic in capitalism, and it is here that is to be found the theoretical origins of the theories of imperialism and colonial exploitation that were to be developed in the years after his death.[28]

It is hard to resist the feeling that Marx was guilty of some confusion and illegitimately used the assumptions on which Say's Law was based to arrive at underconsumptionist conclusions. But Marx's confusion was perhaps not as great as at first appears. Let us look at a passage which is often cited as a direct contradiction by Marx of his own underconsumptionist position, where he writes,

It is sheer tautology to say that crises are caused by the scarcity of effective consumption, or of effective consumers . . . But if one were to attempt to give this tautology the semblance of a profounder justification by saying that the working-class receives too small a portion of its own product and the evil would be remedied as soon as it receives a larger share of it and its wages increase in consequence, one would only remark that crises are always prepared by precisely a period in which wages rise generally and the working-class actually gets a larger share of that part of the annual product which is intended for consumption. From the point of view of these advocates of sound and 'simple' common sense, such a period should rather remove the crises.[29]

This becomes reconcilable with his other statements about the underconsumptionist tendencies of capitalism if it is realized that Marx believed that a failure to satisfy demand or, conversely the appearance of unsaleable gluts of goods in crises, is due to the fact that the structure of commercial arrangements is inherently unstable. This is a vision very much like that of Sismondi, (see Chapter 4 [underconsumption] pp. 50–51) who held that the separation of labour from ownership was a fundamental flaw in the economic system, leading to miscalculation, the misallocation of resources, and an endemic tendency for parts of the economic mechanism to seize up. Marx is impressed by the fact that production processes take place over time, so that after the capitalist has made his original investment in producer goods acquired at particular prices, 'great changes take place in the market . . . since great changes take place in the productivity of labour and therefore also in the *real value* of commodities'. In this way the capitalist's original calculation based on the earlier market prices are nullified, causing 'great catastrophes'.[30] Prices may rise as well as fall as a result of a sudden deficiency in production, as the result, for example, of a harvest failure, so that 'there occurs a stoppage in reproduction, and thus in the flow of circulation. Purchase and sale get bogged down and unemployed capital appears in the form of idle money'.[31] In this way, although money has no independent effect on the circulation of goods and services, there is a chronic tendency in the system for its various parts to get out of phase and to impede each other, causing the whole economy to jam. And if gluts are not caused by a lack of effective demand then increasing the income of the workers will not avert them. Marx perhaps meant to say that the truth of Say's Law will not, given the imperfection of institutions, ensure full employment at reasonable wages. It would be difficult to find many people today who would disagree with such an assertion.

The reproduction schema: disproportionality

Marx's need to provide a theoretical explanation for the 'bumpiness' and destablizing propensities of the capitalist economy is not, as we have seen, well answered by the declining rate of profit. His search for such an explanation led him to expound what is, in effect, an alternative theory of revolution, in the so-called reproduction schema derived from the work of Quesnay (see page 27) which have attracted attention from modern economists for the way in which they appear to anticipate certain modern theories of growth. They show that Marx's conflation of Malthus and Say was not an idle or careless piece of journalism and demonstrate that Marx's own powers of creative economic thinking were greater than some of his more careless passages have led some of his detractors to believe.

For Quesnay, the surplus in the economy arises exclusively in agriculture. The *Tableau Économique* is designed to show how changes in this surplus uniquely determine the distribution of incomes throughout the system and to demonstrate how the market operates to equate all the flows of production, consumption and investment within a given framework and according to a very rigorous logic. Marx greatly admired Quesnay, describing the *Tableau* as 'an incontestably brilliant conception'[32] and his Physiocratic followers as 'the true fathers of modern political economy'.[33] Marx adapted the *Tableau* to analyse a capitalist economy where the surplus is produced in industry. But the purpose of Marx's use of Quesnay's work is quite different from that of the Physiocrats. Like Quesnay he wanted to answer the question of how 'the *capital* consumed in production is replaced in value out of the annual product'.[34] But Marx's account of the complexity of the capitalist mechanism is meant to demonstrate the unlikelihood of any smooth adjustment of the levels of consumption and investment to changes in the level of output. It is meant, not so much to show how capitalism works, but how unlikely it is to work efficiently for very long.

Marx starts out by assuming an economy in which there is no growth.[35] Investment is just sufficient to maintain production at a given level, a state which Marx describes as simple reproduction. The department is divided into two departments, I, producing the means of production, i.e. machines and raw materials, and II, producing articles of consumption. All the various firms in each department are, for the purposes of analysis, aggregated and treated as one. The stability of the economy as a whole depends on the ability of the sectors adequately to fulfil each other's needs, exchanging capital goods for consumer goods. Marx's model shows that the means of production produced in department I must cover its own consumption of capital and also the capital needs of department II. Department II must provide for its own consumption needs and also provide enough for the consumption goods requirements of workers and capitalists in department I. Accordingly, the amount of capital supplied by department I to department II must equal the capital depreciation of the former. This in turn must equal the amount of consumption goods supplied by department II. Again this quantity must be equal to the consumption needs of department I. If department I produces too little capital 'it would be impossible for II to replace its constant capital entirely', if it produces too much 'a surplus would remain unused'.[36] Marx points out that this condition for equilibrium can be met 'only so long as the scale and value-relations in production remain stationary and so long as these strict relations are not altered by foreign commerce'.[37]

But there is another difficulty. Capital is not consumed at a uniform rate. Fixed capital takes longer to turn over than raw materials. While, in any given period, department I can always meet its capital needs from its own resources, department II must constantly lay aside the money acquired from department I against the points in time at which particularly large amounts of fixed capital must be replaced. This means that there will be a chronic tendency for department II's demand for the output of department I to be deficient. This tendency will only be overcome if a cash reserve exists in department II and only if the amount of money set aside each year equals the amount of capital purchased for the periodical and irregular incidence of the replacement of fixed capital, i.e. savings must equal investment in department II.

If there is a sudden jump in replacement requirements in department II the output of consumer goods will fall and there will be an unspendable cash surplus in department I and hence overproduction of the output of department I. Conversely, if there is a fall in replacement requirements in department II there will be a relative surplus of the product of department II.[38] Marx agrees that exports could carry off surpluses, and imports could meet deficiencies, but argues that this 'only transfers the contradictions to a wider sphere and gives them greater latitude'. This shows, writes Marx, that 'A disproportion of the production of fixed and circulating capital . . . can and must arise even when the fixed capital is merely *preserved*'.[39] He is exaggerating, of course, in claiming to have shown that a disproportion *must* arise but, given his assumptions about the blind and irrational way in which capitalists act in pursuit of profit, his model powerfully suggests that it is extremely probable.

This probability is further reinforced once Marx introduces the idea of expanded reproduction, of an economy which is actually increasing its output. Then capitalists in both departments must save some of their profits in order to accumulate them for expanded investment. The problems of balance caused by the irregularity of fixed capital replacements are now complicated by the appearance of new irregular investment outlays in department I, on top of the irregular investment outlays in department II. The likelihood of balance exchange is even further diminished by the fact that the new investment in an expanding economy is constantly changing the organic composition of capital in different industries at different rates. The difficulty of equating saving with investment and production with consumption among industries and between workers and employers means that overproduction and shortages are increasingly likely and the necessary adjustments will only be possible with the aid of what Marx calls 'a great crash'.[40]

Marx's achievement was much greater than this simple summary suggests; the mastery of Quesnay's analysis is, in itself, a demanding exercise, while Marx's painstaking application of this approach to the dissection of his own capitalist model is carried out with an intellectual verve and logical drive that would be sufficient in itself to secure Marx a place in any history of economic thought. It can be objected of course that his division of the economy into departments is much less realistic than in the work from which he drew his inspiration. Quesnay's separation of agriculture from manufacturing is more persuasive than a distinction between consumer and capital goods: coal can be burnt in a kitchen stove as well as in a factory boiler and steel makes cutlery as well as machinery. Nor does Marx, in an era when trade was assumed to be the very core of progress, give any serious consideration to the possible effects of international commerce on the operation of his model. But these are relatively trivial criticism – the model could be refined and it is identifiably a very precocious anticipation, by some seventy years, of the modern techniques of input–output analysis.

More immediately interesting in the context of his ideas as a whole is the way in which it illustrates Marx's powerful grasp of the political economists' fundamental logic. The reproduction schema show that there is nothing *logically* impossible about the expansion and prolonged survival of capitalism. They do not constitute, in short, a refutation of Say's Law. For Marx, the problems of 'underconsumption', breakdown and crisis have their origins elsewhere. By stripping away the veil of prices Marx lays bare the bewilderingly and infinitely complex state of interrelationships on which the operation of the system depends. Marx certainly exaggerates the fragility of these balancing relationships by making no provision in his economy for the reserves of resources, the slackness in management and control, and the general 'fat' which all economies accumulate, and which, in the fluctuations of economic activity from day to day or year to year can be mobilized to cushion shocks and damp the vibrations in the system. Marx's economy rests on a knife-edge; one strike, one ship which fails to come home, one bad harvest will bring the whole edifice down in ruins. The nemesis of capitalism is to be found in its rigidities and the technical improbability of sufficiently rapid, adequate and accurate adjustments.

Nonetheless, the subsequent economic history of the world, suggests that, whatever the shortcoming of much of the detail and many of the assumptions of Marx's economic theories, his intuition that market societies are not self-sustaining but require more and more regulation to ensure honesty in financial dealing, to secure a reliable currency, to finance and control certain kinds of investment and production, and, in general, to secure the full and fruitful employment of resources, *even where most property remains privately owned*, is an extremely powerful and prophetic one. Marx, of course, goes further than this, and his synthesis of Malthus and Say convinces him of the need for planning:

> *To say that there is no general over-production, but rather a disproportion within the various branches of production, is no more than to say that under capitalist production the proportionality of the individual branches of production springs as a continual process from disproportionality, because the cohesion of the aggregate production imposes itself as a blind law upon the agents of production, and not as a law which, being understood and hence controlled by their common mind, brings the productive process under their joint control.*[41]

His analysis stresses that the problems of matching supply and demand are multiplied in an expanding economy: the difficulties of calculation are increased; the division of labour continually enlarges the separation of industry from industry and of supplier from consumer; technical progress increases the gap between investment and the time of its return; and a growing financial structure continually lengthens the chain of transactions between saving and investment. Marx sees that the independent and selfishly guided free activity of individuals cannot sustain such a complex system. Marx finally loses his faith in the 'social process' so vital to his account of the labour theory of value and the declining rate of profit; he no longer believes in Adam Smith's invisible and equilibrating hand.

Marx's double vision

There are thus two approaches to revolution in Marx's writing. On the one hand, there is an account of the way in which the physical constraints on production coupled with the ruthless greed of the capitalists cause a secular fall in the rate of profit which may well have a smooth and continuous outcome in the passage to socialism. This is essentially a price-determined process, in which the equilibrating mechanisms of the market combine the greed of the individual with the restraining forces of nature to manufacture the calm serenity of socialism. On the other hand, there is a vision of the hopelessly complex mechanisms which underlie the veil of price. These constantly founder on shortages of both capital and labour, which are both the cause and consequence of miscalculation. This approach concentrates not on the way in which the market mobilizes resources smoothly for the giant task of increasing the social wealth but on the problem of actually accumulating these resources and then putting them to use. Capitalism is inherently unstable and economic collapse consequently inevitable. So, on the one hand we have the declining rate of profit, on the other 'underconsumption' and disproportionality.

Thus, the analyses of the political economists were as much of a hindrance as a help to Marx. They provided him with a powerful analytical framework in which to array his moral critique of man's self-destructive self-seeking; but equally their preindustrial understanding of technology, their belief in the convergent and decelerating functions of diminishing returns and market equilibrium, and their teaching about the passive function of money prevented Marx from integrating some of his most brilliant insights. His development of a Quesnaysian and macroeconomic analysis of the economy, his insights into the causes of the inherent instability of the free market and industrial system, were each of them enough to ensure a proper place for him in the textbooks. But he was unable to fuse together his idea that the operation of the bourgeois mode of production is 'bumpy', 'lumpy' and discontinuous, with the political economists' assumptions about the smooth, continuous and integrated elements of the market.

But Marx is not prepared to abandon either one or the other. He sees capitalism with a double vision. Superimposed on a violent process in which capitalism tears itself apart as a result of its own structural inadequacies relating especially to the distribution of property, is another image, containing some of the same elements, in which democratic institutions, nurtured and fuelled by economic development itself, increasingly integrate the population of civil society into a progressively egalitarian and rational political system for the management of the material base of civil society.

Paradoxically, this and other ambiguities in Marx were the secret of the spread of his influence and the persistence of his importance. In Germany, which was spectacularly successful in developing an industrial economy in the latter half of the nineteenth century, the members of the German Social Democratic Party were able to adopt Marxism as their official creed, proclaim themselves revolutionaries, and yet pursue a political strategy which depended vitally on the ability to exploit the existing and quasi-democratic institutions provided by the Imperial Constitution. In underdeveloped countries, the idea that capitalism can only be achieved by a leap, by an original confiscation and the violent transfer of property has been an inspiration to revolutionary parties seeking to break out of backwardness. Once in power, the notion that industrialization cannot be expected to proceed autonomously has served to ensure the survival of Marx's work as the legitimization of the State's control of all economic activity. While this dualism has prevented Marx from achieving an uncontested position in the Pantheon of the pioneers of social thought, it nevertheless remains one of the most politically fertile ambiguities in the history of economic ideas.

References and Notes

1. Marx Engels, *Selected Works*, vol. I, p. 39.
2. Ibid., vol. I, p. 105.
3. Ibid., vol. I, p. 381.
4. *Capital*, vol. I, p. 20.
5. Ibid., vol. III, Ch. xv, Sect. 1, p. 242.
6. Ibid., vol. III, Ch. xv, Sect. 2, p. 250.
7. Ibid., vol. I, Ch. xxv, Sect. 3, p. 630.
8. Ibid., vol. III, Ch. xv, Sect. 2, p. 249.
9. Ibid., vol. III, Ch. xv, Sect. 2, p. 254.
10. Mill, *Principles of Political Economy*, Book IV, Ch. iv, Sect. 5, pp. 733–4.
11. *Capital*, vol. III, Ch. xiv, p. 232.
12. Mill, op. cit., Book IV, Ch. iv, Sect. 5. pp. 733–4.
13. Ibid., Book IV, Ch. iv, Sects. 6–8, pp. 735–9; *Capital*, vol. III, Ch. xiv, pp. 232–40.
14. Mill, op. cit., Book IV, Ch. ii, Sect. 5, p. 709.
15. Ibid.
16. Ibid.
17. Marx quotes this sentence approvingly in *Capital*, vol. I, Ch. xv, p. 371.
18. Mill, op. cit., Book IV, Ch. vi, Sect. 2, p. 751.
19. *Capital*, vol. III, Ch. xviii, p. 820.
20. Engels, 'Preface to the English edition'(1886) in *Capital*, vol. I, p. 6. Marx apparently thought that the United States would also reach socialism without serious social upheaval.
21. Ibid., vol. I, Ch. xxxii, p. 764.
22. Ibid., vol. I, Ch. xxiii, p. 568.
23. Ibid., vol. I, Ch. iii, Sect. 2b, p. 121.
24. Ibid., vol. I, Ch. xxv, Sect. 3, p. 633.
25. Ibid., vol. I, Ch. xxiv, Sect. 2, p. 589.
26. Ibid., vol. III, Ch. xxx, p. 484.
27. Ibid., vol. III, Ch. xv, Sect. 1, pp. 244–5.
28. It should not be forgotten that Marx himself never propounded a theory of imperialism. Rather he saw international trade as a force breaking down national and cultural distinctions and uniting the working men of all countries against their class oppressors. Free Trade was the harbinger of *international* revolution.
29. Ibid., vol. II, Ch. xx, Sect. 4, pp. 414–15.
30. Karl Marx, *Theories of Surplus Value*, 3 parts (Moscow 1969–72), Progress Publishers, Part I, Ch. xvii. Sect. 6, p. 495.
31. Ibid., Part II, Ch. xvii, Sect. 6, p. 494.
32. Ibid., Part I, Ch. vi, Sect. 6, p. 344.
33. Ibid., Part I, Ch. ii, Sect. 1, p. 44.

34. *Capital*, vol. II, Ch. xx, Sect. 1, p. 397.
35. What follows is taken from ibid., vol. II, Chs. xx and xxi.
36. Ibid., vol. II, Ch. xx, Sect. 4, p. 411.
37. Ibid., vol. II, Ch. xx, Sect. 4, p. 412.
38. Ibid., vol. II, Ch. xx, Sect. 11, sub-section 3, pp. 471–2.
39. Ibid., vol. II, Ch. xx, Sect. 11, sub-section 3, pp. 472–3.
40. Ibid., vol. II, Ch. xxi, Sect. 3, p. 525.
41. Ibid., vol. III, Ch. xv, Sect. 3, p. 257.

Chapter 15

The socialist model: England

According to Marx, capitalism was to be succeeded by a new mode of production – socialism. But Marx's views on socialism are notoriously incomplete and no full-scale account of socialist economic organization is to be found in his writings. Nonetheless, there are a number of references to the future society in his work and, even if no very clear picture of its nature can be established, they do shed some further interesting light on the nature of Marx's political economy.

I have stressed throughout this book Marx's failure to escape from the analytical ideas suggested to him by the political economists, in spite of his avowed intention to lay clear the 'reality' which lay behind them. It is, therefore, not surprising to find that he saw socialism, not as some entirely new and radically different economic system, but as a 'transformed' version of capitalism, a social arrangement in which the methods and organization of exploitative society are put to a higher and humane purpose. Socialism is capitalism transcended.

Marx's account of socialism is not unequivocal. As we have seen in the previous chapter, his description of the way in which capitalism would break down and be replaced by socialism is ambiguous. Again, as we have also seen, his declaration that the historical role of capitalism is to lay the material foundations for socialism, taken together with other statements about technical advance, imply that socialism would only be installed when abundance had already been achieved and the possibilities of further progress virtually exhausted. But the same pessimism about the extent to which production could be further increased under socialism, coupled with the idea that the first task of socialism was to shorten the working-day, made him point out that productive labour would still occupy a considerable part of the time of the citizens of a socialist society and would entail the continued employment of children. Moreover, his analysis of the productive process led him to conclude that its complexity required careful management in order to match supply with needs and to ensure a smooth flow of output. Planning would therefore be an important part if the new system. On the other hand, the whole purpose of Marx's socialism was the emancipation of man; in it human beings would be free, autonomous and uncoerced. In other words, although the economy was to be planned, no provision was made for institutions to ensure that planning instruction were carried out. Marx appears to have assumed that the resolution of such problems was essentially technical rather than political, because a mankind reintegrated with the world and reunited in the realization of its common humanity would have its understanding and motives transformed; in such a society answers to questions about how to secure the rational allocation of resources and organization of production would be self-evident.

Marx's concept of socialism was intimately connected with his understanding of how the transition to socialism was to come about. This chapter, therefore, complements the immediately preceding chapter. There, the causes of capitalist collapse were considered, here we shall be concerned with the way in which a new society is to emerge from the structure of the bourgeois system even as it degenerates and approaches dissolution. Marx's account of this process is central to his vision of the dynamism of capitalism.

The genetic origins of the socialist mode of production

Marx believed that the nature of socialism could be inferred from the study of capitalist institutions. This belief is connected with his view of the mechanism of social change. Each new social order, or mode of production, Marx thought, sprang from elements embedded in the system which it replaced.

We have frequently referred to the ambiguity of Marx's account of the way in which transitions between modes of production are achieved. On the one hand, he writes as if history and social change proceeded by way of a series of revolutions and disruptive jumps marked by violence and bloodshed. On the other hand, both descriptively and analytically, he often makes explicit allowance for transitions which clearly imply that the passage from one mode to another can be made without any discontinuity. This difficulty does not arise simply from special pleading or bad faith; it is connected with a real theoretical problem. Marx is concerned, in part, to explain and predict 'revolutions'. If revolution is conceived as a complete break in the process of social development, then the theoretical problem is that of specifying the conditions which will lead to the breakdown of a given system. But the 'completeness' of the break with the past makes it difficult to see on what basis it is possible to predict the new social system to which the revolution gives rise. On the other hand, if, in order to deal with this problem, revolution is conceived of as something less than a discontinuity, and the persistence of some determining factors in the old system is posited, then this position may be criticized on the grounds that it does not account for real revolutions, and here the term is being used simply to elevate into a social climacteric something which is better thought of, perhaps, as an accelerated but relatively continuous process of social adaptation. It is with this dilemma that Marx, as we have seen in Chapter 2, was struggling in his account of the emergence of 'capitalism'.

Marx often resorted to a metaphor which helped to resolve, at least imaginatively, the conflict between revolution and organic development: this figure was drawn from the process of pregnancy. Each successive mode of production is related to its predecessor as a child is to its mother, and each new social system is engendered within the matrix of its forerunner, owing its origin and its general characteristics to important elements within the parent mode. The emergence of the new system is like parturition, comparatively sudden, painful and traumatic, issuing in a new, distinct, and now autonomous entity, which is nonetheless clearly and identifiably related to that from which it is sprung. Marx makes this point in its most general form when he writes 'No social order ever perishes before all the productive forces for which there is room in it have developed; and new, higher relations of production never appear before the material conditions of their existence have matured in the womb of the old society itself.' Thus, in the *Communist Manifesto*, some of the productive arrangements of feudal society, the guild organization of handicraftsmen and artisans, and the 'chartered burghers of the early towns' were the embryonic forms of the new capitalist order and 'the means of production and exchange, on whose foundation the bourgeoisie built itself up, were generated in feudal society'[2].

Marx thought that socialism was related to capitalism in the same way that capitalism was related to feudalism. In 1875, discussing the programme of the newly founded German Social Democratic Party, he writes of socialism as it will appear immediately after the revolution: 'What we have to deal with here is a communist society, not as it has *developed* on its own foundations, but, on the contrary, just as it *emerges* from capitalist society; which is thus in every respect, economically, morally and intellectually, still stamped with the birthmarks of the old society from whose womb it emerges.'[3] It was, it will be recalled, this very emphasis on the genetic relationship of socialism to capitalism which was the essential element in Marx's claim that his theory was 'scientific' as opposed to 'utopian'. His conception of socialism was, he contended, based on and derived from the hard and unpleasant facts of capitalist reality.

Marx's account of the effects of the declining rate of profit is a description of the structural difficulties which cause capitalism to collapse. But the same description is also a portrayal of the way in which the outlines of a socialist order are being prepared within the capitalist framework. In the famous Chapter xxxii of volume I of *Capital*, 'The historical tendency of capitalist accumulation', Marx describes how 'the immanent laws of capitalist production' themselves foster

the co-operative form of the labour process, the conscious technical application of science, the methodical cultivation of the soil, the transformation of the instruments of labour into instruments of labour only usable in common, the economising of all means of production by their use as the means of production of combined socialised labour, the entanglement of all peoples in the net of the world-market, and with this the international character of the capitalistic regime.[4]

The technical conditions of production demand rational management independent of national boundaries, and on a scale which requires the displacement of the capitalists by social ownership: 'Centralisation of the means of production and socialisation of labour at least reach a point where they become incompatible with their capitalist integument. This integument is burst asunder.[5] The agent of this sudden change is a working class in revolt: 'a class always increasing in numbers, and disciplined united, organized by the very mechanism of the process of capitalist production itself'.[6] The socialism which succeeds this revolution is not only based on the achievements of capitalism but, by virtue of its internationalism and the development of a working class trained in the cooperative methods required by modern factory industry, better able to carry on the industrial mode of production than is capitalism itself.

The Factory Acts

In the process by which socialism is developed in the womb of capitalism Marx attached great importance to the Factory Acts. It should be noted that the Factory Acts, consisting as they do of the interference by elements of the 'superstructure' with the relations of production which constitute the 'base' of society, and effecting, as Marx himself asserted, an improvement in workers' welfare, might well be thought to be difficult to reconcile either with Marx's theory of social development, in which the 'base' determines the 'superstructure', or with his theory of working class immiseration. Marx apparently thought that this seeming inconsistency could be resolved by resorting to a more 'dialectical' account of the relationship between base and superstructure in which the casual relationships are not simply one way from base to superstructure but are reciprocally related, each conditioning the other. Some such notion doubtless lies behind his declaration that 'Factory legislation, that first conscious and methodical reaction of society against the spontaneously developed form of the process of production, is, as we have seen, just as much the necessary product of modern industry as cotton yarn, self-actors, and the electric telegraph.'[7] Since too, under socialism, man would no longer be the victim of his material circumstances, but the master of them, the beginning of the erosion of the base–superstructure relationship might also be expected in capitalism, and this would account for Marx's allowing that society might *react* 'consciously and methodically' to changes in the base instead of simply adjusting to them as the main elements in his theory suggest. Given the incompleteness of volumes II and III of *Capital* it is difficult to demonstrate this conclusively.

It is probable that Marx himself never succeeded in resolving these obscurities, because of his illness and lack of time; this supposition is given further plausibility by the likelihood that Marx's discussion of the two basic constituents of his theory, the labour theory of value and the declining rate of profit, were completed before he began a more thorough consideration of factory legislation and the structure of capitalist enterprises.

The factory legislation to which Marx refers is made up of the various Acts of parliament passed between 1802 and 1867 (the year of the publication of volume I of *Capital*). These regulated, with varying degrees of success, the length of the working-day and the conditions of employment in mines and factories. Marx was deeply impressed (not always rightly) by the competence, independence and impartiality of the English factory inspectors, medical officers and the various Commissions of Inquiry established for the investigation of social questions in this period. While admitting that 'higher motives' played a part in the work of these critics of industrial conditions, he also writes that 'their own most important interests dictate to the classes that are for the nonce the ruling ones, the removal of all legally removable hindrances to the free development of the working-class'.[8]

The bourgeoisie are obliged, willy-nilly, in order to secure the continued operation of the economic system, and, as Marx hints, as self-protection against the inevitable day when the proletariat comes to power, to see that the working class is not rendered physically incapable or culturally brutalized. In this way the bourgeoisie are the semi-conscious contrivers of their own supersession and help to 'shorten and lessen the birth-pangs' of the new society.

The factory as a model of socialist organization

According to Marx, the function of the Factory Acts is to make explicit and to regularize those aspects of Factory organization which will constitute the framework of socialism. Even the system of disciplinary measures used by factory owners to ensure the prompt rotation of shifts, and to improve the motivation, punctuality and consistency of the work force, is an anticipation of socialist planning methods:

the factory code in which capital formulates, like the private legislatory, and at his own good will, his autocracy over his workpeople, . . . this code is but the capitalistic caricature of that social regulation of the labour-process which becomes requisite in co-operation on a great scale, and in the employment in common, of instruments of labour and especially of machinery.[9]

The industrial revolution, argues Marx, 'is artificially helped on by . . . the Factory Acts'.[10] The shortening of the working-day and the regulations of the employment of children increase labour costs. The employer is consequently forced to substitute machinery for labour at an accelerated rate and to seek for further economies by producing on a larger scale. The Factory Acts accordingly improve productivity and reduce costs.

The Factory Acts also contained sanitary provisions relating to working conditions. Although Marx considered these to be extremely meagre he nonetheless thought that 'on the whole the working population, subject to the Factory Act [of 1850], has greatly improved physically. All medical testimony agrees upon this point, and personal observation at different times has convinced me of it.'[11] This simply underlines the point that for Marx, the factory system was not in principle abhorrent; given the right conditions it showed the present an image of the future.

One of the objections frequently voiced to the employment of young women and children in factories was the sexual temptation to which this work exposed them. Factories were held to break up the family and destroy parental ties. But Marx found, even in these aspects of the factory, pointers to progressive anthropological change. Commenting on a reference in the *Fifth Report of the Children's Employment Commission* to the way in which parents exploited their children by putting them out to work and overworking them in domestic industries, Marx writes that

it was not . . . the misuse of parental authority that created capitalistic exploitation, whether direct or indirect, of children's labour; but, on the contrary, it was the capitalistic mode of exploitation which, by sweeping away the economic base of parental authority, made its exercise degenerate into a mischievous use of power. However terrible and disgusting the dissolution under the capitalist system of the old family ties may appear, nevertheless, modern industry, by assigning as it does an important part in the process of production, outside the domestic sphere, to women and young persons, and to children of both sexes, creates a new economic foundation for a higher form of the family and of relations between the sexes.[12]

The sexual promiscuity of capitalism will be transformed by the factory system into the ethically superior free love of socialism.

Marx also thought that capitalist industrialization entailed the cultural improvement of workers. Although in its earlier stages industry cripples and stunts the worker physically and mentally, in its advanced form it requires, for its development, a highly skilled work force. According to Marx, modern industry 'by means of machinery, chemical processes and other methods . . . is continually causing changes not only in the technical basis of production, but also in the functions of the labourer . . . it necessitates variation of labour, fluency of function, universal mobility . . .'[13] The changing and increasingly demanding technical requirements which characterise modern production process mean that the inability of the ordinary labourer, deprived of access to general and technical education, to adapt himself as industry develops, is a source of waste, and the cause of technological unemployment. Such a situation, argues Marx, is unsustainable:

> *Modern Industry, indeed, compels society, under penalty of death, to replace the detail-worker of today, crippled by life-long repetition of one and the same trivial operation, and thus reduced to a mere fragment of a man, by the fully developed individual, fit for a variety of labours, ready to face any change of production, and to whom the different social functions he performs, are but so many modes of giving free scope to his own natural and acquired powers.*[14]

Socialist man is the necessary product of modern industry.

This truth was, Marx thought, anticipated by the educational provisions of the Factory Acts, which proclaimed 'elementary education to be an indispensable condition for the employment of children'.[15] Moreover, Marx considered that the education received by children employed in factories was superior to that provided privately for the children of the rich. He quotes Nassau Senior to show 'how the monotonously and uselessly long hours of the children of the upper and middle classes uselessly add to the labour of the teacher while he not only fruitlessly but absolutely injuriously, wastes the time, health, and energy of the children'.[16] Factory children, however, 'although receiving only one half the education of the regular day scholars, yet learnt quite as much and often more'.[17]

This high opinion of factory education enabled Marx to make a virtue of something which he regarded as a necessity. Because, as we have argued, Marx was cautious about the possibility of increasing productivity much beyond the level which it had already reached, he thought that, in order to maintain the necessary volume of output under socialism it would still be necessary to employ children. In 1848, the *Communist Manifesto* demanded, not the prohibition of child labour, but only its abolition 'in its present form'.[18] A quarter of a century of residence in England did not change Marx's views and in 1875 he wrote that 'A *general prohibition* of child labour is incompatible with the existence of large-scale industry and hence an empty pious wish'.[19] Indeed, such a step would be retrogressive, for 'from the Factory system budded, as Robert Owen has shown, in detail, the germ of the education of the future, an education that will, in the case of every child over a given age, combine productive labour with instruction and gymnastics, not only as one of the methods of adding to the efficiency of production, but as the only method of producing fully developed human beings'.[20] In a socialist society the employment of children in factories will be both economically inevitable and socially desirable.

The joint-stock company as a model of socialist property rights

But it was not only the productive organization of capitalism that Marx thought foreshadowed the future. He found similar clues to socialist property rights in the commercial organization and credit arrangements of bourgeois society. Writing to Engels in 1858 Marx wrote that the enterprise which was jointly owned by those subscribing for its issued shares was the most perfect form of capitalism and that this form was turning into communism.[21] The idea is not a difficult one. The formation of stock companies meant the 'transformation of the ... capitalist into a mere manager, administrator of other people's capital, and of the owner of capital into a mere owner'.[22] The functions of ownership and control are separated and in this Marx sees the anticipation of the situation in socialism in which the managers of enterprises are the servants of society and ownership is vested in the whole of the community. As he puts it, 'the stock company is a transition toward the conversion of all functions in the reproduction process which still remain linked with capitalist property, into mere functions of associated producers, into social functions ... This is the abolition of the capitalist mode of production within the capitalist mode of production itself'.[23]

Interestingly, Marx did not think that these private enterprises were less important than the various experiments in cooperative enterprises which were tried in this period. They met with varying degrees of success; in manufacturing they were largely a failure, in retailing and wholesaling they have survived to this day, although Marx thought the former more important than the latter. Marx wrote that he thought that the importance of the cooperative movement 'especially the co-operative factories ... cannot be overrated',[24] they represented 'within the old form the first sprouts of the new',[25] but considered that, with the joint-stock companies, they were equally the outcome of capitalist development:

The credit system is not only the principal basis for the gradual transformation of capitalist private enterprises into capitalist stock companies, but equally offers the means for the gradual extension of co-operative enterprises on a more or less national scale. The capitalist stock companies, as much as the co-operative factories, should be considered as transitional forms from the capitalist mode of production to the associated one.[26]

Socialism as 'transformed' capitalism

All this suggests that rather more can be said about the nature of Marx's socialist society than is sometimes supposed. It is true that he does not tell us how the socialist economy is to be controlled, although he frequently refers to the need for 'social' management. But it is very likely that, like Saint-Simon, he thought that the organization of a socialized economy would be like the internal organization of a firm. This, of course, ignores the fact that the internal operations of a firm are carried out with reference to prices continually derived from the market in which it competes. Marx does not tell us what indicators would be used in their place – and there is no evidence that he thought that this was a real problem.

Especially striking is the way in which Marx's theory of the 'transformation' of the joint-stock company lends itself so readily to a social prognosis in which capitalism might simply wither away without a revolution.

Marx's ideas also suggest that he had got no further in his thinking about socialism than had the Utopian socialists to whom he considered himself superior in theoretical achievement. His assumption that socialism would, as an economic organization, be very similar to capitalism, is very close to the ideas which they entertained. Marx acknowledges his debt to Owen, as we have seen, but he also owed much to Saint-Simon, while the gap between his ideas and those of Fourier is not wide. Even Marx's faith in the ability of man naturally and autonomously to engage in reciprocally dependent economic activity without any need for guarantees of good faith has a touch of Proudhon's anarchism.

In general, Marx's ideas about socialism as a system seem to have been arrived at in a fashion cognate with his basic theoretical approach. Marx thought that the understanding of the economic world was to be achieved by undertaking a transformational critique of political economy. This 'revealed' that labour is the true source of value and that capital accumulation was nothing less than the preparation for revolution. Similarly, he saw socialism as 'transformed' capitalism, child labour, factory system, joint-stock companies and all. But in all this Marx is trying, like the Utopian socialists, to retain the rationality, efficiency, productivity and institutional achievements of the market, while trying to escape from its individualistic and competitive assumptions. Socialism is, on this showing, not so much distinct from, as a truncated version of, 'capitalism', and as such it is still as much dependent on the assumptions of the market, as were Fourier's communes.

References

1. Karl Marx, 'Preface to "A Contribution to the Critique of Political Economy" ' in Marx Engels, *Selected Works*, vol. I, p. 363.
2. Karl Marx, 'Manifesto of the Communist Party' in ibid., vol I, p. 39

3. Karl Marx, 'A critique of the Gotha Programme' in ibid., vol. II, p. 21.
4. Capital, vol. I, p. 763.
5. Ibid.
6. Ibid.
7. Ibid., vol. I, Ch. xv, Sect. 9, p. 480.
8. Karl Marx, 'Preface to the first German edition' in *Capital*, vol. I, p. 9.
9. Ibid., vol. I, Ch. xv, Sect. 4, p. 424.
10. Ibid., vol. I, Ch. xv, Sect. 8e, p. 474.
11. Ibid., vol. I, Ch. x, Sect. 6, p. 293, n. 6.
12. Ibid., vol. I, Ch. xv, Sect. 9, pp. 489–90.
13. Ibid., vol. I, Ch. xv, Sect. 9, p. 487.
14. Ibid., vol. I, Ch. xv, Sect. 9, p. 488.
15. Ibid., vol. I, Ch. xv, Sect. 9, p. 482.
16. Ibid. p. 483.
17. Ibid.
18. Marx Engels, *Selected Works*, vol. I, p. 34.
19. Karl Marx, 'A critique of the Gotha Programme' in ibid., vol. II, p. 34.
20. *Capital*, vol. I, Ch. xv, Sect. 9, p. 484.
21. Marx to Engels, 2 April 1858, in *MEW* vol. xxix, p. 321.
22. *Capital*, vol. III, Ch. xxvii, p. 436.
23. Ibid., vol. III, Ch. xxvii, pp. 437, 438.
24. 'Inaugural address of the Working Men's International Association' (1864) in Marx Engels, *Selected Works*, vol. II, p. 383.
25. *Capital*, vol. III, Ch. xxvii, p. 440.
26. Ibid.

Chapter 16

The socialist model: Russia

In the latter part of his life Marx became interested in Russia, a country which was the very anti-type of England, economically backward, politically illiberal, socially and culturally poorly developed. As such, his interest in it, and the adaptations which his knowledge of it forced on his ideas throw into relief the main structural features of his theories. Discussed in a setting quite different from that for which they were originally designed, their fertility and subtle ambiguity emerge with greater clarity.

In order to make the nature of the debate about Marxism in Russia easier to understand, this chapter sketches the nature of Russian social and economic peculiarities and against that background examines Marx's views of the prospects for socialism in Russia. Marx's pronouncements on this issue caused theoretical difficulties for Russian Marxists. The nature of these difficulties reinforce the conclusion that Marx's assumptions about market relations and the unacknowledged role they play in his theory were more important to his ideas than the developmental problems of Russia tempted him to assert. Disappointed by the failure of capitalism to give rise to the revolutionary movements on which he had pinned his hopes in Europe, his desire to encourage Russian radicals with economic ideas significantly different from his own, led him to betray the most powerful elements in his own theory. Russian Marxists succeeded in developing a reasonably powerful 'Marxist' analysis of Russia in spite of Marx.

As we have seen, Marx emphasized that what made his political economy 'scientific' was the stress it laid on the hard and unpleasant facts of economic life as it manifested itself in the contemporaneous and industrialized world. Socialism was, paradoxically, immanent in the cruelty and inhumanity of capitalism itself. By the same token, it followed that without capitalism there could be no socialism. Indeed, writing for the Germany of the mid-nineteenth century, a politically incoherent and still predominantly agrarian country, Marx was explicit in his insistence that Germany could only achieve socialism by passing through the bourgeois stage of social development.

What was true of Germany appeared to apply with equal force to Russia. But, in the 1870s and after, Marx made a number of remarks which suggested it was possible for Russia to jump a stage of economic development and to arrive at socialism without passing through the social dislocation and misery of capitalism. This chapter is devoted to a consideration of Marx's deviation from his own fundamental teaching and to the difficulties which it caused Russian Marxists. These difficulties and the way in which they were resolved, although they take us a little beyond the strict confines of Marx's own writings, are interesting for the way in which they help to illuminate the most important insights and basic ambiguities in Marx's economic ideas.

The Russian economic dilemma

The structure of the Russian economy before the World War of 1914–18 and the Bolshevik Revolution of 1917 was quite unlike that of the industrialized or industrializing countries in Western Europe. Russia was an overwhelmingly peasant society. On the eve of the First World War only 5 per cent of its population were employed in industry. Moreover, the northerly latitude, soil, and incidence of rainfall in Russia condemned Russian agriculture to very low levels of output by comparison with the more favourably situated European States to the west. The poverty of the very large agrarian sector was the key element in a vicious circle of backwardness. Low agricultural output meant that there was little surplus available for reinvestment either in agriculture itself, or to finance industry, which might have provided more productive employment. The overall poverty of the economy was compounded by the rapid growth of the population. In 1913 the Russian population of about 170 million was increasing by about 3 million each year; that is to say, the increase in the population every two years was roughly equal to the number of those employed in industry. In terms of income per head Russia was the poorest of any major power in Europe, and, economically, was in a state of chronic crisis.

Russia was, moreover, by virtue of her geographical position, forced to play a major role in international affairs. She bordered in Europe on three empires, the Turkish, Austro-Hungarian, and German, whose territories covered an area of great political instability. The open nature of the Central and East European plain, which offered no readily defensible natural boundaries, and the problems of controlling an empire which included a large number of non-Russian subject peoples, accentuated the military needs generated by Russia's role as a great power. In the nineteenth century, as now, Russia was obliged to make defence the largest single item in the budget, and this meant that, fiscally, the government was faced with a permanent emergency – disproportionately large resources had to be exacted from an impoverished population.

Her economic problems and the consequent pressure of State demands on resources played a large part in determining the character of the Tsarist regime. Since its primary need was to extract the surplus from the peasantry in order to maintain the army and sustain the military operations in which Russia was frequently engaged in Eastern

Europe, the Caucasus and Central Asia, control and coercion were at the centre of its administrative preoccupations. Until 1861 a large part of the peasant population was unfree and the nobility, themselves mostly impoverished and culturally largely indistinguishable from the serfs they owned, played an important part in maintaining order in the countryside. But attempts by the tiny educated section of the aristocracy to secure the institutionalization of government and their own participation in political decision-making were firmly and ruthlessly resisted. The regime maintained a censorship, and parliamentary freedoms were denied. After the abortive 'revolution' of 1905 the situation changed, but, right until the fall of the Romanovs in 1917, the Tsar asserted his right to rule independently of any system of advisers, and the ministers he appointed were responsible to him and not to the pseudo-parliament set up in 1906. Until the end the Tsar remained an autocrat, autonomous and arbitrary.

In the sixty years before the Bolshevik Revolution the authorities made several concerted attempts to deal with the economic backwardness of the country. The initial impetus came from the debacle of the Crimean War (1853–55). A spate of reforms followed in the 1860s when the peasants were emancipated, the whole of the State apparatus, legal, financial and military, was overhauled and the building of railways encouraged. The increased demand for grain from the industrializing areas of Western Europe coupled with improved fiscal arrangements gradually effected a small but critical change in Russia's trade balance, and by the late 1880s Russia was on the way to establishing an industrial sector which had previously been confined to a feeble iron industry, food processing and textiles. In the 1890s the pursuit of a vigorous policy of subsidization, foreign borrowing and ruthless taxation enabled the authorities to secure an unprecedented rate of growth in industrial output, and by the outbreak of the First World War commercial relations had made appreciable inroads into an agriculture which, until the improvement of communications, had never been far removed from the conditions of a subsistence economy. Thus, by 1917, although still a poor country, Russia had seen economic innovations and changes which had no parallel in history, and made economic and social change a topic of discussion not only for radicals but also for conservative administrators and government advisers.

The Russian radical response: populism

Although the Tsarist government controlled the expression of opinion by a system of censorship, this system was at times sufficiently laxly applied to make it possible for some kind of political debate to be carried on in the press. Under Alexander II, the Tsar in whose reign from 1855–81 the administrative structure of the empire underwent a major review and reorganization, the public expression of political views was, for a time, and by Russian standards, exceptionally free. These conditions enabled a number of journalists to carry on a lively discussion, albeit in guarded terms, of the reforms prepared by the regime and the social and economic problems from which they were thought to have arisen.

The most famous of the journalists of this era, and a man who more aptly epitomizes the Russian radical tradition than any other, was Nikolai Gavrilovich Chernyshevsky (1828–89). Exiled in 1864, Chernyshevsky, who contrived to publish a novel even after he was imprisoned in 1862, produced throughout the first part of Alexander II's reign a flood of articles which set the tone for Russian radical thought until the Revolution. Only ten years younger than Marx, it is not surprising that, having been brought up on a very similar intellectual diet of Hegel, Feuerbach, the French socialists, and John Stuart Mill, Chernyshevsky should have propounded notions that were, in some respects, not very different from those typical of Marx's own ideas. There is, at all events, no evidence that he derived them from Marx.

On one particular point Chernyshevsky's analysis of economic development was very different from that offered by Marx in *Capital*. This was his belief that the very backwardness of Russia might enable her to arrive at the socialism described in the work of Western radicals, without passing through the exploitation and social degeneration which industrialization seemed to have brought to England and France. A key part was to be played in Russian development, on this view, by the survival in the Russian countryside of the communal organization of agriculture. The commune, or *obshchina*, to give it its Russian name, is of vexed origin, but in structure and function it was related to the manorial organizations of Western mediaeval agriculture. The use of primitive farming methods and the allocation of strips of the village fields required cooperation among the peasants. A time had to be agreed for harvesting and for turning out livestock into the stubble, and the fields rotated according to an agreed arrangement. The land available to the village had also to be allocated to families by need so that each household had enough land to maintain its members. In Russia it was also employed by the State as a tax device and as a means of political control, and it was used and strengthened by the authorities, especially after the Emancipation of 1861, both to ensure a supply of labour to noble farmowners and to secure the collection of the redemption payments which were imposed upon peasants as the price of their emancipation. To Chernyshevsky, however, the village commune seemed to provide a real and already existing basis onto which could be grafted the fantasies of Fourier; what, in advanced Western Europe, had yet to be constructed, was already available in the actually existing commune.

Chernyshevsky provided no account of how these communal and 'socialistic' organizations were actually to be employed for these higher purposes, nor how the autocratic State was to be transformed into one in which these communal arrangements would provide the basic structure of society. Nor was Chernyshevsky the first, as he himself pointed out, to draw attention to the commune and its possible role in avoiding capitalism. No Russian radical, however, wrote more extensively about economics, and his subsequent savage treatment by the authorities earned him the reverence of the Russian revolutionary movement as a martyr to its cause. He was greatly admired by Lenin and is still regarded by the Soviet authorities as the most important pre-Marxist thinker in Russia.

His influence helped to ensure that for a generation after he had been silenced by the regime in 1862, the most striking characteristic of Russian radical thought was the hope that Russia might achieve socialism without passing through a social and economic development analogous to that of the West. By the 1870s there was a considerable and troublesome body of Russian radicals, mostly very young, either in exile, or at foreign universities, or engaged in clandestine political activities and occasional terrorism in Russia itself. They called themselves indifferently socialists or 'populists', a coinage meant to indicate their concern for the 'people', using a word which, in the Russian context, meant, unequivocally, the peasantry. These 'populists' then, were socialists, who, unlike their orthodox and 'scientific' Marxist counterparts in the West, instead of seeing in urbanization and industrialization the path of escape from 'the idiocy of rural life',[1] sought to save the peasants from 'progress', as it was understood in England, France and Germany. For most of them, the corner-stone of their belief that Russia was destined to tread a path to socialism that was uniquely her own was constituted by the existence of the Russian field commune.

Marx and Russian populism

In *The Philosophy of History* Hegel writes off the history of the 'Slavonic nation', in which he includes the Russians, on the grounds that 'hitherto it has not appeared as an independent element in the series of phases that Reason has assumed in the World'.[2] This view of the Russians as a culturally inferior and backward people was widespread among Germans, and shared by Marx. Moreover, German radicals, like those of the rest of Western Europe, regarded the Tsar with particular hatred as the principle guarantor of the ancient regime in Eastern Europe, both within his own territory, and as a willing helper in the preservation of social order in the repressive Prussian and Habsburg Empires. Again, the Russian suppression of the Poles in 1831 and of the Hungarians in 1849 were black days in the calendar of every revolutionary. Marx had a more personal reason for a dislike of all things Russian; in 1842 Nicholas I had himself taken a hand in seeing that the Prussian authorities expelled Marx from Germany for the virulence of his attacks as a journalist on the Russian regime.

Marx's early acquaintance with radical Russian aristocrats like Herzen and Bakunin in the 1840s and 1850s only served to convince him that Russian revolutionary ideas were as backward as the culture from which they sprang. Marx's suspicion of Russian radicalism was further strengthened as a result of his bitter squabble with Bakunin and his anarchist supporters about the structure and policy of the *International Working Men's Association* which Marx helped to found in 1864. But the failure of Western Europe to fulfil its revolutionary promise, especially after the suppression of the Paris Commune in 1870, led Marx to look at the efforts of the Russian radical terrorists with a more benign eye. The First International brought him into contact with Russians whom he found more sympathetic. In 1870, some Russian exiles in Geneva formed a Russian section of the International and Marx agreed to be their representative on the General Council of the International.

It is from about this time that Marx begins to take a more serious interest in the political and economic problems of Russia. He had been pleased, and, at the same time, surprised, when, after the publication of volume I of *Capital* in German in 1867, it was widely read and reviewed in Russia. Indeed, the first language into which *Capital* was translated was Russian, and some knowledge of Marx's ideas on industrial development was part of the intellectual equipment of every Russian revolutionary for years before there was any politically organized body of Russians who could fairly be described as Marxist.

But the comparative popularity of Marx's work in Russia did not mean that those who read it understood it in the way which Marx had, at least originally, intended it to be understood. Rather, the most common approach to *Capital* was to treat it as a *description* of the process of industrialization while ignoring its pretensions as an account of the universally valid laws of socioeconomic change. Populists found it quite easy to assimilate Marx's account of the miseries of the working conditions of the British proletariat to their own *prescription* of radical and socialist change which was to be based on existing Russian agrarian institutions. Indeed, on balance, one might say that the effect on Marx of the work of populist thinkers proved to be greater than the effect of Marx on the populists themselves; it was Marx who became a populist rather than the populists who became Marxists.

Quite clearly, Marx's theory as set out in *Capital* implies that the customary and traditional social and agrarian practices of a country like Russia, constituted a 'feudal' system doomed to be supplanted by the 'capitalism' of railways and industry; according to the Marx of 1867 the populists' hope of an alternative path of development for the Russian economy was without substance. In 1875, however, Engels, who was in general less inclined to make concessions to Russian radical theories than was Marx himself, published an article in which he was less than categorical in his dismissal of their views. The general point he has to make is a hostile one and he declared that 'communal ownership in Russia is long past its period of florescence and to all appearances is moving towards its disintegration',[3] but the saving force of the phrase 'to all appearances' is later strengthened by the admission that 'the possibility undeniably exists of raising this form of society to a higher one, if it should last until circumstances are right for that . . . without it being necessary for the Russian peasants to go through the intermediate stage of bourgeois small holdings'.[4] According to this line of argument the principal precondition for avoiding 'the intermediate stage' was that there should be a proletarian revolution in the West the leaders of which would then be able to assist materially in the establishment of socialism in Russia. This relatively cautious attitude was reinforced in a piece signed by both Marx and Engels in 1882 in which they asked

Can the Russian obshchina, *though greatly undermined, yet a form of the primaeval common ownership of land pass directly to the higher form of communist common ownership? Or on the contrary, must it first pass through the same process of dissolution such as constituted the historical evolution of the West?*

The only answer to that possible today is this: if the Russian Revolution becomes the signal for a proletarian revolution in the West, so that both complement each other, the present Russian common ownership of land may serve as the starting point for a communist development.[5]

In 1877 Nikolai Konstantinovich Mikhailovsky (1842–1904), the most important of contemporary Russian radical journalists, and a man on whom, in some sense, Chernyshevsky's mantle had fallen, attacked Marx for his 'theory of fatal historical inevitability'. Mikhailovsky held that to subscribe to Marx's views obliged a Russian to view with indifference the social cost which industrialization had imposed on the working population of the United Kingdom and which the same process, was even then, through the construction of railways, beginning to exact from the Russian people. In a reply (not in fact published until 1886) Marx went even further in the revision of his earlier teaching, claiming that he had not been properly understood. He pointed out that in the second German edition of *Capital* of 1873 he had referred to Chernyshevsky as 'the great Russian scholar and critic' and as a 'master mind'[6] and declared that

In order to be able to assess the economic development of Russia on the basis of sound factual knowledge, I learnt Russian and for many years studied the relevant official and other publications. The conclusion which I have reached is this: if Russia continues on the path which it has taken since 1861[7] *then it will miss the finest opportunity ever afforded by history to a people, and therefore will be obliged to go through all the disastrous vicissitudes of the capitalist system.*[8]

Of course, wrote Marx,

If Russia strives to become a capitalist nation after the Western European pattern – and in recent years she has been at great pains to move in this direction – she will not achieve this without first transforming a good part of her peasants into proletarians; and then, once sucked into the maelstrom of the capitalist economy, she will have to submit to the inexorable laws of this system just like other mundane peoples.[9]

But Mikhailovsky was wrong, claims Marx, in trying 'To change my historical sketch of western European capitalist development into an historiosophical theory of the universal process of development'.[10]

It will be recalled (see Chapter 2) that in *Capital* Marx had argued that capitalism was to be distinguished from commercialization and had pointed out that the existence of a propertyless proletariat had produced in Rome not the institutions characteristic of the modern world but slavery instead. He now deployed these arguments again and came to the somewhat obscure conclusion that

Events of striking similarity, but which are played out in different historical circumstances, thus lead to quite different results. If these developments are studied for themselves and then compared with each other the key to these phenomena is easily found, but not by using the universal key of a general historiosophical theory of which the chief virtue lies in its suprahistoricity.[11]

In other words, while refusing to commit himself, Marx made it quite clear that he was not prepared to exclude the possibility of the correctness of populist hopes and predictions – ideas that he once dismissed as 'Utopian'.

But in 1882, just two years before his death, Marx went even further in his apostacy from his own doctrines. A number of populists including Georgii Valentinovich Plekhanov (1856–1918), who was to become the most authoritative of Russian Marxist thinkers, had become disillusioned with populist ideas, convinced that the peasants lacked the inclination and the commune the viability necessary for a social revolution of the kind Chernyshevsky had hoped for. From Geneva, Vera Zasulich, a terrorist with a famous attempted assassination of a Russian police chief to her credit, wrote on behalf of a number of her colleagues to Marx for advice:

You know better than anyone else, how extraordinarily pressing this question is in Russia . . . especially for our socialist party . . . Recently we have often heard it said that the village commune is the archaic form which history . . . has condemned to extinction. Those who hold forth in this fashion call themselves your pupils in the truest meaning of the word: 'Marxists'. . . . You will, therefore, Citizen, understand how much your opinion on this question interests us and what a great service you

would do us if you were to set out your views on the possible fate of our
village commune and on the theory of historical necessity, which states
that all the countries of the world must pass through all the phases of
capitalist production.[12]

Marx spent some time trying to compose a satisfactory answer to this
letter, and four drafts, three of them much longer than the final version
as actually sent, are extant. What he finally told Zasulich was that a
'nervous illness' prevented him from providing a full and publishable
explanation but that he hoped that a few lines would be sufficient to
clear her mind of any doubt about 'the misunderstanding of my so
called theory'.[13] He goes on to identify the origins of capitalism with the
expropriation of the peasantry. He claims, however, that in the French
translation of *Capital* (1875), which he has personally supervised, the
'historical inevitability' of capitalism is expressly limited to Western
Europe.[14]

Chernyshevsky had argued, in an article with which Marx was
familiar,[15] with direct reference to Hegel's ideas about the dialectical
nature of progress, that, in general, social development was one of a
transition from the archaic form of communal ownership to the modern
form of private ownership, and that the triad of advance would be
completed by the socialistic reinstatement of common ownership.

As far as Russia was concerned, his argument that it was possible to
omit the stage of private ownership, or capitalism, lay in the fact that the
archaic form still survived in Russia and would therefore need little
adjustment to conform to the needs of socialism. In a passage
reminiscent of this and other populist arguments, Marx went further
than he had gone before and now abandoned the idea that a socialist
revolution in the West was a precondition for the transformation of
Russia. 'In the West', he wrote,

the problem was one of changing from one form of private ownership to
another form of private ownership.[16] *But when it came to the Russian*
peasant the question was, on the contrary, that of changing their
common ownership into private ownership.

The analysis in Capital *thus provides no proof – either for or against*
the viability of the village commune, but the special research which I
have made into this subject and for which I obtained original source
material, has convinced me that these village communes constitute a
fulcrum for the regeneration of Russia: but in order that they may
operate in this way, they must first be freed from the disruptive
influences, which are attacking it from all sides and the normal
conditions for their natural development secured.[17]

The 'disruptive influences' were those advanced by his populist friends,
fiscal pressure from the government, and, a paradox in the mouth of
Marx, the competitive pressures of the market being built up by the
construction of railways. The degree to which Marx's ideas had

diverged from those of his followers is powerfully illustrated in one of the drafts of his letter to Zasulich, where he writes, 'The Russian "Marxists" of whom you speak are quite unknown to me. The Russians with whom I am personally acquainted, have, as far as I know, quite opposite views'.[18]

Thus Vera Zasulich and her group of friends, who were to form the first organized group of Russian Marxists, started with a cold douche from Marx himself. The letter of Zasulich was not published until 1924 so that the degree to which Plekhanov and the Group for the Emancipation of Labour might be said to have been publicly discouraged is not to be exaggerated. Nonetheless, Russian populists certainly felt no hesitation in describing themselves as socialists and they had the authority of Marx himself for so doing. When Marx died in 1883, Russian socialism was a tangled skein of ideas, and it took a fierce debate to reinstate a 'classical' Marxist interpretation of the Russian economic situation.

Russian populists and Russian Marxists: Danielson and Struve

The most important of the radical populist economists was Nikolai Francisovich Danielson (1844–1918). It was Danielson who was principally responsible for the translation of *Capital* into Russian, an enterprise which had brought him close contact and friendship with Marx himself. It was his book, *Sketches of our Post-Reform Economy* (1893), which sparked off the Russian debate on Marxism which was to rescue it from the confused state in which it had been left by Marx's last exchanges with his Russian friends.

After the reforms of Alexander II, most of which were implemented in the 1860s, the authorities successfully, albeit expensively, encouraged the steady expansion of the railway system, and with it the development of a weak but significant industrial sector. Successive ministers of finance gradually improved the fiscal system and by the late 1880s heavy indirect taxation combined with the improved transport system was beginning to squeeze out the surplus from the peasantry more effectively than ever before. In 1891 and 1892 famine, in any case endemic in an impoverished agrarian economy, struck Russia with particular force, and there were widespread epidemics of typhus which attracted world-wide interest and concern. Danielson's book aroused a great deal of attention because it offered a coherent analytical account of Russia's economic problems, in particular attributing the famine to the fatal weakening of Russian agriculture which has been brought about by the inroads of capitalism.

The first part of Danielson's book had been published as an article in 1880; Marx read and approved of it. Some of the ideas which Marx was turning over in his mind when he was drafting his letter to Zasulich were taken from Danielson's essay. Danielson's book contains many turns of phrase taken from Marx himself and it is easy to see why Danielson should have thought himself a Marxist even though his conclusions were so different from those of Marx's *Capital*. Danielson's argument was that the imperial government was pursuing two contradictory policies. On the one hand, the arrangements for the emancipation of the peasants in 1861, had, through the *obshchina* ensured that the means of production, the land, remained in the hands of the producers, the peasants. On the other hand the government, by taking the peasantry and using the proceeds to encourage capitalism, was creating conditions which, by commercializing relations in the countryside, would destroy that security for the peasant which, according to the Imperial Decree of 1861, the emancipation of the peasants was designed to achieve. Independent producers were being put out of business, and forced to hire themselves out to others as the means of production became concentrated in a smaller number of hands. But, instead of leading to the development of the economy on Western lines, the result of all this could only, according to Danielson, be disastrous. The industry which the government was promoting by subsidies was not able to compete with the foreign industries established before them. They were unable to count on foreign markets for success and were thus obliged to turn to the internal market. But part of the prosperity of the Russian peasant, such as it was, depended on the fact that, apart from agriculture, which the climate only allowed him to pursue for six months of the year, he also engaged in the hand production of many items of domestic consumption, shoes, eating utensils, agricultural tools and so on. The new industries, however, lowered the amount of 'socially necessary labour time' embodied in these products so that the peasants were unable to compete with the output of the new factories. The cheapness of the newly marketed goods therefore impoverished the peasants who were driven to cultivate the soil even more intensely in order to compensate in some measure for the fall in their income. This simply led to the impoverishment of the soil and crop failures of the kind witnessed in 1891 and 1892. In this way the new industries actually destroyed the market on which they depended and therefore were based on a contradiction which could only bring ruin on the entire economy. Danielson, in short, was an underconsumptionist and, as such, an inheritor of that tradition of radical political economy initiated by Sismondi. It is not surprising, therefore, that Marx should have sympathized with his views.

Danielson's antagonist in the ensuing debate, and the man who did more than any other to reinstate Marx's original teaching and a non-populist analysis of Russia's economy was Peter Bernhardovich Struve (1870–1944). Struve was a brilliant if mercurial young intellectual whose career was to take him from Marxism to liberalism and later to a renewed belief in the teaching of the Russian Orthodox Church. But in the 1890s he was one of the moving spirits in a semi-public debate on the economic development of Russia half-tolerated by the authorities, partly because the Marxists seemed to suggest that the government's policy of forced industrialization which was now beginning to produce unprecedented rates of economic growth, was a highly desirable one. In his review of Danielson's book Struve mounted a whole-scale attack on the populist idea that there was some other way of reaching socialism than through capitalism. He identified the ideas of Danielson and those who thought like him with the Utopian socialism attacked by Marx in the *Communist Manifesto*. Their analysis, wrote Struve,

represents an idealization of the peasant natural economy and of communal ownership. This national socialism was and remains decidedly utopian in character. What are the forces on which it relies – the much vaunted 'communal spirit' of the peasantry and the socialist sympathies of a small band of representatives of the intelligentsia – compared to those forces that are released by the absolutely unavoidable transition from a natural economic organization to the money economy?[19]

In 1894 Struve presented his views in more extended form in a book entitled *Critical Remarks on the Question of Russia's Economic Development*. The key to Struve's application of Marxism to Russia was in his examination of Marx's notion of 'capitalism'. As we have emphasized, Marx tried, unpersuasively, to distinguish between the market as the motor of economic change and some other, less clearly specified, force which he thought to be embodied in the sociological conditions of a given epoch. As we have shown, in spite of his explicit denials of the fact, his analysis rested on assumptions drawn from the market, and the nature of 'capitalism' is nowhere fully explained. Struve goes straight to the root of the matter and writes that political economy is '. . . unthinkable without exchange: *it appears only together with exchange, the further development of which to a significant extent determines all the other aspects of politico-economic life'.*[20]

Struve does not reduce capitalism to the market in quite the reductionist manner which we have proposed in the second chapter, but he is quite clear that it is exchange relations which are fundamental to social change and that capitalism is, in spite of Marx, simply itself a product of them. In a section of the third chapter of his book specifically devoted to the meaning of the word, he tries to suggest that, if it is to have any use as a term, it must be something narrower than simply the 'commodity economy', 'i.e. modern mass production of goods mainly for distant and undefined markets'.[21] On the other hand, capitalist production, understood as 'the economic and technical centralization of heavy industry with the general application of basic capital – machinery – and with a considerable number of workers employed in every undertaking . . . represents . . . the highest point of the commodity economy'.[22]

The reason for Struve's hesitancy is that he is opposing Danielson's own reduction of capitalism to the market[23] because he wants to make it clear that the first pains of monetization and commercialization of relations in the countryside are not all that there is to capitalism. Struve notes that the propensity to identify heavy industry and the existence of a large proletariat with capitalism, and at the same time to equate the latter with the monetization of the economy leads to the belief that commercialization makes no sense without the existence of the kind of commercial and industrial achievements typical of Western Europe. The part is mistaken for the whole by the populists, who are then able to claim that the introduction of railways and the intensification of monetary relations is without a proper economic foundation in Russia. Struve's point is that the exchange economy is a dynamic system and that its development must be encouraged to reach the capitalistic stage – which he sees as a loose term simply denoting advanced industrial-ization. To drive the point home he makes it quite clear that socialism itself 'is only practicable in so far as it reproduces capitalism in negative terms'.[24] For a socialist

capitalism ... means the whole contemporary economic structure, based on the private ownership of the land and the means of production and founded on the principle of economic freedom: and socialism is conceived as a similar socio-economic order in which the opposite principles are realized: no private ownership of land or the means of production, production itself is socialized and distribution regulated.[25]

'The existence of socialism', writes Struve, 'is bound up with capitalism'.[26]

The populists then, had argued, with Marx's support, that the introduction of monetized exchange relations which they identified with capitalism could only lead to disaster. Struve pointed out that Marx's ambiguous remarks (he did not know about Marx's letter to Zasulich), in his letter replying to Mikhailovsky, dated from the end of the 1870s, that economic development had gone much further since then, that railways had been built, a protectionist policy established, and that a crisis had developed in agriculture. There was now no going back: 'From the moment that the railways had been revealed as a factor in socio-economic evolution superior to that of the critically thinking intelligentsia and even – alas – the *obshchina*, from that moment, to prolong the debate about the economic development of Russia, relying on Marx's letter, was pointless.'[27] Struve is able to cite Engels specifically in support of this argument so suggesting that Marx's letter was of less than general significance.[28] With the market re-established, and capitalism identified with the intense development of the exchange economy, the way was clear for the propogation of a Marxist analysis of the economic development of Russia.

Lenin's economic ideas

As we have already indicated, Struve was not the first Russian seriously to try to adapt Marxism to the analysis of the peculiar economic conditions prevailing in Russia. Vera Zasulich's colleague, Plekhanov, was in fact the first to do so, in an attack on populist ideas published abroad in 1884. But it was Struve's enthusiasm which aroused interest in Marxism and which helped to bring the ideas of Plekhanov and others to a wider audience than they had hitherto enjoyed. Among the younger urban intelligentsia some sort of Marxism was almost *de rigeur* by the turn of the century.

One of those who came into the ambit of Struve's influence was Vladimir Ilyich Ulyanov (1870–1924), better known by his revolutionary pseudonym, Lenin. Struve and Lenin had an uneasy but extensive friendship which was only terminated with the former's defection to liberalism at the end of the decade. Until then Struve did a great deal to encourage Lenin, supplying him with translation work and books when the latter was arrested and exiled to Siberia until 1900. Lenin's most important academic production, *The Development of Capitalism in Russia* (1899), was read and corrected by Struve in proof, and its title was also Struve's idea. In fact, the book itself appears to have been one which Struve himself intended to write as a sequel to his *Critical Remarks*. At all events, Lenin's effort is an amplification of Struve's thinking about the development of the commercialization of Russian agriculture.

Lenin's message was that the populists' struggle against capitalism was hopeless because it was already established among the peasantry. Struve's logic-chopping about the exact nature of capitalism is simplified again into the market and Lenin declares that ' "The internal market" for capitalism is created by the development of capitalism itself, which deepens the social division of labour and differentiates the direct producers into capitalists and workers. The degree to which the internal market is developed is the degree to which capitalism has developed in the country'.[29]
He wrote that Russia in an important economic sense is *not* backward; capitalism has arrived already;

The structure of socio-economic relations among the peasantry . . . displays the presence of all those contradictions, which are peculiar to every commodity economy and to every capitalist economy: competition, the struggle for economic independence, the bidding up of land prices (for sale and rent), the concentration of production in the hands of a minority, the squeezing out of the majority into the ranks of the proletariat, and their exploitation by trading capital and the hiring of workers.[30]

Lenin claims that the commercialization of agriculture creates not merely a 'differentiation' of the peasants into richer and poorer, but leads to the creation of Marxist classes, a rural proletariat and a rural bourgeoisie, 'a class of commodity producers ... and a class of agricultural hired labourers'.[31] The *obshchina* is not an alternative to capitalism but is simply eaten up by it, as, he notes, Marx himself had predicted.

Lenin's book, which represents several years' hard work on the statistics which were becoming more and more copious at this period, is well documented and represents a very considerable contribution to the understanding of changes in the Russian agricultural sector. But from then until his death in 1924 Lenin's writings offer no serious advance on Marx's economic ideas. Even after the October Revolution what he has to say about technology, or planning, amounts to little more than a series of slogans.

Underlying these slogans, however, are some assumptions which, in the light of what we have had to say about the ambiguity of Marx's own economic ideas, will perhaps seem not so surprising. In August and September 1917, in the midst of the political turmoil of the period immediately preceding the October Revolution, Lenin found time to produce a pamphlet called *The State and Revolution*. In it he sets out his ideas on economic organization and control in the socialist stage. From Marx's *Critique of the Gotha Programme* he deduces that the structures of capitalism are more durable than a socialist might be expected to suppose: 'under communism there remains for a time not only bourgeois right, but even the bourgeois state, without the bourgeoisie'.[32]

Eventually this bourgeois state, i.e. the institutions inherited from the capitalist era, will wither away because, according to Lenin, the socialist discipline which is to be enforced in the immediate aftermath of the socialist revolution by armed workers will be internalized by all citizens and develop into habitual behaviour which it will no longer be necessary to police. But the point to be made here is that Lenin's socialist society even after the State has withered away still looks very much like capitalist society – as it does in Marx. Lenin has no distinctive ideas about how to proceed beyond it. In fact, according to him, the problem is simple, because the solution has been prepared by capitalism itself;

Accounting and control – that is mainly *what is needed for the 'smooth working', for the proper functioning of the* first phase *of communist society.* All *citizens are transformed into hired employees of the state, which consists of the armed workers.* All *citizens become employees and workers of a* single *country-wide 'syndicate'. All that is required is that they should work equally, do their proper share of work, and get equal pay. The accounting and control necessary for this have been* simplified *by capitalism to the utmost and reduced to the extra-ordinarily simple operations – which any literate person can perform – of supervising and recording, knowledge of the four rules of arithmetic and issuing appropriate receipts.*[33]

Lenin had a vision of the capitalist society as something simply controlled and managed by a skein of financial threads; and it was those financial threads, the apparatus of capitalism, which were to serve socialist purposes – indeed, were vital to them:

Capitalism has created an accounting apparatus *in the shape of the banks, syndicates, postal service, consumers' societies, and office employees' unions.* Without big banks socialism would be impossible.

The big banks are the 'state apparatus' which we need *to bring about socialism, and which we take* ready-made *from capitalism; our task here is merely to* lop off *what* capitalistically mutilates *this excellent apparatus, to make it* even bigger, *even more democratic, even more comprehensive . . . A single State Bank, the biggest of the big, with branches in every rural district, in every factory, will constitute as much as nine-tenths of the* socialist *apparatus. This will be country-wide book-keeping, country-wide accounting of the production and distribution of goods, this will be, so to speak, something in the nature of the skeleton of socialist society.*[34]

He even goes so far as to suggest that the ownership of the means of production is not as important as the way in which income is distributed: 'The important thing will not be even the confiscation of the capitalists' property, but country-wide, all-embracing workers' control over the capitalists and their possible supporters. Confiscation alone leads nowhere . . . Instead of confiscation we could easily impose a *fair tax.*'[35]

Thus on the very morrow of the revolution Lenin was proposing that nationalization should be less than complete and that an income tax would be enough to ensure the establishment of socialism – a view which does not differ essentially from that held by modern European social democrats.

In short, Lenin seems to have thought that the Bolshevik revolution would simply lead to the passing into the hands of the party of the market economy as a going concern. This view may have been naive – but it is one for which, as we have seen, there is extensive support in the works of Marx himself.

Soviet economic policy 1917 to 1929

In our discussion of Lenin we have already strayed some way from the consideration of Marx's text. However, for the sake of completeness, and because it illuminates the structure underlying Marx's thought, this section and the next will deal briefly with the relationship between Marxism and Soviet economic policy until Stalin's establishment of the modern Soviet command economy beginning with his forced collectivization in 1929.

The Civil War appeared to belie all Lenin's optimistic suppositions about the ease with which the economic apparatus of the Russian Empire could be taken over by a handful of revolutionaries. The period from 1917 to 1920 was one in which Russia was hardly governed at all and the Soviet regime, fighting for its very existence against internal resistance and Allied intervention, fell back in its economic policy onto the impoverisation and direct requisitioning which war demands. Industrial production collapsed, city dwellers fled to the countryside, markets withered away, and food for the army and the towns was sequestered by force. The Soviet authorities, making a virtue of necessity, abandoned the use of money, abolished the central banking apparatus, and embellished their series of heroic makeshift measures – payment in kind, the use of the army to get in the harvest – with the title of War Communism. In the euphoria which attended their success over the Whites, many even came to believe that the moneyless system of direct and forcible control which had enabled the Bolsheviks to survive the war could be rendered permanent. But by 1920 the country was exhausted and the peasants responded to sequestration by simply refusing to sow more than was sufficient for their own needs.

In 1921 market relations were reintroduced, and state-owned enterprises put onto a commercial footing. Much of retailing was in private hands and the largest sector of the economy, agriculture, remained privately owned. Lenin abandoned any belief that he may have harboured about the possibility of a great leap forward and referred constantly, in the years immediately preceding his death in 1924, to the need to run the economy commercially, to foster efficiency and to look to the United States as a country whose business methods were to be emulated. He died knowing that socialism had not yet been established in Russia.

Along with the re-establishment of internal markets, the Soviet Union sought commercial contacts abroad and concluded an Anglo-Soviet trade agreement. In 1924 an extensive and successful effort was made to reform and stabilize the currency and the rouble was backed by gold and made convertible. In 1924, Sokolnikov, the People's Commissar for Finance, referring to the stabilization of currencies which was taking place throughout central Europe at that time, even claimed that 'We, as members of a European whole, notwithstanding all the peculiarities of our political position, notwithstanding that with us a different class is in power, have been drawn into this European mechanism of economic and financial development'.[36]

It is true that, in this period, there was extensive and important discussion about the nature and extent of economic planning and the first efforts were made to establish the relationships between the economic variables which would determine the rate of growth. But even the first Five Year Plan which was drawn up in this period relied heavily on market relationships and price manipulation rather than direct allocation and, although the Five Year Plans were to be brandished as slogans by Stalin in the 1930s, they were never implemented, but were simply the cover for the improvised measures of forced industrialization and agricultural dragooning reminiscent of the Civil War which were introduced by Stalin in 1929. Until that point, the Soviet economy was one in which market relations predominated; the road to socialism still appeared to lie through the development of some sort of capitalism. This was not to say, of course, that the survival of the market was viewed by the Soviet authorities with anything other than regret; the point is that their doctrines provided them with no clear workable alternative.

Stalin and Marx

In 1929, Stalin, having broken the back of left-wing opposition to himself within the Communist Party, embarked on a new and violent economic policy in the course of which he also disposed of the right-wing elements in the party whose support he had hitherto enjoyed. The exact motivation of Stalin's policies remain enigmatic; they need not concern us here. In general, it was clear that the kind of incentives provided by the market for the peasants, given the expensive nature of the goods provided by Russian industry, and the unpropitious state of world trade, meant that the resources provided by the agricultural sector were insufficient to enable the Soviet economy to grow at the speed which her international position and Bolshevik ambition demanded. Stalin's policy of collectivization, or the re-enserfment of the peasantry, and his decision to force industrialization by dint of political pressure, terror, and direct physical control, can be described as a radical departure from Lenin's New Economic Policy. 1929 marks a greater caesura in Russian history than does 1917. For the first time since the emancipation of the peasants in 1861, except for the period of crisis after the First World War, the Russian government abandoned the market as the chief institution of economic development.

It has often been contended that Marx's economic ideas have little or no connexion with the practice of the Soviet Union. The fundamental importance of market concepts to the Marxist analysis suggests that this is too sweeping a dismissal of the practice of Lenin's New Economic Policy. But how is Marx, except by virtue of his Utopian ideas of substantive justice, to be connected with the voluntarism and savagery of economic development, with its slave labour camps and decimation of the peasantry, in Russia in the 1930s? Was it only cynicism and hypocrisy that allowed Stalin to claim that his actions were legitimized by *Capital*?

This is not the place to examine this problem in detail – this is a book about Marx, not Soviet economics. But one or two points should be made. In particular, the extraordinary readiness with which Marxist analyses were applied to the new Soviet departure in economic management is perhaps to be attributed to the 'double-vision' of Marx's economic insight discussed in Chapter 14.

In the 1930s the Soviet Union was, as it still is, heavily dependent on its agricultural sector; the harvest was and is the factor which vitally affects all economic activity. In spite of the industrialization drive before the First World War the economy still possessed, in the shape of a rudimentary railway network and the basic elements of a metal industry, only a bare framework for future growth.

After the Revolution of 1917 the Bolshevik leaders had seen their role as one of holding the line until the proletarian insurrection had achieved the overthrow of the bourgeois governments of Western Europe. Their hopes that the Soviet economy would be helped and transformed by large injections of capital and technical assistance from well-disposed and socialist-controlled industrial economies gradually faded as stability and order reasserted themselves in post-war Germany. By 1924 it was quite clear that socialism would have to be constructed 'in one country' without outside help; the Russians looked inwards. Most Russians were peasants – only the peasants could provide the resources for the creation of an industrial and proletarian Soviet Union. In the earnest debates on the future of the Soviet economy which marked the mid-1920s, discussion hinged on this point – how could the agricultural sector be induced to produce and transfer to the feeble industrial sector the raw materials and food needed to improve the rate of growth?

The New Economic Policy of market incentives failed because the peasants, in effect, were on strike. At the prices offered they were simply not prepared to market their output in the required quantities. The income they would have derived from their sales was too small in terms of what they could buy with it from the inefficient industrial sector; the peasants preferred to eat their own output rather than exchange it for shoddy goods. The peasants' failure to respond was, from the point of view of the Soviet economic administration, an implicit condemnation of the market as an institution. Price-induced exchanges would not correspond with the real delivery of resources required from the agricultural sector. When the market failed, the Soviet government brought about by force what the spontaneous calculation of self-interest by the Russian peasant had thwarted.

The political economists' vision of a truth hidden behind the veil of money now became an actuality – the economy was disconnected from market forces, both domestic and foreign. Resources were allocated and distributed internally largely by direct command and external trade carried on mainly by barter. The currency and the banking system became matters of secondary importance. Prices ceased to reflect relative scarcities, especially with respect to industrial supplies, and were used, either as accounting devices or else, quite crudely, to tax the wage-earner by setting them so as to bleed off surplus cash in the pockets of consumers. Economic initiative was reserved for the central authorities and taken in terms of what were considered in Moscow to be the most pressing social and national needs; values were fixed and imputed by planners as political decisions, not derived from the market.

Marx's writings could be used to sanction the management of the economy in this way for a number of reasons. First, Marx's economic thought is suffused with the unexamined assumption that economic progress is identical with mechanization and urbanization. He has comparatively little to say about agriculture. His long discussion of land rent[37] is designed to show only that it should not be considered as a category distinct from the surplus value produced in industry – indeed, it is, according to Marx, derived from it. As far as agricultural organization was concerned, Marx merely supposed that it would be assimilated to that of industry with regimented armies of labourers working the land like a disciplined factory labour force. The peasants were a doomed class and the establishment of capitalism entailed their extinction. There was nothing in Marx to suggest that Stalin's suppression and exploitation of the peasantry and his recruitment of them to the industrial and urban work force was anything more than forcing the pace of a natural and inevitable process.

Secondly, Marx's treatment of the price and market mechanism as the mere reflex of more fundamental economic processes encouraged the unsophisticated belief among socialists that the proper disposition of resources is something easily achieved and that it requires not very sophisticated apparatus. There is no proper price theory in Marx and there is no discussion of the nature or effect of governmental monetary or fiscal policy. Nor, again, does Marx give any real thought to international trade and the effects which two or more economies engaged in exchange exert on each other. In striving for economic autarchy Stalin would have found no discouragement in the economic doctrines of Marx.

Stalin's Russia brings the history of Marx's economic ideas full circle. Marx had started the analysis of capitalism by seeing it as a vast mass of goods offered for sale in the market, changing hands against money. He had used political economy to get at the basic elements in the structure of production and exchange. In doing so he had penetrated to a world which was poor in capital, rich in labour and in which exchange was the residual and secondary effect of these factors – the world of late eighteenth- and early nineteenth-century England. In this economy, against a background of relatively stagnant and increasingly inadequate agriculture, strenuous efforts were being made to mobilize the population, to drive it into the towns, and to set it to producing the capital which would allow for the reproduction of the system by providing yet more employment for yet more labourers. It was an economy which was industrializing but which was not yet industrialized. As such, seen from the vantage point of the 1860s in England or the 1930s in Russia, it was an underdeveloped economy racked by the *need* to develop.

Marx had drawn his inspiration from writers whose work was based on the characteristics of an economy as yet fundamentally undisturbed by the Industrial Revolution. He had used their ideas to analyse a productive system which, two or three generations later, had been transformed by the steam-engine and mechanical engineering. Paradoxically, but unsurprisingly, he had carried over enough of the assumptions of Smith and Ricardo into *Capital* to make it possible to find his economic ideas apposite in a country which was, as was the Great Britain of 1776 in relation to the economic achievements of the nineteenth century, underdeveloped.

References and Notes

1. Karl Marx, 'Manifesto of the Communist Party' in Marx Engels, *Selected Works,* vol. I, p. 38.
2. Hegel, *The Philosophy of History*, p. 350.
3. Frederick Engels, 'On social relations in Russia' in Marx Engels, *Selected Works*, vol. II, p. 54.
4. Ibid.
5. Preface to the Russian edition of *The Communist Manifesto of 1882* in *Communist Manifesto. Socialist Landmark. A new appreciation written for the Labour Party by Harold J. Laski, together with the original text and prefaces* (London, 1948), George Allen and Unwin, p. 104.
6. *Capital*, vol. I, p. 15.
7. The date of Alexander II's proclamation of the emancipation of the Russian serfs.
8. Marx Engels, *MEW*, vol. XIX, p. 108.
9. Ibid., vol. XIX, p. 111.
10. Ibid.
11. Ibid., vol. XIX, p. 112.
12. Ibid.
13. Marx to Vera Ivanovna Zasulich, 8 March 1881, in ibid., vol. XXV, p. 166.
14. Ibid., vol. XXXV, p. 166. In fact in the French translation, while the expression 'Western Europe' is used, it is not *expressly* limited to that part of the world.
15. N. G. Chernyshevsky, 'Kritika filosofskikh preubezhdenii protiv obshchinnogo vladeniya' in *Polnoe Sobranie Sochinenii*, vol. IV. (Petrograd 1918) pp. 304–333.
16. Note again the preoccupation with ownership rather than technological forms. Chernyshevsky's argument is similar.
17. Marx Engels, *MEW*, vol. XXXV, p. 167.
18. Ibid., vol. XIX, p. 397.
19. P. B. Struve, 'Zur Beurtheilung der Kapitalischen Entwickelung Russlands', *Socialpolitisches centralblatt*, vol. 3, No. 1, (October 2,

1893) pp. 1–3. Cited in R. Pipes, *Struve, Liberal on the Left, 1870–1905* Harvard University Press (Cambridge, Mass. 1970), p. 90.

20. P. B. Struve, *Kriticheskie zametki k voprosu ob ekonomicheskom razvitie Rossii* (St. Petersburg 1894), p. 74. Italics in original.
21. Ibid., p. 126.
22. Ibid.
23. Danielson writes quite simply 'A money economy is a commodity economy which in turn is a capitalist economy'. See *Ocherki nashevo poreformennovo obshchestvennovo khozyaistva* (St Petersburg 1893), pp. 70–1.
24. Struve, op. cit., p. 128.
25. Ibid.
26. Ibid.
27. Ibid., p. 180.
28. Ibid., p. 180, n. 1.
29. V. I. Lenin, *Razvitie kapitalizma v Rossii, Polnoe Sobranie Sochinenii*, 5th edn (Moscow 1971) vol. III, p. 60.
30. Ibid., vol. III, p. 165.
31. Lenin read Marx very carefully and his knowledge and understanding of his writings is undoubtedly the greatest single factor in the filiation of Marxism in the Soviet Union. And, in spite of a certain creative attitude towards the 'political' implications of Marx's work, even Lenin's pamphlet on imperialism *(Imperialism, the Highest Stage of Capitalism; A Popular Outline*, Petrograd 1917) is little more than an adaption of work by Hobson, Hilferding and Bukharin and has no direct relevance to the domestic economic problems of Russia discussed in this chapter.
32. V. I. Lenin, 'The State and Revolution' in *Selected Works* 3 vols. (Moscow 1967), Progress Publishers, vol. II, p. 343.
33. Ibid., vol. II, p. 345.
34. V. I. Lenin 'Can the Bolsheviks retain State Power' in *ibid.*, vol. II, pp. 397–8.
35. Ibid., vol. II, p. 399.
36. Sokolnikov, *Sotsialisticheskoe khozyaistvo*, No. 5, 1924, p. 6. Quoted in E. H. Carr, *A History of Soviet Russia*, vol. IV *The Interregnum 1923–1924*, p. 125.
37. See *Capital*, vol. III, Part VI, 'Transformation of surplus-profit into ground-rent'.

Epilogue

In this book I have maintained that Marx's work is

(a) an attempt to give a total and coherent account of the whole world, physical and social, in defiance of the philosophical assertion that mind and matter are mutually exclusive;

(b) the development of a theory derived from Hegel and Feuerbach according to which 'scientific' theories like those of Adam Smith are merely the epiphenomena of the material world, so that political economy can be read as an account, albeit distorted, of the 'real' laws of social development;

(c) the application of this theory in an attempt to 'decompose' market relationships so as to establish the nature of the 'real' phenomena which lie behind the superficial manifestations of exchange and price;

(d) in particular, the dissection of political economy in order to show that the labour theory of value is both a theory of price and also a disguised theory of exploitation and, similarly, that the law of the declining rate of profit is simultaneously the explanation of the trend of capital accumulation and a concealed theory of revolution

Put in this way the relevance of Marx's theories to the world of the twentieth century may appear to be obscure. But the purpose of trying to relate Marx more securely to the intellectual tradition within which he wrote is to make it easier to approach what is otherwise a very esoteric text and hence facilitate a surer grasp of the elements of the great analytical engine which he constructed; without such an understanding no confident assessment of modern Marxism can be made nor will the perennial fascination of Marxism be understood.

The history of posthumous Marxism and a detailed account of its intellectually generative power in economics and politics as disparate as those of, say, Cuba, France and China, would require a preliminary discussion of the economic, social and cultural background of these places at a length for which even one more book would hardly be sufficient. Here I wish only to touch on the central notion underlying all kinds of Marxism, a notion which, as I have argued in this book, forms the core of Marx's own ideas.

The crux of Marx's teaching is to be found in his critique of commercialized society. It is this which ensures its continued attraction for both mature economies and as yet incompletely developed countries. As I have argued, it is misleading to see Marx as an account of 'capitalism' if by that is meant simply the anatomy of industrialized economies; this simply blinds us to the real fertility of his theories. Rather it is his critique of the social effects of individualism and the revolutionary results of submitting customary, traditional and familial values to the test of the market which is central to his vision.

It is this which explains why what Marx intended primarily as an explanation of the economic structure of nineteenth-century England can be so easily read as a *programme* for any agrarian society facing the task of modernization. By making his analysis partly historical and by searching for the transition to 'capitalism' in the pre-industrial world of the sixteenth-century Marx offers, as well as a guide to the inner workings of commercial society and its inherent instability, an account of how economic development is brought about.

By stressing that what *underlies* economic growth is *capital accumulation* and that the most powerful force in this process is the systematic violation of property rights, Marx's theory powerfully suggests that growth can be driven on more rapidly by the open recognition of the need for confiscation independently of the slower and more surreptitious hypocrisies of the market. By stating that the inevitable and unwilled goal of capitalism is the emergence of a socialist society in which scarcity will have been abolished and in which social justice will be inherent in the natural order of things, Marx provides a legitimization for policies which cut across established cultural traditions of economic and social intercourse; the masters of one-party states with backward economies and unwilling populations can claim to be operating in terms of a social good which transcends the transient opinions of an as yet unenlightened and largely peasant majority. Marx above all provides a way of transferring the problems of economic development from the commercial to the political level and at the same time offers intellectual weapons with which to fight political resistance to a programme of rapid and violent change.

In industrialized and commercialized societies, Marx's theories enjoy a continued resonance deriving from his acute insight into the paradoxes and social evils which stem from individualism and competition and from the use of the commercial system to provide an index of welfare and human comparison. These societies are managed by politicians and administrators nurtured in the liberal faith of individual and market freedom. Yet government no longer exists simply to ensure good order and the supervision of the rules of market competition; in every modern economy the State is a powerful engine of social management which not only operates independently of market values but by its decisions actually alters the framework of values within which private individuals operate. Governments now not only control and meliorate the excesses produced by uncontrolled competition; they are themselves price-setters and by their actions determine how the system of price incentives is to operate.

But if the market is to be controlled, from whence are to be derived the values with reference to which this control is to be exercised? Publicly financed medicine, education, defence, various other public services and even large sections of productive industry now absorb a considerable proportion of the national product. Governments make their investment and spending decisions in a variety of more or less satisfactory ways but are uneasily aware that the criteria they employ are all insecurely based on patched-up compromises between guesses about the supposed 'needs' of society and what can be politically contrived. It is no longer the government but the market that is the residual element in social calculation. But governments have no surer way of arriving at tests of welfare and utility than that provided by the market they know to be unreliable. As a result, social managers are thrown back onto their own intuitions about the relative political weight of the various sections of the community and make hopeful calculations from the mass of data now gathered in untold numbers of surveys and research projects. It is not possible to claim that the development of modern industrialized economies is anything more than the chance outcome of sets of often inconsistent information and incoherent political bargaining. All this is reflected in the demoralization of modern political and economic theories which confess their inability to offer any certain guide to social action.

In examining Marx and his own sometimes perverse, sometimes muddled, but often brilliant and always impassioned attempt to 'transform' the market and search for some better and more humane way of ordering society, we do well to observe, respectfully, that this was the earliest, most extensive, and in some sense, the bravest attempt to offer a theoretical solution to a problem which is perhaps now the most pressing general issue in politics. It still awaits its resolution. Where Marx failed no one else has yet succeeded.

Further reading

The volume of work on the themes dealt with in this book is enormous and all that is intended here is an indication of some of the books and articles which may be of the most use as immediate further reading.

The best introductory life of Karl Marx is Werner Blumenberg, *Karl Marx* (London 1972). There are a number of others but the best of the longer biographies is perhaps Maximilien Rubel, *Karl Marx, Essai de biographie intellectuelle* 2nd edn (Paris 1971). In English, the fullest recent account is David McLellan, *Karl Marx, His Life and Thought* (London 1973, Macmillan).

The most complete and uniform edition of Karl Marx's writings in English is *Karl Marx and Frederick Engels Collected Works*, publication of which commenced in 1974 and had reached 42 volumes by 1987 (Lawrence and Wishart, London; International Publishers Co. Inc., New York; Progress Publishers, Moscow). Translations referred to in the text include *Karl Marx, Early Texts*, translated and edited by David McLellan (Oxford 1971, Blackwell); The *Economic and Philosophic Manuscripts of 1844 by Karl Marx*, edited with an introduction by Dirk J. Struik (New York 1964, International Publishers); Karl Marx and Frederick Engels, *The German Ideology* (London 1965, Lawrence and Wishart); Karl Marx, *The Poverty of Philosophy* (Moscow 1955, Progress Publishers); Harold J. Laski, *Communist Manifesto, Socialist Landmark* (London 1948, George Allen and Unwin); Karl Marx, *Grundrisse, Foundations of the Critique of Political Economy (Rough Draft)*, translated with a foreword by Martin Nicolaus (Penguin Books, Harmondsworth 1973); Karl Marx, *A Contribution to the Critique of Political Economy*, edited by Maurice Dobb (London 1971, Lawrence and Wishart); Karl Marx, *Capital, vols I–III*, (Moscow edition) published in Britain by Lawrence and Wishart (1967–71), which follow the original German editions of 1887–94; a new translation is also available (Harmondsworth 1976–81, Penguin Books) with an excellent introduction by Ernest Mandel; Karl Marx, *Theories of Surplus Value* (Vol.IV of *Capital*), 3 parts (Moscow 1969–72); Karl Marx and Frederick Engels, *Selected Works*, 2 vols (London 1958–9). Useful collections of translated extracts can be found in David McLellan, *The Thought of Karl Marx* (London 1971, Macmillan), which also provides a commentary; Karl Marx. *Selected Writings in Sociology and Social Philosophy*, edited by T.B. Bottomore and Maximilien Rubel

(Harmondsworth 1963, Penguin Books); *Marx on Economics*, edited by Robert Freeman (Harmondsworth 1962, Penguin Books). Ben Fine's *Marx's Capital* provides a brief but thorough and readable introduction to the core of Marx's economics, highlighting Marx's methodological debts to Hegel and Feuerbach and his economic debts to Ricardo and Smith.

There are several general books on Marx's ideas which will be found helpful. George Lichtheim, *Marxism, An Historical and Critical Study*, 2nd edn (London 1964, Routledge & Kegan Paul), is sometimes idiosyncratic in its arguments but it is a stimulating attempt to place Marx within 'Marxism' historically, and covers the whole period from 1789 to 1948. M. M. Bober's *Karl Marx's Interpretation of History*, 2nd edn (Harvard University Press 1948) first appeared in 1927 and is accordingly rather dated; it is nonetheless very useful for its thorough marshalling of Marx's text as it was known before the publication for the first time of Marx's earlier 'Hegelian' writings in the 1930s. H. B. Acton, *The Illusion of the Epoch, Marxism-Leninism as a Philosophical Creed* (London 1962, Cohen and West) and John Plamenatz, *German Marxism and Russian Communism* (London 1954, Longman), contain classic critiques of Marx's ideas, and reference should also be made to the latter's *Man and Society, A Critical Examination of some important Social and Political Theories from Macchiavelli to Marx*, 2 vols (London 1963, Longman). Shlomo Avineri's *The Social and Political Thought of Karl Marx* (Cambridge 1970), is a brilliant attempt to provide a fully coherent account of an Hegelian Marx. Finally, *Marx for Beginners*, by the Cuban cartoonist Rius (London, Writers & Readers, 1978) covers Marx's philosophy, politics and economics, and is both highly readable and more serious that its appearance suggests.

Readers seeking a simple introduction to economics could do no better than to start with a history of economic thought like William Barber's short and clear *A History of Economic Thought*, 2nd edn (Harmondsworth 1967, Penguin Books). Sir Eric Roll's *A History of Economic Thought*, 4th edn (London 1973, Faber & Faber) was written when the author's sympathies were Marxist but is more, rather than less, useful because of that. Ken Cole, John Cameron and Chris Edwards, *Why Economists Disagree – The Political Economy of Economics* (Harlow 1983, Longman) examines the foundations of the three main schools of economic thought: 'subjective preference' theory (orthodox neoclassical); 'cost of production theory' (Keynes and Sraffa) and Marxian 'abstract labour theory'. Mark Blaug's brilliant *Economic Theory in Retrospect* 2nd edn (London 1968, Heinemann), is written for those with a mathematical training but is not inaccessible to the innumerate, while its chapter on Marx is extremely valuable. A very good short introduction to the particular period of economic thought with which we are concerned in this book is provided by Donald Winch, 'The emergence of economics as a science, 1750–1870', in *The Fontana Economic History of Europe* (London 1973), vol. III, Sect. 9.

Sir John Hicks, *A Theory of Economic History* (London 1969, OUP), is a stimulating and excellent analytical introduction to the history of economic development. There are good essays in *The Cambridge Economic History of Europe* of which those of E. Carus-Wilson. 'The woollen industry', and Robert S. Lopez, 'The trade of medieval Europe: The south' in Vol. II, *Trade and Industry in the Middle Ages* (Cambridge 1952), are good illustrations of 'precocious' economic growth. On English economic history see Christopher Hill, *Reformation to Industrial Revolution* (Harmondsworth 1969, Penguin Books); T. S. Ashton, *An Economic History of England. The Eighteenth Century* (London 1955, Methuen); and, by the latter author, the best short account of the most important economic phenomenon in modern history, *The Industrial Revolution 1760–1830* (London 1968, OUP). R. M. Hartwell's *The Industrial Revolution and Economic Growth* (London 1971, Methuen), contains helpful and readable surveys of the most recent literature. Maurice Dobb, *Studies in the Development of Capitalism* (London 1946, Routledge & Kegan Paul), is an attempt to fill out Marx's sketch of capitalist development with an account of the development of the modern world into the twentieth century. A non-Marxist account is to be found in David S. Landes, *The Unbound Prometheus. Technological Change and Industrial Development in Western Europe from 1750 to the Present* (Cambridge 1970, CUP).

On the Scottish Historical School see Gladys Bryson, *Man and Society: The Scottish Inquiry of the Eighteenth Century* (Princeton, 1945). A. L. Macfie, 'The Scottish tradition in economic thought', *Scottish Journal of Political Economy*, February 1965, vol. 12, pp. 1–22. A particularly valuable introduction to Adam Smith is that written by Andrew Skinner for his edition of *The Wealth of Nations* (Harmondsworth 1979, Penguin Books). The logical beauty of Smith's ideas is nicely dissected and displayed in W. A. Eltis, 'Adam Smith's theory of economic growth', *Essays on Adam Smith*, edited by Andrew Skinner and Thomas Wilson (Oxford 1975). On Physiocracy see Ronald L. Meek, *The Economics of Physiocracy. Essays and Translations* (London 1962, George Allen & Unwin). Ricardo's complete works have been edited in 11 vols by Piero Sraffa and Maurice Dobb (Cambridge 1951–73, CUP). See especially Sraffa's introduction to vol. I.

For the German cultural background to Hegel's philosophical origins see W.H. Bruford, *Germany in the Eighteenth Century*, 2nd edn (Cambridge 1965). There is no commentary on Hegel known to me which deals with his work in the way suggested in Chapter 5, as a misconceived theory of psychological development. A standard work is J. N. Findlay, *Hegel: A Re-examination* (London 1959, George Allen and Unwin). Raymond Plant's *Hegel* (London 1973, George Allen and Unwin), while giving a different account of Hegel provides a general introduction to his political ideas and is especially helpful in placing Hegel in his historical context. Paul Chamley, *Economie politique et philosophie chez Steuart et Hegel* (Annales de la Faculte de Droit et des Sciences Politiques et Economiques de Strasbourg. no.12 Paris 1963), links Hegel with Scottish economics and makes some extravagant claims for Hegel's own economic ideas. Shlomo Avineri's *Hegel's Theory of the Modern State* (Cambridge 1972) brings out very clearly the economic assumptions in Hegel's political writings. Although the general conclusion of Robert Tucker's *Philosophy and Myth in Karl Marx* (Cambridge 1965), are questionable, the explanation of the connexion between the ideas of Hegel, Feuerbach and Marx which it provides is brilliant and persuasive. Sidney Hook's *From Hegel to Marx. Studies in the Intellectual Development of Karl Marx* (London 1936, Victor Gollancz), is also still valuable for its interpretation of Marx's debt to Hegel. A useful account of Marx's relationship to Hegel, more sympathetic to Marx than Tucker's book, though no less questionable in its conclusions, is Bertell Ollman, *Alienation, Marx's Conception of Man in Capitalist Society* (Cambridge 1971). John Plamenatz, Karl Marx's *Philosophy of Man* (Oxford 1975), is an important non-Marxist and philosophical analysis of Marx's Hegelian notions.

On socialism, G.D.H. Cole's *Socialist Thought*, 5 vols in 7 (London 1953–60, Macmillan), although written in haste and sometimes inaccurate, is still a mine of information. Charles Gide and Charles Rist, *A History of Economic Doctrines*, 2nd English edn (London 1948, Harrap), gives an old-fashioned and French view of its subject but is valuable for the way in which it brings out the economic content of the ideas of the Utopian socialists. See also *A Short History of Socialist Economic Thought* by Gerd Hardach and Dieter Karras (London 1978, Edward Arnold).

For an illustration of the way in which economic assumptions are embedded in traditional British political thought see C. B. Macpherson's *The Political Theory of Possessive Individualism. Hobbes to Locke* (Oxford 1962). John Rawls' *A Theory of Justice* (Oxford 1972), the most important of recent general statements of liberal political thought, shows how little the preoccupations of modern political thought have changed in the last 300 years; market assumptions, or assumptions functional for economic competition are still axiomatic.

The discussion of Marx's general theory in Chapter 8 can be followed up in the books by Plamenatz, Bober, Acton and Avineri cited above, and also in Alfred G. Meyer, *Marxism. The Unity of Theory and Practice. A critical Essay* (Cambridge, Mass. 1970, Harvard University Press). An introduction to the general problems of social theory can be found in Alan Ryan, *The Philosophy of the Social Sciences* (London 1970, Macmillan).

Paul M. Sweezy, *The Theory of Capitalist Development* (London 1946, Dobson), is still a very good introduction to Marx's more specifically economic doctrines by a sympathizer. Marx's prophecies are examined in F. M. Gottheil, *Marx's Economic Predictions* (Evanston

1966, Northwestern University Press). Also useful is P. N. Junankar's *Marx's Economics* (Oxford 1982, Philip Allan).

Most of the more recent work on Marx's economics has been undertaken by writers who are neo-Marxists in the sense employed in the foreword to this second edition. I include them here for the sake of greater completeness and because none of us should believe that we have a monopoly of the truth.

For the neo-Marxist in recent years, it is the labour theory of value which has attracted most attention. The debate on 'the transformation problem' – how labour values are used by the market to determine prices and surplus value is translated into profits is best entered by way of the much earlier work of Eugen von Bohm-Bawerk, whose classic attack on Marx, *Karl Marx and the Close of his System* (first published in German in 1896) is conveniently issued in one volume with Rudolf Hilferding's defence of Marx, *Bohm-Bawerk's criticism of Marx*, by Augustus M. Kelly (Clifton, 1973). The modern debate in English owes much to Piero Sraffa's difficult *Production of Commodities by Means of Commodities* (Cambridge University Press, 1960). Ironically, this classic work was intended as a critique of orthodox neo-classical economic theory, not of Marx, and drew heavily on the tradition of Ricardian political economy, developing a theory of price determination based solely upon the method (i.e., the technical coefficients) of production. The neo-Ricardian school uses Sraffa for its resolution of the 'transformation problem'; see especially Ian Steedman *Marx After Sraffa* (New Left Books, London, 1977) and Geoff Hodgson *Capitalism, Value and Exploitation* (Martin Robertson, Oxford, 1982).

The neo-Marxist position appears to be that the labour theory of value is an attempt to develop the tools necessary for an analysis of the 'laws of motion' of capitalism, and that, consequently, value is a relationship and an abstraction, rather than an object and the basis of price determination. This approach is reviewed and defended by Sue Himmelweit and Simon Mohun 'Real Abstractions and Anonymous Assumptions', in *The Value Controversy*, edited by Ian Steedman and Paul Sweezy (Verso/NLB, London, 1981), although in general this book takes a neo-Ricardian position. The orthodox Marxist rejoinder is *The Value Dimension – Marx versus Ricardo and Sraffa*, edited by Ben Fine (RKP, London, 1986). See also the same author's 'The Labour Theory of Value', in *Economic Theory and Ideology* (Edward Arnold, London, 1980) and A.K. Sen 'On the Labour Theory of Value: Some Methodological Issues' in *Cambridge Journal of Economics*, Maurice Dobb Issue 2.2, 1978. For an earlier history of the labour theory of value see Ronald Meek *Studies in the Labour Theory of Value* (Lawrence and Wishart, 1956).

On the Declining Rate of Profit see Ben Fine 'On the Law of the Tendency of the Rate of Profit to Fall', in his *Theories of the Capitalist Economy* (Edward Arnold, London, 1982) and Ben Fine and Lawrence Harris *Rereading Capital* (Macmillan, London, 1979) which offers an orthodox defence of Marx's economics. Critiques of this position can be found in Geoff Hodgson 'The theory of the falling rate of profit', *New Left Review*, no.84, 1974, and in the debate in the *Cambridge Journal of Economics* in June 1978, December 1979 and March 1980. The general status of 'tendencies' within marxist economics is questioned by Cutler, Hindess, Hirst and Hussain in *Marx's Capital and Capitalism Today Vols I and II* (RKP, London, 1977 and 1978); Lawrence Harris presents a critique of this work and a defence of Marx's scientific method in 'The Science of the Economy', *Economy and Society*, vol.7 no.3, pp. 285–320, 1978. On the declining rate of profit see also Angus Walker 'Karl Marx, the declining rate of profit and British political economy', *Economica*, November 1971, new series, vol.xxxviii pp. 362–77. This owes something to B.A. Balassa, 'Karl Marx and John Stuart Mill', *Weltwirtschaftliches Archiv*, 1959, vol.83, pp. 147–63, and to Bernice Shoul 'Similarities in the work of John Stuart Mill and Karl Marx', *Science and Society*, 1965, vol.xxix, pp. 270–95. On Mill's economics generally see Pedro Schwartz, *The New Political Economy of J.S. Mill* (London 1972, Weidenfeld and Nicolson).

The relationship between socialism and the operation of markets is considered by Geoff Hodgson *The Democratic Economy* (Penguin, 1984) and Alec Nove's *The Economics of Feasible Socialism* (George Allen & Unwin, 1983) – both taking the view that market relations should operate extensively; this position is contested by Ernest Mandel 'In Defence of Socialist Planning' *New Left Review*, 159, 1986; see also Robin Murray 'Ownership, Control and the Market', *New Left Review*, 1987.

In general, *Capital* is in many ways a much less abstruse book if it is read after the study of Adam Smith's *The Wealth of Nations*, David Ricardo's *Principles of Political Economy* and John Stuart Mill's *Principles of Political Economy*.

In contrast with his analysis of capitalism, Marx wrote very little on the nature of the socialist economy, but for an overview see Ben Fine's 'Marx on Economic Relations Under Socialism', in Betty Matthews (ed.) *Marx 100 Years On* (London 1983, Lawrence and Wishart).

For a sketch of the basic Russian economic problems see A. Baykov, 'The economic development of Russia', *Economic History Review*, December 1954, vol. vii, pp. 137–49. Martin Malia's *Alexander Herzen and the Birth of Russian Socialism 1812–1855* (Cambridge, Mass. 1971, Harvard University Press), gives a clear account of Russia's own proto-Marx. Richard Pipes, *Struve, Liberal on the Left 1870–1905* (Cambridge, Mass. 1970, Harvard University Press) provides much more than its title promises; it is an excellent account of the intellectual history of the last third of the nineteenth century in Russia and deals extensively with the reception and influence of Marx. On Lenin and Hegel see Lewis Feuer, 'Lenin's fantasy. The interpretation of a Russian revolutionary dream' *Encounter*, December 1970, vol. xxxv, No.6, pp. 23-35. For the economic history of Russia in this period see Alexander Gerschenkron,

'Russia: patterns and problems of economic development, 1861–1958', in *Economic Backwardness in Historical Perspective* (Cambridge, Mass. 1966, Harvard University Press), pp. 119–51, and also Alec Nove's *An Economic History of the USSR* revised edn (Harmondsworth 1982, Penguin Books). The latter's 'Lenin as an economist' in *Lenin*, edited by Leonard Schapiro and Peter Reddaway (London 1967, Pall Mall Press), pp. 187–210, draws together Lenin's basic ideas about economics.

Index

Index

Index

Index